In the Name of Allah

In the Name of Allah

Understanding Islam and Indian History

RAZIUDDIN AQUIL

PENGUIN
VIKING

VIKING
Published by the Penguin Group
Penguin Books India Pvt. Ltd, 11 Community Centre, Panchsheel Park, New Delhi 110 017, India
Penguin Group (USA) Inc., 375 Hudson Street, New York, New York 10014, USA
Penguin Group (Canada), 90 Eglinton Avenue East, Suite 700, Toronto, Ontario,
M4P 2Y3, Canada (a division of Pearson Penguin Canada Inc.)
Penguin Books Ltd, 80 Strand, London WC2R 0RL, England
Penguin Ireland, 25 St. Stephen's Green, Dublin 2, Ireland (a division of Penguin Books Ltd)
Penguin Group (Australia), 250 Camberwell Road, Camberwell, Victoria 3124, Australia (a division of Pearson Australia Group Pty Ltd)
Penguin Group (NZ), 67 Apollo Drive, Rosedale, North Shore 0632, New Zealand (a division of Pearson New Zealand Ltd)
Penguin Group (South Africa) (Pty) Ltd, 24 Sturdee Avenue, Rosebank, Johannesburg 2196, South Africa

Penguin Books Ltd, Registered Offices: 80 Strand, London WC2R 0RL, England

First published in Viking by Penguin Books India 2009

10 9 8 7 6 5 4 3 2 1

The views and opinions expressed in this book are the author's own and the facts are as reported by him which have been verified to the extent possible, and the publishers are not in any way liable for the same.

ISBN 9780670082612

Typeset in Aldine401 BT by Eleven Arts, New Delhi
Printed at Chaman Offset Printers, Delhi

For
Professor Partha Chatterjee

Contents

Preface ix

1. Islam and Indian History 1
2. Sufi Traditions and the Emergence of Islam in the Subcontinent 25
3. Muslims and Kafirs in the Delhi Sultanate 49
4. Islam and Heresies in Mughal India 76
5. Recommending Right and Forbidding Wrong 109
6. Violating Norms of Conduct 133
7. The Sufi-Bhakti Milieu: Later Transformations 157
8. Reason and Faith in Islam 192

Notes 215
Timeline 253
Glossary 256
Select Bibliography 266
Index 279

Preface

This book emerges out of a research project conducted at the Centre for Studies in Social Sciences, Calcutta (CSSSC). The aim of the project was to move away from the rather constricted framework of the agenda-driven conventional history of medieval India to think of the larger questions on Islam and medieval Indian history, questions which are of serious concern to contemporary reflections on how to make sense of a complex past and its controversial inheritance. It was also, in a measure, inspired by Partha Chatterjee's critical appreciation of the creative energies of a people who have lost in the race of modernity, the terms of which were dictated by an aggressive West. I have immensely benefited from Professor Chatterjee's encouragement and guidance for the major part of the research for this book, and I wish to dedicate this volume to him as an expression of my deep sense of gratitude for his kindness and generosity.

Earlier versions of several chapters were experimented with in workshops, seminars and conferences over the years and I would like to thank the organizers and participants in these events for giving me the opportunity to share my work as well as tolerating raw ideas. I would particularly like to mention Amit Dey, Arvind Sinha, Bodil Frederiksen, David Curley, Dilbagh Singh, George Thadathil, Gyan Pandey, Ipshita Chanda, Isabel Hofmeyr, Jon Hyslop, Kavita Panjabi, Lakshmi Subramanian, Manas Ray, Nirmal

Kumar, Pius Malekandathil, Preben Kaarsholm, Rajat Datta, Ritwika Biswas, Shirin Maswood, Susanta Ghosh, Tapati Guha-Thakurta and Yogesh Sharma.

Several scholars have seen one or more chapters in draft versions. I have especially tortured Anjan Ghosh, Himadri Banerjee, Indrani Chatterjee, Kumkum Chatterjee, Mubarak Ali, Muzaffar Alam, Narayani Gupta, Richard Eaton, Satish Saberwal, Shail Mayaram, Shinder Thandi, Sumit Guha and Werner Menski. As usual, Partha Chatterjee read a very early draft of the whole manuscript and suggested interesting ways to deal with crude formulations. Tilottama Mukherjee has also helped polish early drafts of most of the chapters.

My ever-growing list of friends was always there for support in times of crisis and anxieties, whether caused by a 'Jihadi' blast in the name of Allah or American/Western onslaught for 'divine' justice, and I remember with thanks Anuradha Chanda, Arupjyoti Saikia, Najmul Hoda, Padmanabh Samarendra, Rekha Natarajan, Shashank Sinha, Sohel Firdos and Sunandan Chakraborty. The 'South India Lobby' at CSSSC, though always dwindling and somewhat shaky, has helped in resisting the dominant propositions and I would especially like to thank Ramesh Bairy, Sanal Mohan and Udaya Kumar for their crucial support.

Thanks are also due to Abhijit Bhattacharya, Arshad Rizvi, Malvika Gulati, Prabir Basu, and Sujata Mishra for their many courtesies at different stages of research for this book. I take this opportunity to pay my tributes to the unsung heroes of CSSSC, who make things happen at this extraordinary institution. I especially remember Biswanath Nag, Debo Prosad Mitra, Jayati Nayak-Yagnik, Priyanka Basu, Sambhu Nath Nag, Sanchita Bhattacharyya, Soumitra Chatterjee and Surajit Bose. Their useful little inputs together proved to be of great value.

I should not forget to thank Sugata Marjit and Surajit Mukhopadhyay, Director and Registrar respectively of CSSSC, for their support and encouragement while working on the manuscript during these past couple of years.

Last, but not the least, it has been a pleasure to work with the editors at Penguin Books.

July 2009 Raziuddin Aquil
Kolkata

1

Islam and Indian History

A proper appreciation of the history of Islam in the Indian Subcontinent—from the early inroads made into Sindh in the eighth century to the establishment of the Delhi Sultanate in the thirteenth century, and through the middle ages up to the present day—requires detailed and dispassionate investigation. The social, economic, political, religious and cultural transformations that have taken place during this period in the region would be the subject of such a study. This means developing an understanding of not only the medieval period, which was largely under Muslim political domination, but also of the pre-Muslim or early-medieval period as well as that of colonial rule. Importantly, this study needs to be conducted without secularism, communalism, separatism, or any other modern ideology dictating the terms and issues. In a sense, modern understandings of Muslims and of their medieval past have more to do with contemporary politics in the Subcontinent than any historical experience marked by violence and bloodshed.

The coming of Islam to the Indian Subcontinent opened the floodgates of immigration and migration, and trade and cultural relations with Iran, Central Asia and the Middle East. India's integration with the Muslim world witnessed the transmission of fresh political ideas (though presented in an Islamic idiom), which had evolved over centuries in ancient Greece, Iran and of course, India. In many ways, this was a case of a set of political ideas re-emerging in a new garb.

The Sultanate and Mughal periods witnessed the continuation of political practices and institutions at the local level with slow and gradual changes being imposed from above. Certain administrative institutions such as the posts of *iqtadar*s or *muqtai*s (provincial governors) were introduced with the advent of Islam, and later, under the Mughals, modifications in the *mansabdari* system in the ranks for nobles and administrators were put in place. Muslim rulers did not bring about any revolution in 'Hindustan', used here in the modern sense of the whole of India; yet, their presence did play an important role in the Islamization or Persianization of the political culture. The various connotations of the *shariat* (Muslim law) and compromises with requirements of the time forced rulers to adopt policies suited to the context, occasional pressures from the Sunni Muslim theologians notwithstanding.

Muslims did not always announce their arrival in a particular region with widespread bloodshed. Compared to the irruptions of the Mongols and several other accounts of political conquests during medieval times, the Turkish invasion of Hindustan and the advent of the Mughals did not result in large-scale violence and demographic dislocations. Also, though some temples might have been destroyed in the wake of confrontations, mainly to announce the end of the prevailing political order, it must be noted that scholars of *prachin* (ancient) temple architecture in many parts of India have dated the construction of these temples during the heyday of Muslim power in the Subcontinent—between the thirteenth and eighteenth centuries. Popular notions about the general desecration of Hindu temples under Muslim rulers simply do not take into account facts about the construction and maintenance of many prominent Hindu shrines through the middle ages (more on this later).

The Turks, Afghans and Mughals, amongst other sets of Muslim immigrants from Central Asia, Iran and the Middle East, were essentially urban people and wherever they settled down in the Subcontinent, new cities and towns emerged. In some cases, following the change in political regimes as well as a dominant Muslim presence, a pre-existing city was renamed and transformed into a Muslim stronghold. Also, the prolonged interaction between Muslim urban centres and a predominantly Hindu rural hinterland led to the gradual diffusion of Islam in this region. As Richard Eaton has shown, the large-scale expansion of Islam in eastern Bengal must be attributed to this process of cultural accretion over centuries and not to the use of political power for forced conversion.[1] On the other hand, huge settlements of Muslim communities on the Malabar and Coromandel coasts in southern India emerged as part of the Indian Ocean trade network. Arab, Persian and other Muslim merchants settled down in coastal towns and mixed up with the 'locals' to evolve new cultural forms.[2] These communities were not generally influenced by Muslim politics in northern India. Further, a pre-modern world system extensive across Eurasia possibly existed in the thirteenth century CE, prior to the formation of the modern world system. Despite all the initial destructions, the Mongol empire eventually played an important role in binding together the Chinese, Indian, Muslim and European regions in the first half of the thirteenth and early fourteenth centuries, but this is beyond the scope of the present work.

In addition, given the religious diversities and sectarian divisions amongst Muslims, a colossal, monolithic or uniform Islam backed by state power could never establish itself in the Subcontinent. Instead, interactions between various strands of Islam and diverse Indic religious traditions led to the emergence of new forms of religiosity, cults and sects, the most prominent being Sufism, Bhakti and Sikhism. Besides these, there were also a large number of 'syncretic' traditions in different regions, which did not strictly conform to any organized religion in spite of political pressures on them to identify with Islam or Hinduism. Given the diversities of opinion on religious matters and occasional conflicts and tensions, rulers took positions (which in modern political parlance would be referred to as 'pluralism') that were often not in line with the totalizing rhetoric of certain Sunni Muslim quarters. Arguments were many, but violence was certainly not the order of the day.

However, despite this space that existed in medieval India for accepting difference and critiquing orthodoxy, the period did not witness the kind of strides as were made in the West during the same period. The innovations in military technology (artillery, gunpowder, cannon, cavalry), craft (metal ware, pottery, weaving), agriculture (through the introduction of the Persian wheel and new crops), food habits, clothing, etc., did bring about some transformations in the life of the people of the Subcontinent, but beyond these, there was a veritable lack of initiative to turn things for the better. Enthusiastic secular historians have attributed many advances to the Mughal emperor Akbar and his intellectuals and scientists, but these seem to have been very limited. The initial spectacular success of the Mughal military regime actually turned into stagnation, which proved to be the nemesis of the Mughals in India. The inability of the *jagir* or the landholding-based Mughal military system to change needs further exploration, especially as we now know the consequences of their indifference to emerging techniques of warfare and governance.

Even as our present knowledge about medieval Indian Muslim communities and their cultural contributions remains a subject of debate, the surviving material heritage—including large numbers of exquisite paintings, grand architecture, vast literature in Persian and in vernacular languages, and complex musical and dance forms—presents a very different picture from the gory accounts of violence, rape and murder told by political groups that aim to demonize Islam and Muslims. Large sections of Muslims too remain unsure of how to lead a life in harmony with the times while still conforming to the religious path shown by Prophet Muhammad in seventh-century Arabia. On the other hand, despite pressure from orthodox elements, Muslim communities have adapted to the changing requirements of time and place, though the more they change, the more they are made out to be the same! It will be interesting to see how Muslims negotiate with the challenges of modern times (for more on this issue, see the concluding chapter).

As noted in the last section, Islam in India has been involved in complex negotiations throughout its long history—neither has it been marked by bloodshed all along, nor has it simply been about peace and harmony. A more informed understanding therefore requires a dispassionate unravelling of the complexities of this issue. Modern scholars' commitment to divergent political positions and competing ideological strands has meant, however, that many such complexities have not been adequately dealt with. This is especially true of conventional medieval Indian history, an area dominated by a set of historians identified as 'secularists' and 'pluralists'. These scholars de-emphasize, even condemn aspects of Sunni Islam that they consider to be inimical to the ideal of tolerance that is to be upheld in the Indian situation and are uncomfortable with the language of violence frequently deployed by Hindu right-wing fringe elements. They are driven by their concern to safeguard the secular character of the modern Indian state and the nation's social diversities from communal and separatist elements, who seek to portray a gloomy history of the medieval period. The secularists' sanitized version of medieval Indian history thus leaves out many important themes and issues, which, in turn, are highlighted and abused by other sets of historians.[3] This inability to rise above the considerations of contemporary politics and ideological demands remains a major challenge to the study of Islam in medieval India.

It is worthwhile to note here that since separatist ideologies cut people off from alternate ideas and followers of other ideologies, they are obviously detrimental to scholarship. Separatist ideas are also socially undesirable because they lead to conflict. However, separatist ideologies have thrived in the past, as they do even now. This too must be recognized in order to understand historical reality accurately. In political terms, communalists with wide popular appeal need to be taken seriously and confronted in an acceptable idiom.

In this book, I will attempt to explain a few significant themes of Muslim history and culture in northern India that have remained largely unexplored in medieval history, with the aim of understanding the roots of the politics of Islam in the Subcontinent. To clarify, 'medieval India' is referred to in this work in the broadest sense of the term, covering the period from the thirteenth to the eighteenth centuries.[4] Also, the focus of the discussion in this book is on northern India. Regrettably, regional trajectories will remain neglected here, as is generally the case in medieval Indian historical scholarship.

Moving on from the discussion on the dominant secularist scholarship, we will now focus on some recent works that study Islam in the Subcontinent. The issues that this scholarship has explored include competing forms of the shariat in *adab/akhlaq* literature (political treatises), differences among the *ulama* (theologians, custodians of Hanafite Sunni Islam), divergent and proactive Sufi traditions, the dominance of Persian in medieval India, and the spectacular rise of the vernacular in the wake of Mughal decline. Unfortunately, architecture and paintings, which showcase the grandeur of not only the Mughals but also of 'lesser' dynasties in popular memory, remain outside the purview of this work.[5]

As Muzaffar Alam has shown recently, a clear-cut distinction existed between the meaning of shariat laws for Muslim jurists and for philosophers and intellectuals who wanted to break free from the clutches of Sunni Muslim orthodoxy, as is reflected in the two sets of writings on Muslim political ideas—akhlaq and adab. The shariat in the early adab writings—treatises on principles and practices of government, generally referred to as 'mirrors for princes'—was informed by jurists, thus making its scope narrow and theological. Early texts on norms of governance in the Islamic tradition that conformed to the shariat in the legal sense include *Ahkam-us-Sultaniya* of Abul Hasan Al-Mawardi (d. 1058), *Siyasat-nama* or *Siyar-ul-Muluk* of Nizam-ul-Mulk Tusi (d. 1092) and *Nasihat-ul-Muluk* of Imam Ghazali (d. 1111). Though these authors wrote from divergent doctrinal and intellectual positions and drew on ancient Greek and Iranian texts as well, for all of them, '[the] defence of the *shari'a* and keeping alive of religion and true faith were among the most important duties of an Islamic king.'[6] In other words, for all of them, the shariat, as interpreted by the ulama, was to be the guiding principle for governance. (We will return in chapter five to a more detailed discussion of the ulama's role in guiding Muslims on the straight path of Islam, and also in recommending right and forbidding wrong in the light of the early sources of Islam, especially the Quran and the Traditions of the Prophet, the *hadis*.)

Returning to the discussion on political ideas, according to Alam, early Indo-Muslim writings on governance such as Fakhr-i-Mudabbir's *Adab-ul-Harb* (*c.* early thirteenth century) and Ziya-ud-Din Barani's *Fatawa-i-Jahandari* (*c.* mid-fourteenth century) extended the 'mirrors for princes' genre. Though Barani's invocation of hereditary principles and the appropriation of non-Islamic Iranian or Indian political traditions is noteworthy, it is reiterated, especially by secularist historians, that the political theorist was basically serving 'the narrowly sectarian interests of the early Islamic regime in India'.[7] This position on Barani's work, particularly the dismissal of his controversial *Fatawa-i-Jahandari* as unimportant, needs to be reconsidered and revised. As we shall see below, Barani was not the typical Sunni fanatic that he is made out to be. The context in which he produced his work needs as much attention as his informed assertion that the religious laws of Islam were not enough to govern the predominantly non-Muslim population of the Delhi Sultanate.[8]

The more inclusive akhlaq texts, which emerged in the post-Mongol period, are marked by their distinct departure from orthodox Sunni positions on the regulations of the shariat, as is the case in adab writings. In other words, whereas the approach of adab texts is theological and narrow, akhlaq literature offers philosophical and broad-based political advice to rulers. Khwaja Nasir-ud-Din Tusi's (d. 1274) classic work, *Akhlaq-i-Nasiri*, is a significant early example of this kind of literature. Using a translated summary of Ibn Miskawayh's Arabic work *Tahzib al-Akhlaq* or *Kitab al-Taharat*, Tusi included sections on the management of family (*tadbir-i-manzil*) and politics (*siyasat-i-mudun*) as part of practical wisdom (*hikmat-i-amli*) required for rulers. In doing so, he 'drew on Hellenic philosophical writings and blended them with his own "Islamic" view of man and society'.[9]

The version of *Akhlaq-i-Nasiri* prepared by Tusi and dedicated to the fourteenth-century non-Muslim Mongol ruler of Maraghah in Azarbaijan envisaged the role of the ideal ruler, or philosopher-king, of the city/state as one that would 'harmonize the conflicting interests of diverse social and religious groups' of people. Religion did occupy an important place in this political ideal, but the connotations of the shariat were broadened to ensure that religious differences among the subject population did not determine state policy in such matters as justice. Thus, no discrimination was to be made between people on the basis of their religions. The responsibility of the ideal ruler in Nasirean ethics was to maintain the well-being of people of different social and religious backgrounds and not of Muslims alone.[10]

The Mughal rulers' ability to cater to the interests of their heterogeneous subjects in the Subcontinent was possibly informed by political ideals included in the Nasirean akhlaq. Not only was Nasir-ud-Din Tusi's text widely read in Mughal India, but later recensions of the book were also in circulation. The *Akhlaq-i-Jalali* of Jalal-ud-Din Dawwani (d. 1501), the *Akhlaq-i-Muhsini* of Husain Waiz Kashifi (d. 1504–05) and the *Dastur-ul-Wizarat* or *Akhlaq-i-Humayuni* of Qazi Ikhtiyar-ud-Din Hasan Husaini inspired generations of Mughal Persian writers and Husaini's *Akhlaq-i-Humayuni* is a particular example of the Nasirean tradition of political theory. However, the Islamic orthodoxy's reading of the shariat was never completely abandoned during Mughal rule and appears in texts prepared during the late sixteenth and early seventeenth centuries. Indeed, the line between adab and akhlaq gets blurred in the *Akhlaq-i-Hakimi* of Hasan Ali ibn Ashraf Munshi Khaqani, as well as in the expanded version, *Akhlaq-i-Jahangiri*, prepared by his grandson, Nur-ud-Din Qazi Khaqani. However, the impact of akhlaq literature on Mughal norms of governance may be found in such later texts as the *Ain-i-Akbari* of Abul Fazl, the *Mauizah-i-Jahangiri* of Muhammad Baqir Najm-i-Sani and also in a large number of Mughal edicts.

The complicated question of a language of power in a situation where several languages were competing for favour, particularly from the rulers, also needs further examination. The Mughals are said to have evolved a political culture compatible with diverse Indian religious and cultural identities and found Persian to be the most appropriate language for communication and for sustaining such a political ideal, which they felt would not be possible through Sanskrit, Prakrit or any Indic vernacular. As a result, not only did images and metaphors from the world of Persian poetry come to influence the lifestyle of Muslim political elites by the time the Mughals came to power, but Persian also became 'known to literate Indians from the banks of the Indus to the Bay of Bengal,' and 'served as an important vehicle of liberalism in the medieval Muslim world'.[11] The history of Persian literature in the 'pre-Mughal' or 'Sultanate' period (thirteenth to early sixteenth centuries) too needs to be studied more intensively in this context.

It is generally assumed that the extraordinary rise of Persian as the dominant language was facilitated by the Iranian contacts of the early Mughals, the immigration of liberals into Hindustan because of the intolerant Shi'ite rule of the Safavids, the Mughal patronage of Persian language and literature, especially through the position of the *malik-us-shuara* (poet laureate) at the Mughal court, and the Persianization of the royal household and political elite.[12] However, as indicated earlier, the emphasis on the emergence of Persian as a language of power in the context of the

Mughal–Safavid relationship tends to ignore the political patronage given by the Turkish Sultans and Afghan rulers of pre-Mughal India to literary production in Persian, as well as Sufi literature, which existed in a variety of genres (*maktubat*, *malfuzat*, *tazkiras*, devotional poetry, as well as mystical philosophy). Portions of Indo-Persian literature from the Sultanate period will be studied later in this book.[13] The extraordinary story of the marginalization and silencing of the Turkish language in medieval India, despite the fact that sections of the dominant ruling elites, including the Mughals themselves, claimed to be ethnic Turks, will, unfortunately, remain untold here.

The role of Sufis, not only as conduits of power but also as legitimizers of the policy of acceptance and accommodation at the social level, needs serious reconsideration. Even as 'orthodox' (*ba-shara*) Sufi traditions were concerned with restricting deviations from the foundational categories of Islam and ensuring the continuation of Muslim rule in the Subcontinent, their belief in unity within multiplicity contributed to religious synthesis and cultural amalgamation. This complex and contentious belief was elaborated as the *wahdat-ul-wujud* doctrine (literally, unity of being), which was originally propounded by the thirteenth-century Iberian Sufi, Ibn-i-Arabi. Also, the presence of some influential Sufi orders (*silsilas*) such as Chishti (from Chisht, now in Afghanistan) and Qadiri (owing spiritual allegiance to the twelfth-century saint of Baghdad, Sheikh Abdul Qadir Jilani) ensured that rulers did not give into the Islamic orthodoxy's demand that non-Muslims be given the option of *imma'l islam-imma'l qatl*, that is, Islam or death, even if they were capable of carrying out the discordant agenda.

However, there were limits to the Sufi policy of assimilation, which emerged when their power, additional benefits and authoritative position in society were at stake, or when their role as Islamizers was emphasized. This is clearly seen in medieval Sufi accounts (tazkiras or biographies), where the late-twelfth-century founder of the Chishti order in Hindustan, Khwaja Muin-ud-Din Sijzi is shown to be involved in miraculous encounters with his opponents at Ajmer in northern India, one of these encounters being with its Rajput ruler, Prithviraj Chauhan. As the historiography of medieval India remains hostage to the demands of a 'secularist' agenda, many of the above issues remain largely neglected.[14]

The primacy accorded to the Mughal regime, especially the reign of Akbar, and more generally, to political processes in the late sixteenth and seventeenth centuries, is typical of the 'pluralist' scholarship on medieval India,[15] which refers to the earlier period only to downplay its significance. This is particularly so in the case of a very critical phase of the 'Indianization' of Islam under Afghan rulers in the late fifteenth and early sixteenth centuries, which receives only passing attention.[16] Also, the grand narrative of the pluralists is not entirely applicable to regions such as Bengal and the Deccan.[17] Much of southern India too remains marginalized in such Mughal-centric scholarship. Further, the frequent deployment of Persian sources and the general acceptance of the hegemony of Persian in Mughal India have meant that the significance of vernacular traditions remains neglected. The fact that Urdu and other regional languages emerged in a big way during the period of Mughal decline in the eighteenth century shows that the fate of these linguistic traditions hinged on Mughal fortunes. This was also perhaps the cause for the retardation of Awadhi language and literature, which coincided with the coming of the Mughals in the early sixteenth century. All these issues raise the question of the actual extent of the diffusion of Persian before and after the advent of the Mughals. The adoption of Persian by Hindu secretarial castes such as Kayasthas and Khatris, and Persian translations of Sanskrit scriptures may also have provided incentives to people in general to learn the language, but, as Alam has noticed, Persian was 'not entirely sensitive to local languages and local usages'.[18]

In contrast to the rulers, the Sufis' contributions to the evolution and development of the vernacular and their social roles in medieval India have long been recognized. Attempts to show that the medieval Indian state, rather than Sufism, was crucial in bringing together major communities of the region by creating conditions for a 'composite culture' are not fully substantiated.[19] In contrast, the critical role played by the Sufis in what is loosely referred to as synthesis or syncretism was significant and is often invoked by modern scholars when confronted with uncomfortable evidence in 'political' accounts. Yet, when the limitations of the Sufis' interventions are encountered, historians refrain from handling the question of their role in conversion and Islamization. Sufi tradition has long celebrated leading Sufi sheikhs' contributions to the emergence and spread of Islam in the Subcontinent. Examples of this can be found in authoritative texts such as the *Siyar-ul-Auliya* of Amir Khwurd, *Siyar-ul-Arifin* of Sheikh Jamali, *Akhbar-ul-Akhyar* of Abdul Haqq Muhaddis Dehlawi, *Mirat-ul-Asrar* of Abdur Rahman Chishti and *Khazinat-ul-Asfiya* of Ghulam Sarwar, besides a host of other Sufi writings of considerable value. These texts were written over a span of six hundred years, from the fourteenth to the nineteenth centuries, and cannot be wished away as useless accounts of Sufi exploits. It may be difficult to corroborate the Sufis' claims in all cases, but the fact remains that they did try to take credit for being the harbingers of Islam in the region. This is further supported by the collective memory of Muslim communities across the Subcontinent, who believe that their ancestors embraced Islam under the influence of Sufi masters and warriors (*ghazi*s and *shahid*s) directly, or through a long process of acculturation around their shrines. A rather defensive, secular scholarship ignores all this to declare that the Sufis were never interested in the propagation of Islam. It also avoids the question of how Islam spread in the region if neither the medieval state nor Sufi institutions contributed to the process.[20] Secularist/pluralist writings would also like to do away with any suggestion of the ulama sodality taking part in shaping the character of political Islam, either in medieval India or in modern times.

Though Muzaffar Alam has tried to move away from this thinking, his treatment of Barani's views on political ideals for the Delhi Sultanate is eventually not very different from that of Mohammad Habib.[21] It is important to recognize that what Habib wrote from his 'secular' perspective half a century ago or earlier was the demand of his time. However, if scholarship is to grow with time, there is a need to expand beyond the confines of a limited field of questions. Only an entrenched orthodoxy can block or resist the rethinking and re-evaluation of sources that were used, and in some cases, even abused by historians of previous generations.

Thus, a fresh reading of Barani's *Fatawa-i-Jahandari* reveals that instead of advocating the total annihilation of infidels, the author was actually calling for the dominance of Islam over infidelity. His arguments thus pertained to the realm of power relations; anywhere else, in his scheme of things, the Turkish Sultans were not supposed to discriminate between Muslim and non-Muslim subjects in such matters as providing protection and meting out justice. As mentioned earlier, important in this connection is Barani's view that just the shariat could no longer serve as a practical political framework. The author also proposed the formulation of an almost secular *zawabit-i-mulki* (state regulations) by an assembly comprising public intellectuals of the Sultanate. On the other hand, Barani's call for endowing extraordinary powers to the Sultan reminds one of Giorgio Agamben's 'state of exception' where hapless non-Muslims were liable to be killed without any ritual or ceremony.[22] The two propositions, justice to all and advocating the subduing of non-Muslims, sound like a contradiction in terms and reveal the complexities of the politics of the period. In a rather simplistic treatment of Barani's advice to rulers on the art of government, modern scholars condemn the author as a 'high born' racist courtier, Sunni fanatic and a frustrated old man, whose words are not important for understanding Sultanate politics.[23] Such an attitude is also clear in the attempt to downplay and even ignore the Naqshbandi Sufi, Sheikh Ahmad Sirhindi's activism in the early seventeenth century. However, the fact remains that the charismatic figures of Sirhindi and Shah Waliullah (who flourished in the eighteenth century) continue to inspire almost all forms of Islamic movements in the Subcontinent even now.[24]

At this point, a discussion on statecraft in a comparative framework would be a worthwhile exercise. Recent writings, for instance, Michel Foucault's insightful observations on transformations in political ideals and practices in the period between the sixteenth and eighteenth centuries,[25] would be particularly applicable to this case. This is also because Western texts used by Foucault and the medieval Persian sources that we are considering here both appear in the 'advice to princes' variety and 'art of government' forms. They have much in common—the 'origins' of all these texts go back to the Abbasid Caliphate (*c.* 750–1250 CE)[26] and, indeed, to ancient Greece, Iran and India.[27] Mention may be made here of the significant impact of Indian statecraft, as delineated in celebrated texts like the *Arthashastra* and *Panchatantra*, on early medieval Middle Eastern conceptions of government. One can refer in particular to Foucault's reading of Machiavelli's *The Prince*, written in 1505 (almost the same time when Ikhtiyar-ud-Din Husaini compiled his *Akhlaq-i-Humayuni*). A principal debate in this book is about the question of rationality being attached to the art of government—a position that sought to move away from 'theological foundations and religious justifications' of kingship.[28] Reminiscent of tensions in Persian writings about the power of the Sultan and shariat-driven juridical theories of sovereignty, some of the Western treatises also outlined, very much in line with the akhlaq text of Nasir-ud-Din Tusi, the range of the ruler's jurisdiction as including the art of self-discipline (adhering to moral values), the proper management of the family or household (involving economy) and politics or ruling the state (governing the population). Thus, a re-reading of these sources could also open interesting possibilities for looking at norms of governance and political practices in a comparative framework. Such a view could go beyond Central Asia, Iran and the Middle East, to Renaissance Europe, even if the state in 'pre-colonial' India under Muslim sovereigns was not 'governmentalized' in the Western sense and the specific details of their rule remained peculiar to South Asian Islam. As Arjomand has noted, scholars exposed to Indo-Persian statecraft and to Greco-Muslim conceptions of practical philosophy would find themselves 'fairly comfortably at home in the political culture' of Renaissance Italy and late-sixteenth-century France, despite 'divergence in the reception of Aristotle and political trajectories of medieval Islamic and West European Civilizations'.[29]

Thus, medieval India witnessed contestations for power and prestige between what may be referred to as institutions of authority such as rulers, nobles, ulama, Sufis and leaders of non-Muslim religious traditions, who deployed a range of resources, from linguistic tropes and religious justifications to personal charisma and brute force, to gain power. Committed to the cause of secularism and other contemporary ideological concerns such as certain forms of Marxism, modern scholars are reluctant to address these issues head on. The above discussion on aspects of literary and cultural production, political patronage and interconnections between religion and politics points to the possible uncovering of newer areas in the study of medieval Indian history.

Coming back to the discussion on Sufism, the rhythm of Islam in early medieval northern India can be studied using Sufi sources from the Sultanate period (thirteenth and fourteenth centuries) that have been largely neglected so far. These sources point to the role of Sufis in politics, as well as their interactions with non-Muslim religious leaders. It is clear that their world was politically unstable: the Sultanate kingship was unsteady; the Mongol advance threatened northern India directly; and non-Muslim chiefs waited for their moment and their victory could be dreadful news for Muslim lives and religious places. Many of these anxieties continued into the fifteenth and a major part of the sixteenth century, a period particularly noted for ambiguous relationships involving attractions and repulsions in matters of religion, not only at the level of the elite, but also in the realm of 'popular' culture. The appropriations and exclusions of religious ideas were often marked by critical questioning, compromises and accommodation. Sufi-Bhakti interactions, as we shall see in chapter seven, were not an innocent and happy mixing of Islam and Hinduism as some modern historians would like to portray them.

In this milieu of uncertainty and insecurity, while rulers were wary of the ulama's occasional bigotry and fanaticism, the bonds of shared religion did hold the Muslim ruling class together in a region inhabited by a vast Hindu majority. The rulers needed the Sufi masters' support for legitimizing their authority, but the latter's response was variable: ranging from keeping their distance from rulers zealously to providing active support in military campaigns. The Sufis' otherworldliness notwithstanding, contemporary accounts are full of worldly difficulties they faced with various 'others': Sultans, ulama, rival Sufi masters, Hindu kings and masses of unbelievers. Collective opinion believed in their charitable endeavours, paranormal powers, understanding of Islamic law, and, above all, in their moral integrity, a feature that enabled them to hold their own against all others.

The response of the Sufis to their predominantly Hindu environment too was divergent. Alongside difficulties, the great masters received widespread devotion from people across social strata and religious affiliations, and their popularity rested on their easy accessibility and use of the vernacular. For drawing converts to Islam, their charismatic influence received much credit in oft-repeated hagiographies. However, a master who employed yogic practices in his own religious experience could advise lesser men to stay clear of Hindu mystics for though the latter's conception of God could be considered acceptable, they were *not* Muslim. And given the uncertain political scene, some Sufis were clearly hostile to Hindus. We will examine the Sufis' negotiations with their Indian environment in some detail later in this book.[30]

Turning to the *Fatawa-i-Jahandari*, Barani's career and context in general also need careful study as it would be inaccurate to say that his thoughts were unique. His contemporary and near-contemporary authors such as Sayyid Ali Hamadani and Fakhr-i-Mudabbir also proffer similar formulations. Also, many of the views expressed in these works appear to be canonical as they are attributed in many cases to the second rightly-guided caliph, Umar ibn al-Khattab. It is important to keep in mind that the evolution of ideas in classical Islamic thought has shown two different, yet interdependent facets.

On the one hand, the doctrinaires, mainly jurists (*mufti*s) and judges (*qazi*s), who have interpreted regulations in a restrictive way, seek to develop a programme which, if not one of persecution, is at least vexatious and repressive. From time to time, a sovereign, either through Islamic zeal or because of a need for the support of Muslims, carried out measures to the doctrinaires' satisfaction. Also, sometimes, there were outbursts of popular anger against *zimmi*s (protected people of the book), which in some cases, arose because of the higher social status they enjoyed as a result of their being in the higher ranks of administration, especially that of finance.[31] Several examples can be given in the medieval Indian context of the articulation of such protests, for instance, by Barani, Abdul Quddus Gangohi, Abdul Qadir Badauni and Sheikh Ahmad Sirhindi. But, on the other hand, practice often fell very short of the programme of purists, which was hardly ever implemented. Moreover, the different schools of jurisprudence were rarely all in agreement and some of them reiterated rules without intending any practical effect.

With these caveats in mind, reconsidering the *Fatawa-i-Jahandari* of the mid-fourteenth-century courtier and intellectual Ziya-ud-Din Barani will also be useful for uncovering his views on *kafirs*[32] and Hindus. Who were the kafirs (the infidels) in the medieval Indian context? How did Muslims characterize idol-worshipping non-Muslims? Did they know and identify them as Hindus? Were these Hindus categorized as kafirs or as zimmis? If there were any ambiguities in categorization, in what contexts did the categorization change from kafirs to zimmis, and vice versa? How much *jizya*, discriminatory tax, was demanded, from whom and when, and who collected it? How many temples were destroyed, by whom and when? How many temples could survive, were maintained and constructed in medieval India? What does the construction of temples mean for Islamic iconoclasm and monotheism? Did all Muslims think alike on the question of classifying non-Muslims and on the treatment to be meted out to them? If not, what were the different views? To what extent were Muslim rulers receptive to the differing 'agendas' of different groups of people? What were the limitations of the political authorities? Was the shariat inadequate to address the problems faced by Muslim rulers in a predominantly non-Muslim region? Even if the proverbial 'gates of *ijtihad*' or fresh interpretation of Islamic law were not closed and the shariat could potentially be re-interpreted to deal with new questions in a new setting, could it be implemented as the law of the land? To what extent did ruptures within Indian Islam—struggles between different *mazahib* or schools of jurisprudence; sectarian divisions; differences between ulama and Sufi orders; and between traditionalist and rationalist Muslims—limit the scope for creating conditions in which a monolithic Islam could construct and deal with a non-Muslim 'other'?

These and many such questions of crucial import for the study of Muslim attitudes towards non-Muslims need to be addressed and resolved. On the other hand, the equally important question is, how did the vast majority of non-Muslims/Hindus respond to the advent of Islam in India? What were the strategies they adopted when successive generations of Turks, Afghans and Mughals wielded considerable political power, or how did they perceive Muslim rule? What were the factors which allowed for non-Muslims to join the political process? What were the opportunities offered to them? Or were they completely unaffected, silent all the time, and shut off from politics? If not, what were the sites of interaction? Did Muslims and Hindus consider themselves as separate communities? Did religious identities exist? If yes, in what forms? Finally, can the formation of community identities be understood only in terms of colonialism and modernity, or there can be some alternative ways of looking at the problem? Our ignorance about these questions does not prove their irrelevance. Many of these issues may have contemporary resonance and, indeed, are legitimate research questions. We will return to some of these issues in chapter three.

Two Mughal emperors, Jalal-ud-Din Muhammad Akbar (ruled 1556–1605 CE) and Alamgir Aurangzeb (ruled 1658–1707 CE), have particularly attracted attention in recent discussions on the nature of medieval politics and its repercussions on communal relations in India. Modern opinion on their religious policies and actions are polarized: for the Hindu communalists, the re-imposition of the discriminatory tax, jizya, by Aurangzeb in 1679 is generally regarded as a turning point in the history of the Mughal empire in India that led to the alienation of Rajputs, Marathas and Hindus in general, and also hastened the disintegration of the Mughal empire.[33] On the other hand, for Muslim separatists, the 1679 imposition of jizya was caused by a growing spirit of opposition to the empire among Hindus, leaving Aurangzeb with no option but to appeal to the loyalty of the Muslims by reverting to a more specifically Muslim state.[34] Thirdly, battling communal polarization and biased readings of history, secular nationalists have once again followed hackneyed stereotypes. For them, Akbar was 'good', liberal, secular and compassionate; and Aurangzeb, 'bad', narrow-minded and bigoted. Also, in this blatantly 'present-minded' scholarship, modern ideological concerns such as secularism and nationalism, etc., are projected backward in time to present a sanitized picture of medieval India, and a ruler such as Akbar is even called the originator of the idea of Indian nationalism![35]

A more empirically sustainable approach requires a study of the religious policies of the two emperors in their contemporary political and social contexts. Akbar's well-known religious policy of 'peace with all' (*sulh-i-kul)* may be situated in the context of his attempts at winning wide political support for the empire. His initial abolition of inequitable measures such as the pilgrimage or jizya tax occurred in the 1560s, when he was endeavouring to recruit Rajput nobles into imperial service. However, when he had to resort to the use of force against his Rajput opponents, as he did at Chitor in 1568, Akbar issued a 'proclamation of victory' (*fath-nama*), exulting in his having waged a *jihad* (holy war) against infidelity. In the 1570s, while trying to attract Indian Muslims to the imperial cause, he re-imposed the discriminatory jizya tax on non-Muslims, and even had himself declared the 'king of Islam' in the manifesto (*mahzar*) of 1579, which was signed by leading ulama. According to reports, in some cases, the ulama were forced by the emperor to do so. When such drastic measures still failed to prevent the outbreak of serious rebellion among his Muslim nobles in 1580–81, Akbar abandoned his 'pro-Islamic' policy and returned to a conciliatory posture on religious matters.[36] The need here is to guard against the pitfalls of an instrumentalist kind of reading of evidence, that is, to assume that Akbar and Aurangzeb were compelled to do what they did as if they had no larger agenda or policy.

Yet, beyond the question of discord and hostility between Hindus and Muslims, and the growth of a spirit of religious particularism, both of which are regarded by communalists as the primary factors that prompted the re-imposition of jizya by Aurangzeb, it is also necessary to take into account political and economic developments in the empire, religious trends at the court, and, in particular, the controversy regarding the nature of the state, which had continued, with some changes, since the establishment of Muslim rule in India. Further, we need to consider the political conditions of the Deccan, which had begun to deteriorate sharply from 1676 onwards, as well as the emperor's perception that some striking declaration was needed to rally Sunni Muslim opinion in the face of the Marathas' alliance with the Shi'ite state of Golconda. As one of such moves, the jizya was re-imposed.[37]

Comparisons of the composition of the nobility under Akbar and Aurangzeb—comprising Turanis (Central Asians), Iranis (Persians), Indian Muslims (*sheikh-zadas*), Afghans, Rajputs, Marathas and other Hindus—also lead to interesting insights into the divergence of actual Mughal politics and later perceptions of it. This is especially true in the case of the suggestion that Aurangzeb's adopting a hostile attitude towards the Rajputs led to their widespread rebellion, which, in turn, sounded the death-knell of the Mughal empire. Such generalizations are not supported by evidence, which actually points to the increased presence of non-Muslim (particularly Rajput and Maratha) nobles of high rank in Aurangzeb's service.[38]

Also, with regard to the issue of the desecration of temples mentioned earlier, contrary to popular notions, very few temples were actually demolished in medieval India under Muslim rule. Temples were attacked in the context of violent campaigns for political conquest and as a statement of regime change, that is, non-Muslim rulers were no longer in a position to patronize or maintain religious institutions in regions brought under the direct control of a Muslim ruler.[39] Subsequently, however, patronage to these places of worship came in the form of revenue-free land grants issued by Muslim kings, including Akbar and Aurangzeb. Even under a most Muslim-friendly rule like that of Aurangzeb, during times of peace, an old temple could not be demolished even if attempts were otherwise made to prevent the construction of new temples (according to a supposed juridical decree). Finally, if surviving historic temples in our time are any indication, it would seem that not only have so many places of worship of non-Muslims been spared, but many were also actually built in the medieval period.

A recent study has also shattered the myth of a bigoted Aurangzeb being against such cultural forms as music, which allegedly declined because of a ban imposed by him in accordance with the tenets of orthodox Sunnite Islam. Katherine Brown has questioned the received wisdom on Aurangzeb's alleged suppression of music and showed how the ruler's possible distancing from certain musical forms or instruments for a period did not affect musical practices and cannot be stretched to prove another example of a Mughal policy shift towards puritanism and intolerance. As a matter of fact, not a single Indo-Persian treatise on music, written between 1660 and 1750, mentions any restrictions on music during Aurangzeb's reign. Neither do they refer to any large-scale departure or dismissal of musicians from the imperial court. Ignoring this and other such evidence of Aurangzeb's interest in music and its patronage by his sons and nobles, historians have uncritically subscribed to the notion that emperor had banned music and ordered its boycott as a corrupt and un-Islamic art form.[40]

Let us return to some of these issues with reference to the religious debates in Akbar's *ibadat-khana* (literally, hall for prayer) and more generally, with regard to the Quranic injunction on recommending right and forbidding wrong. For this purpose, we will refer to Abdul Qadir Badauni's report in his *Muntakhab-ut-Tawarikh*, which serves as a counter-narrative to Abul Fazl's celebratory account of Akbar's reign. Badauni, a traditionally inclined noble of Akbar's court, participated and sometimes even moderated discussions in the ibadat-khana and found much of the discussion there not only heretical, but also aimed at pleasing the emperor who was disgusted with the Islamic orthodoxy and therefore willing to listen to any voice of reason (see chapter four). The orthodoxy's attempt at safeguarding tradition is further illustrated in a classic text on adab composed by Abdul Haqq Muhaddis Dehlawi (see chapter five). Abdul Haqq enjoyed a considerable reputation as a leading scholar of the Traditions of the Prophet in Mughal India and was, just like Badauni, a witness of and participant in the discussions on Islam. The discussion of their work in later chapters will reveal the range of themes debated in Mughal India in the latter half of the sixteenth and first half of the seventeenth century, and also bring to the fore strategies deployed by various interested parties. In chapter six, I will examine the actual possibilities that existed of defying Sunni Muslim norms of conduct. Thus, we will seek to answer the question: were Islamic theoretical positions mere ideals to be reiterated by the ulama even as deviance from or violations of religious and social norms might have been the order of the day?

The interaction between Islam and other religious traditions in medieval India led to many different kinds of responses. The origins and development of the religious ideas of Guru Nanak, the founder of Sikhism, may be located in the Sufi-Bhakti complex of late-fifteenth- and early-sixteenth-century north India. This is most clearly reflected in the inclusion of the devotional songs of a large number of saint-poets belonging to diverse mystical traditions in the Sikh scripture *Guru Granth Saheb*, which was first compiled in the late-sixteenth century. Later editions, including the final authoritative version prepared in the eighteenth century, have persisted with compositions of religious leaders outside the fold of the hierarchy of Sikh Gurus, and include poems by a leading thirteenth-century Chishti Sufi sheikh of Punjab, Farid-ud-Din Ganj-i-Shakar, popularly known as Baba Farid. This is despite the fact that the formation of the *khalsa* had already occurred. The khalsa was the religious community of the Sikhs with strict markers of identity that was founded when Mughal-Sikh conflicts through the seventeenth and eighteenth centuries completely vitiated relations between Sikhism and Islam. Large-scale confrontations over political power transformed Sikhism from a syncretic religious tradition drawing heavily on beliefs and practices from Islam to outright hostility towards the latter. Sikh tradition both laments and celebrates the 'martyrdom' of the Gurus following recurrent clashes with the Mughals. Despite political violence and the standardization of Sikhism as a religion of the book, independent of both Islam and forms of Hinduism, Guru Nanak's image as a holy man comparable to a Sufi sheikh survives in popular Muslim tradition.

This is particularly important as examples included here are from a literary tradition, Urdu, which is often condemned as the communal or ghettoized language of Islam in the Indian Subcontinent.[41] A more dispassionate reading of Urdu literature and history will reveal a remarkable attempt to explore the possibility of a middle ground in social and political relations between Muslims and others in India. This could be as true for liberals as for conservatives.[42]

The ability to reach out and connect with the audience in an acceptable language of the time has been one of the distinguishing features of Sufi traditions through the ages. As we shall see in chapter seven, despite sustained onslaughts from secular-rationalists and reform-minded Islamists (Wahhabi/Deobandi), devotional Islam has been able to survive because of its capacity to adapt to changing social and political contexts. Historically, this has been characterized by a kind of 'double-movement' in which Sufic Islam gets entrenched in the dominant culture of the time and place even while being mindful of the terms of reference of Islam as derived from the Quran and the hadis, the Traditions of Prophet Muhammad.[43] Sufi traditions are also distinguished from Islamist groups by their sensitivity towards historical Islam, as is represented by the veneration for saints and by their attempts to safeguard customs and traditions of earlier times, thus allowing for concessions in certain situations, such as tolerating religious and cultural differences. In the following chapters, we will return to some of these issues, which are of crucial importance for an informed understanding of the history of Islam in India. Such an exercise can facilitate a better appreciation of the Muslim question in the Subcontinent, as many different forms of Islam and Muslim religiosity are here to stay. It is best to negotiate with them with care, sensitivity and understanding.

2

Sufi Traditions and the Emergence of Islam in the Subcontinent

Sufism began as a spiritual revolt against the worldliness and rampant materialism of the Ummayad and Abbasid Caliphates within the first couple of centuries of the emergence of Islam (seventh and eighth centuries CE). Famous early figures of the movement include Bayazid Bustami, Rabiya Basari and Hasan Basari, who led simple, ascetic lives and aspired to achieve union with God through meditation and other spiritual disciplines. The early mystics of Islam, who were often charismatic leaders with popular appeal, eventually organized and the movement became institutionalized in silsilas, which, over time, branched into quite a few competing strands. Beginning with the influential mystic circles of Baghdad, Sufi networks were established in lower Iraq, Iberia, Egypt, north-eastern Iran and Central Asia between the ninth and twelfth centuries. Even as genealogies, distinct rituals and norms, and self-conscious attempts to follow the path laid down by Prophet Muhammad remained the defining features of these silsilas, they were also noted for their adaptation of and compromise with the dominant social and religious milieu in the areas where they spread. In some cases, their departures and deviance pushed them out of the pale of the accepted limits of transgressions in Sunnite Islam. Thus, the Sufi movement not only grew into an established system of faith and worship in Islam, but also had popular appeal in Islamic societies even before the emergence of the Delhi Sultanate in the thirteenth century.[1]

Of the various Sufi orders that emerged, four enjoyed considerable importance in India. Two of these, the Chishtis and Suhrawardis, flourished in the Sultanate period, while the Qadiri and Naqshbandi orders gained importance in the Mughal period. To start with, the living Sufi master (referred to as *sheikh, khwaja* or *pir*) guided followers at his dwelling place (*khanqah/ jamatkhana*), but later, the shrines (*dargah*s) of the Sufi masters of earlier generations grew in importance and became places of pilgrimage, eventually forming a sacred geography of Sufism, called *wilayat*, which led to struggles and competition for control of territory, followers and resources. The leading early figures of the Chishti order were Muin-ud-Din Chishti Ajmeri, Qutb-ud-Din Bakhtiyar Kaki, Sheikh Farid-ud-Din Ganj-i-Shakar (who is venerated in the Sikh tradition as Baba Farid), Nizam-ud-Din Auliya and Naṣir-ud-Din Chiragh-i-Dehli. A comparable figure in the competing Suhrawardi order was Baha-ud-Din Zakariya, who was based in Punjab.

What distinguished Sufism from other forms of Islam was the belief that a human soul could achieve union with God. This belief was later formulated as the doctrine of 'wahdat-ul-wujud' (unity of existence, or monism as a reality) by Ibn-i-Arabi. This doctrine often brought Sufis into conflict with the Islamic orthodoxy of the Delhi Sultanate (represented by the Hanafite Sunni ulama or theologians),[2] who asserted that since God was unique, to suggest that a human soul could achieve union with God was to imply that there was no distinction between God and human beings. For this reason, even before Islam came to India, 'heterodox' Sufis were persecuted elsewhere for heresy. The examples of Bayazid and Mansur Hallaj come to mind, though it is possible that the persecution of the latter had more to do with a political intervention that went awry than his heretical spiritual ideas. Sufis were also targeted by the ulama for their occasional indifference to formal religious practices such as regular congregational prayers (*namaz/salat*) and their focus on meditation and spiritual exercises, including the use of music. The legitimacy of listening to music during *sama* or *qawwali* was a major difference between the ulama and Sufis, an issue that will be discussed at length later.

The Sufis also played a significant role in the growth and development of vernacular literature (Urdu, Hindi, Deccani, etc.). By contrast, the court culture was crucial to the spread and dominance of Persian as the language of power and government. The Sufis' contribution to the spread of poetry and music is equally notable and the Chishtis even used song and dance techniques of concentration for achieving spiritual ecstasy. Sufism, therefore, contributed greatly to the development of both Indian folk and classical culture.

The belief in wahdat-ul-wujud and several techniques of meditation brought the Sufis spiritually very close to certain strands of non-Muslim religious traditions already existing in the Indian Subcontinent. For example, the Advaita Hinduism stream believed that the *atma* (human soul) and *parmatma* (God) were one and the same, a theory similar in principle to wahdat-ul-wujud. Similarly, the Sufis found much to learn from Hindu disciplines such as yoga, which influenced their meditation techniques. Mention may be made here of the popular practice of *pranayam* (breath control) and the rare, but more spectacular *chilla-i-makus*, that is, hanging oneself upside down from a tree at the mouth of a well—a spiritual exercise which was generally conducted in private and in the darkness of the night.[3]

If Sufis learnt from non-Muslim traditions; local, Indic traditions were also powerfully affected by the principles of Islam as represented by the Sufi saints. (Here, it is important to note that 'local', 'foreign' and 'Indic' are sensitive categories which must be used with care.) The teachings of Kabir and Guru Nanak both show the clear imprint of Sufi Islam. The criticism of idol worship, of 'useless' ritual, the emphasis on human equality, and the worship of, and excessive devotion towards one God, can all be traced to Sufism. In the case of Sikhism, whole sections of the *Guru Granth Saheb* consist of Sufi poetry. However, it is interesting to remember that Sikhism transformed from a syncretic, devotional movement inspired by Sufi Islam into a sect hostile to Islam for political reasons (discussed in chapter seven). The history of disturbed relations between Islam and Sikhism notwithstanding, Sufism's greatest contribution to Indian culture is considered to be the example it set for religious and cultural co-existence. Indian Sufi orders showed that Muslim and non-Muslim religious traditions could prosper side by side and learn from each other, providing, from the point of view of the contemporary demands of secular politics, a shining example of fruitful syncretism.

Their closeness to non-Muslim traditions helped the Sufis play an important role in the Islamization of the Subcontinent, even if many of them were not working with an explicit agenda of this sort. Yet, the presence of Sufis was the main factor in the conversion of significant sections of the Subcontinent's population to Islam. To start with, khanqahs and dargahs became centres where Muslims and non-Muslims gathered for worship, meditation or spiritual experience and sought blessings and benediction from Sufi masters. The process of conversion started with devotion towards a particular Sufi, which led to syncretic sects, symbolizing only half or partial conversion. Eventually, there emerged communities of Muslims who professed Islam formally, but continued with their local customs, practices and traditions, which were condemned by the puritanical, reformist Islamic orthodoxy. Reformist movements have gained ground particularly from the eighteenth and nineteenth centuries onwards (see chapter seven). However, it may be noted here that Indian Sufism made a significant contribution through the reformist Naqshbandi Sufi Sheikh Ahmad Sirhindi's development of the idea of *wahdat-us-shuhud* (unity of witness) in opposition to the more widely accepted wahdat-ul-wujud (more on this later).

The ulama's attitude towards the Sufis was traditionally hostile, for the former considered many Sufi ideas and practices heretical from the point of view of their own interpretation of the shariat. The ulama in India were concerned with guarding orthodoxy rather than spreading Islam and their contact with non-Muslims was limited and unproductive. Yet, the role played by the Sufis in conversion and Islamization was not counted as important by the ulama because they thought that the quality of Islam practised and preached by the Sufis was inadequate and inferior. In fact, the ulama attacked many Sufi practices, condemning them as un-Islamic. For this, they also often used political power (for more on the social and political role of the ulama, especially in relation to the Quranic injunction on recommending right and forbidding wrong, see chapter five).

The relationship between Sufi orders and the state is also considered to have been distant. Orders like the Chishtis refused to accept money or support from rulers. They believed that involvement in politics led to materialism and worldliness, which they wished to avoid. However, this attitude varied across silsilas and even differed between Sufis of the same order. Whereas the Chishtis recommended aloofness from the state, the Suhrawardis had no qualms about associating with the Sultans' court. Even the Chishtis of the Deccan accepted patronage from the state. The Naqshbandis and the Qadiris were also known for their political involvements during the Mughal period, though the representatives of the two silsilas displayed remarkable divergences in their approach to contemporary social and political issues.

Much of what has been said above about the Sufis of the Delhi Sultanate and of medieval India generally, has been derived from modern historical writings based on Sufi sources in the Persian and vernacular languages. Sufi literature includes (i) malfuzat (discourses of a Sufi compiled by a disciple, *murid*, generally during the lifetime of the Sufi), (ii) maktubat (letters, written by a Sufi to his disciples), (iii) mystical treatises on Sufism prepared by Sufi sheikhs, (iv) compilations of Sufi poetry, and (v) tazkiras (hagiographies of Sufis, compiled generally after the death of a Sufi). Important information on Sufi activities can also be found in court chronicles and general histories, particularly on matters relating to the Sufis' relations with rulers.[4]

In this chapter, we will study literature on Sufi masters of the Sultanate period based in upper north India, chiefly

Chishti malfuzat and tazkiras that celebrate the role they played in the spread of Islam in the Subcontinent. In particular, we will focus on their role in politics and their interactions with non-Muslim religious leaders, including yogis, gurus, Brahmins and sanyasis. These sources use the words 'kafir' (infidel), '*ghayr-muslim*' (non-Muslim) and 'Hindu'; accordingly, we shall refer to these categories as infidels, non-Muslims and Hindus. Further, Sufi narratives do not always match those that were written outside their circles. Non-Muslim traditions have a very different representation both of this period and of encounters with Muslim mystics.[5] Besides, within Islam, many people, especially the 'official' ulama, were ready to denounce the Sufis. The moderate amongst them criticized the 'bad' quality of Islam practised and occasionally preached, if at all, by the Sufis. Moreover, the Muslim mystic movement was far from homogenous. The Chishtis' religious ideas and notions about the social roles of their *khwajagan* (leading preceptors from the past) did not have many takers amongst the Suhrawardis, and later, the Naqshbandis. Within the Chishti silsila itself, the attitude of individual Sufi masters differed on many important aspects, from the importance given to sama as part of the mystical practice of *zikr* (remembrance of God) to their attitudes towards conversion and Islamization. The rest of this chapter is an attempt at making sense of a portion of Sufi literature pertinent to the history of the Delhi Sultanate.[6]

The study of the Sultanate period has been marginal to the concerns of most medieval historians. A common excuse for this neglect is the alleged lack of sufficient source material; but there have also been other factors. This lack of attention has also stemmed from certain basic assumptions, which have been shaped by contemporary ideological issues. For instance, the celebration of the achievements of Mughal emperor Akbar during the dark medieval age of 'intolerance' and 'fragmented' polities has meant that the history of the earlier Sultanate period has been de-emphasized.

The few studies that exist on the Delhi Sultanate are largely based on court chronicles and political histories. These accounts are resolutely centred on the activities of the Sultans and present a 'top down' view of history.[7] Sufi literature, on the other hand, offers rich data on social and political processes, and presents a view from below of disgruntled elites and depressed commoners. A valuable portion of this literature, which was in circulation during the mid-fourteenth century and was subsequently used by authorities such as Amir Khwurd, Sheikh Jamali and Abdul Haqq Muhaddis Dehlawi, has been dubbed as 'forged' and denied any historical value.[8] The abundance of miracle stories attributed to the Sufis in this literature is an important reason for the neglect of these sources. But then, such tales are found in the so-called genuine texts too.[9] Most historians also prefer to put this literature aside in the belief that the Sufis, in general, and Chishtis, in particular, kept away from the politics and government of their times.[10] Finally, for nearly four decades, the history of religion or ideas was a neglected stream because of the dominance of Marxist historians in medieval Indian historiography. The historians of this 'school' saw the Sufis as 'parasitic' and extraneous to the political economy of the time and hence their literature was considered to be of little value. We shall appraise some such observations later in this chapter.[11]

A new chapter began in the history of the Subcontinent with the eastward expansion of Islam in the last decade of the twelfth century and the establishment of a series of Islamicate Sultanates. The Ghurid forces of Muiz-ud-Din bin Sam, referred to as the *lashkar-i-islam* in early sources,[12] overran Ghaznavid Punjab. The Rajput resistance was smothered at Tarain in 1192.[13] The Muslim army went on to occupy large swathes of territory in upper north India[14] and eliminated the symbols of Rajput power and prestige in the region. Remarkably, there was no general massacre and no major demographic dislocation. As much as the chroniclers celebrated the conquest of new territories, the conquerors preferred minimum use of force and violence. Though iconoclasm may have been a motivating factor for some soldiers, places of worship were generally plundered for their wealth. Alternatively, their despoliation was aimed at hammering home the point that the old regime was overthrown and that it could no longer protect the people and their religious places.[15] The general public was thus made aware that the Turks and their Sultan had established a new Islamic order. Indeed, the minaret attached to Delhi's congregational mosque, which later became known as the Qutb Minar, was subsequently perceived as a victory tower. Among the prime targets of Ghurid campaigns were Muslim Ghaznavids as well, but the Muslims of the Sultanate period particularly liked to remember how they defeated the infidels.

Given their inaccurate understanding of the Sultanate as an Islamic state, the ulama wanted the Sultans to present Hindus of the dominion with the choice of death or Islam. The ulama's pressurizing was ignored—a measure that speaks of the rulers' attempts at rapprochement with non-Muslims. The Turks had realized that it was difficult to rule a mainly non-Muslim population using a narrow interpretation of the shariat. Instead, they tried to evolve a broad, 'secular' or non-theocratic state law, *zawabit-i-mulki*,[16] while still maintaining public protestations of respect to Muslim divines and their institutions.

The enthronement of Sultan Qutb-ud-Din Aybak (ruled 1206–10) at Lahore coincided with the election of Chenghis Khan as the great leader of the Mongols.[17] It is important to mention here that the Mongol hordes and Chenghis were not Muslims, a common misconception caused by the title 'Khan'. They practised forms of animism or shamanism, but their descendants and followers later embraced Buddhism, Islam and Christianity, not necessarily in that order. The Mongol irruption witnessed large-scale devastation in Central and West Asia over the next fifty years, that is, the first half of the thirteenth century.

Major centres of Islam like Bukhara and Baghdad were sacked. The Subcontinent did not witness any major attack, though Punjab and Sindh were exposed to the threat. Escaping the wrath of the Tartars, Islam prospered in the Sultanate with the name of the caliph being included in the *khutba* (Friday sermons) and the *sikka* (coins). This period also witnessed the large-scale immigration of Muslims, including a number of Sufis.

Sufi institutions like the khanqah (hospice) and dargah (shrine) have greatly contributed to shaping the harmonious culture of the Subcontinent. The presence of Chishti Sufis particularly ensured that force was not used to convert the general population to Islam. Though the Islamic orthodoxy strove for the total annihilation of kafirs, the seemingly liberal approach of the Sufis proved more appealing to the early Sultans. The rulers themselves detested the arrogance of the ulama and felt that the Sufis' position on the treatment to be meted out to Hindus, and generally on matters related to the shariat, was more apt. The Sultanate thus had a fairly 'secular' and broad-based polity, though religious institutions did play important roles. Controversial religious issues that had the potential to create difficulties occasionally came to the fore, but in the end, sanity prevailed. The Sultans were careful to avoid violence and hostility. The extent to which there was theoretical support for Muslims to live in peace with others remains to be explored; though, as mentioned in chapter one, the akhlaq texts did show that it was possible for a Muslim polity to deploy justifications for its political measures based on broader historical experience. As a result, Hindus were given the status of zimmis or *ahl-i-kitab*, People of the Book, like Jews and Christians and later, Zoroastrians, in the matter of collecting jizya from them, but they were condemned as kafirs as well, especially in hostile contexts. Theoretically speaking, zimmis are to be protected and kafirs, eliminated. To grapple with the seeming contradiction in how the infidels of the Subcontinent were treated, we need to know the authors and the context in which they wrote. Ziya-ud-Din Barani (a companion of Sultan Muhammad Tughluq and disciple of the Sufi sheikh, Nizam-ud-Din Auliya), who eventually emerged as a major historian and political theorist, took an extremely provocative position on these questions. He not only wanted kafirs to be subdued and humiliated, but even wanted to suppress 'low-born' Indian converts to Islam. Apparently, not all his ideas were considered practical even in his circle. We shall return to Barani's political ideas in the next chapter.

In a way, it augured well for the history of Islam in India that reportedly, one of the first Muslims born in the capital, Delhi, after the Turkish conquest went on to become a Chishti Sufi with a reputation for syncretic proclivities: Sheikh Hamid-ud-Din (d. 1274).[18] The sheikh was a disciple and *khalifa* (spiritual successor) of Muin-ud-Din Chishti Ajmeri.[19] Muin-ud-Din, in turn, is said to have dreamt of Prophet Muhammad directing him to go to Hindustan from Medina. The khwaja's arrival coincided with the Turkish conquest of northern India.

Sufi tradition claims that Muin-ud-Din had prophesied a Ghurid victory in the second battle of Tarain because the Chauhan ruler, Rai Pithaura or Prithviraj, was reportedly harassing the sheikh and his disciples at Ajmer, in the state of Rajasthan in western India. Later traditions also assert that the Sufi sheikh displayed miraculous powers to subdue the Chauhan ruler. Amir Khwurd, who wrote in the mid-fourteenth century, too refers to the sheikh's miraculous powers. According to him, when Muin-ud-Din reached Ajmer, Rai Pithaura was the ruler there. The ruler and his officials resented the sheikh's presence in the area, but the latter's eminence and power to perform miracles prompted them to resist. Meanwhile, a disciple of the sheikh who was in the service of the Rajput king began to be treated in a hostile manner and the sheikh sent a message to the king on his behalf. Pithaura apparently refused to accept Muin-ud-Din's recommendation and took exception to the sheikh's alleged ability to know the secrets of the Unseen. When the Sufi master, called '*badshah-i-islam*' by the biographer, heard this, he commented: 'Pithaura has been captured alive and handed over to the army of Islam' (*pithaura ra zinda giraftim wa dadim ba lashkar-i-islam*). At about the same time Muiz-ud-Din's army reportedly arrived from Ghaznin and defeated the Rajputs.[20]

Amir Khwurd also utilized material in the malfuzat, or Sufi discourses, which highlighted Muin-ud-Din as a preacher and Islamizer with considerable charismatic power. Amir Khwurd wrote that infidelity and idol worship were widespread in Hindustan before the arrival of the sheikh and that people here worshipped stones, trees, animals and even cow dung. The hearts of the inhabitants of Hindustan were reportedly sealed in the darkness of infidelity. The author claimed that with the coming of the saint, the dark clouds of ignorance gave way to the spiritual light of Islam. Addressing the Sufi master as the true *muin* or helper of the faith, the Chishti biographer claimed that the credit for the conversion of the people of Hindustan goes to the sheikh and to those whose further preaching transformed this enemy land, *dar-ul-harb*, into the abode of Islam, *dar-ul-islam*.[21]

Theoretically, dar-ul-islam is a territory where the shariat prevails as the supreme law of the land, guaranteeing a privileged position to the members of the community of Islam, the *umma*.[22] Others like the zimmis could stay in the dominion with the assurance that their lives would be protected and that they would have some amount of freedom to practise their religions. In the Indian case, the position of the Hindus in the Sultanate remained ambivalent even though the Sultanate was far from a shariat-driven Islamic state. Occasional rhetoric notwithstanding, no concerted effort for a complete political and religious transformation was undertaken and Sufis were also satisfied with the respect and spiritual authority that they enjoyed in the dominion. The veneration showed by the people, even if they did not formally convert to Islam, was gratifying enough.

We will return to the question of the Sufis' attitude towards conversion later, but Muin-ud-Din's popularity amongst non-Muslims needs to be mentioned here. The fact that infidels visited the sheikh's tomb every year and offered large sums to the keepers of the shrine is extolled by Sufi biographers. In early Muslim perception, however, the sheikh was the harbinger of the faith in the region of Ajmer. This image of the sheikh is also reflected in non-Sufi literature of the period. Referring to Sultan Muhammad Tughluq's visit to Muin-ud-Din's tomb in the second quarter of the fourteenth century, the chronicler Isami, in his *Futuh-us-Salatin*, called the sheikh the refuge of the faith of Islam.[23] Evidently, the sheikh's charisma, both as living master and as he lay in his grave, won him a large following, and his khalifas spread out in all directions. Hamid-ud-Din, the child born in Delhi, went to live in a village near Nagaur, a district not far from Ajmer. He cultivated a small plot of land, became a vegetarian, and seemingly led a life that conformed to his Hindu environment.

Muin-ud-Din Chishti chose the more sophisticated Qutb-ud-Din Bakhtiyar Kaki (d. 1235) for the cosmopolitan wilayat of Delhi.[24] Bakhtiyar Kaki was born in Ush on the banks of the Jaxartes in Central Asia. He reportedly met Muin-ud-Din first during the course of his travels to the Abbasid capital, Baghdad, where he became his disciple. Following his pir (preceptor) Muin-ud-Din, who is styled in Sufi literature as 'the Sultan of Hind', Bakhtiyar Kaki reached Delhi during the reign of Shams-ud-Din Iltutmish (ruled 1211–36). The ruler welcomed the sheikh and invited him to live in the city. Though initially hesitant, Bakhtiyar Kaki finally agreed, but had to compete for space in the spiritual geography of the city. Besides the ulama, quite a few eminent Sufis of various lineages had already settled there. Many had just arrived, following the Mongol invasion of Central Asia and Iran. Bakhtiyar Kaki found his most powerful antagonist in Sheikh-ul-Islam Najm-ud-Din Sughra, a Sufi from his own order. (Najm-ud-Din and Bakhtiyar Kaki's pir were disciples of the same sheikh, Usman Harwani.) Najm-ud-Din did not take kindly to Bakhtiyar Kaki's growing popularity and influence in political circles.

To prevent this tension from escalating, Muin-ud-Din, on a visit to Delhi, asked his disciple to accompany him to Ajmer.[25] The news of the saints' departure was perceived as a sign of calamity by Sultan Iltutmish and the people. They followed the sheikhs for miles, crying and wailing. Touched by the grief of the ruler and the ruled alike, Muin-ud-Din asked Bakhtiyar Kaki to remain in Delhi.[26] As the patron saint of the city, Bakhtiyar Kaki enjoyed prestige and authority, and in a measure, influenced the Sultan's style of governance. The Sultan, whose authority as the head of the hierarchy of theologians and jurists was undisputed, followed his contemporary Abbasid caliph, al-Nasir's approach of using a prominent Sufi order as the official organization of popular Islam under the ruler, thus combining the pietistic legality of the ulama with the spiritual adventures of the Chishti Sufis.[27] No wonder then that Sufi institutions like khanqahs and jamatkhanas flourished along with mosques and *madrasa*s.

The weakness of the rulers and the supremacy of the nobles were two important features of the period following Iltutmish's death. Within a decade of his death, the nobles put four of his descendants on the throne and removed them at will. The next twenty years saw his slaves exterminate his dynasty by executing all the male members of his family. One of his slaves, Ghiyas-ud-Din Balban, ruled from Delhi for over forty years, beginning from about the middle of the thirteenth century—acting first as *naib* (deputy) of the puppet Sultan Nasir-ud-Din Mahmud (ruled 1246–66)[28] and subsequently ascending the throne of Delhi as Sultan (ruled 1266–87). When Balban came to power, the Mongols had already ravaged a major part of the Muslim world. Having sacked Punjab, they were threatening to take Delhi. It was finally Balban's aggressive anti-Mongol policy that protected the Sultanate from Mongol depredations.[29]

The suppression of 'rebellious' elements in the region and the protection of trade routes were some other of Balban's achievements, which brought great prestige to the throne.[30] If Ziya-ud-Din Barani is to be believed, the Sultan also thwarted political upheavals in the capital by providing a veneer of divinity to his rule. He called himself the shadow of God on earth, *zillullah*, and proclaimed that kingship was the vice-regency of God, *niyabat-i-khudai*. Tracing his genealogy to the mythical

Afrasiyab, the Sultan emulated the customs and ways of life of the pre-Islamic Sassanid rulers of Persia. Elaborate court rituals, including *sijda* (prostration) and *paibos* (kissing of feet) were introduced and forcibly implemented. Given the anarchy following Iltutmish's death, Balban's measures restored the authority of the crown.[31]

Balban was a devotee of Sheikh Farid-ud-Din Ganj-i-Shakar, khalifa and spiritual successor of Bakhtiyar Kaki.[32] Ali Asghar, himself a descendant of Farid-ud-Din, recorded in his early-seventeenth-century text, *Jawahir-i-Faridi*, that the saint had married Balban's daughter Bibi Huzaira and had six sons and three daughters with her.[33] Writing earlier, in the middle of the fourteenth century, Amir Khwurd had noted that the sheikh had several wives and five sons and three daughters.[34] The saint's favourite son, Nizam-ud-Din (not to be confused with his khalifa, Nizam-ud-Din Auliya) had reportedly joined Balban's army and died fighting Mongol invaders in Punjab.[35]

Farid-ud-Din was succeeded by his illustrious disciple, Nizam-ud-Din Auliya, who eventually turned Delhi into a major Chishti centre.[36] Nizam-ud-Din is an important member of the first cycle of Chishti saints, following Muin-ud-Din Ajmeri, Qutb-ud-Din Bakhtiyar Kaki, and Farid-ud-Din Ganj-i-Shakar. Nizam-ud-Din's successor, Nasir-ud-Din Chiragh-i-Dehli (d. 1356),[37] was the last of this chain of the 'great' Chishti tradition, which is known to have played a crucial role in shaping the political and cultural traditions of the Delhi Sultanate. In terms of modern, secular politics, they are particularly valued for their religious tolerance and broad-mindedness. It is their seemingly liberal attitude, coupled with their perceived ability to perform miracles and their consequent popularity, which brought them into conflict with the Islamic orthodoxy, and in the case of Nizam-ud-Din, with the rulers as well.

Though Nizam-ud-Din's differences with the powerful Delhi Sultan Ala-ud-Din Khalji (ruled 1296–1316) were amicably resolved, the saint's encounters with Qutb-ud-Din Mubarakshah Khalji (ruled 1316–20) and Ghiyas-ud-Din

Tughluq (ruled 1320–25), are particularly celebrated in Chishti tradition. Even as Nizam-ud-Din was concerned about the political instability of the period, the rulers were evidently angry over his indifference towards the court (*darbar*) and its rituals. For the saint, to visit the court would have amounted to accepting the superiority of the ruler over his own claim to authority in his wilayat. Indeed, the Sufis' claim to power and authority in society was a continuous irritant for kings and ulama alike. In such a situation, the Sufis had to defend their actions in the light of the shariat. As mentioned earlier, biographical accounts, in turn, reasserted that they occasionally resorted to paranormal powers to defeat their opponents. Their reported victories only contributed to their authoritative position in society.[38]

Nizam-ud-Din was made to defend his interest in music (sama/qawwali) in the light of the hadis. Conservative ulama insisted that he follow the Hanafite interpretation, which forbids listening to music.[39] In such a condition, the sheikh was reduced to cursing his detractors. In Chishti legend, the saint's righteousness was established when the Sultans and their supporters were eliminated in quick succession. While a close confidante, Khusrau Khan killed Qutb-ud-Din Mubarakshah Khalji, Ghiyas-ud-Din's death in an accident on the outskirts of Delhi was suspected to be the handiwork of his own son, who enthroned himself as Sultan Muhammad Tughluq (ruled 1325–51). Ghiyas-ud-Din, who was returning from a campaign in the east, had apparently sent a *farman* (imperial order) asking Nizam-ud-Din to leave the city. The saint responded in his characteristically humorous way: *hunuz dilli dur ast*, that is, 'Delhi is far away yet' (for the ruler).[40] The king never returned to the city. For Chishtis, Nizam-ud-Din had already cursed Ghiyas-ud-Din and bestowed kingship on Muhammad Tughluq.[41]

A number of scholars have shown how the Sufis, including the Chishtis of the Sultanate period, did get involved in politics.[42] Some of them avoided visiting the Sultan's court, perhaps because they considered it below their dignity to visit the court and follow its rituals.[43] A few may also have felt that a tactical distance from the rulers helped them deal with the hostile non-Muslim population. It is important to note that three of the five 'great' Chishti saints—Farid-ud-Din's preceptor, Qutb-ud-Din Bakhtiyar Kaki, his successor, Nizam-ud-Din Auliya, and the latter's disciple, Nasir-ud-Din Chiragh-i-Dehli—all settled down in Delhi. The other places they chose to stay in were strategically located on much-trodden trade routes like Ajodhan (renamed Pak Pattan, now in Pakistan) on the Multan–Delhi road, where Farid-ud-Din established his hospice. Caravans and armies headed for India passed through Ajodhan and carried the saint's fame far and wide. The centres of political power in Bengal and the Deccan too witnessed an influx of Muslim religious personnel led by charismatic Sufis, who helped consolidate the Muslim presence in regions where they settled down. The Chishtis never settled in forests or lonely places, and like Sufis in general, were supposed to reside amongst the people of their wilayat, look after their welfare and educate them into the ways of Islam.

A measure of their involvement in the politics of the time is that the Sufis sometimes accepted cash grants from rulers to pray for their success. Sheikh Farid-ud-Din received money from Ulugh Khan, later known as Balban, even if it was immediately distributed amongst the dervishes.[44] Farid-ud-Din's successor Nizam-ud-Din Auliya took five lakh *tanka*s from the usurper of the Delhi throne, Khusrau Malik, and distributed the sum amongst the public.[45] This issue was a source of tension between the Sufi sheikh and Sultan Ghiyas-ud-Din Tughluq, who had removed Khusrau Malik to establish his own dynasty. The Sultan demanded that the usurper's money be recovered from Nizam-ud-Din Auliya and the Sufi's response that the money belonged to the public, among whom he had distributed it, displeased the Sultan. Even if the latter was antagonized, Nizam-ud-Din's actions were a crowd-puller in Delhi and attracted many more followers to the Chishti order.

Further, during military campaigns, soldiers would take detours to visit Sufi hospices or shrines to seek blessings. Sources refer to Nasir-ud-Din Mahmud's army visiting Farid-ud-Din at Ajodhan.[46] Also, Sufi sheikhs were consulted about the fate of Muslim armies campaigning in the region. Ala-ud-Din Khalji, it is said, sought Nizam-ud-Din's spiritual assistance for knowing the fate of his campaign in southern India—the Sufi master had predicted its victory.[47] Later, it is said, he spoke to his audience about the enormous booty collected by Malik Naib and suggested that it be used for public welfare.[48] Some Sufis even aided the Muslim control of newly conquered territories by sending their khalifas with the army.[49] Others allowed their sons to join the army and fight a jihad against infidels, as with Farid-ud-Din's son, Nizam-ud-Din. Yet others went to report on the campaign.[50]

Most Sultans, members of the royal family and court officials were murids of the sheikhs, who, it is said, bestowed kingship on a person of their choice and snatched it when dissatisfied with his performance. Also, there are a number of anecdotes in the sources concerning the opposition and disrespect shown by rulers, ulama and other notables, which provoked the sheikh's wrath. The saint's curse could allegedly cause the antagonists' sudden, and often painful, death.

Such episodes from the life of a Sufi saint like Nizam-ud-Din Auliya, narrated over time with much embellishment, have contributed to his popularity. Chishti hagiographies highlight Nizam-ud-Din as a healer and protector of people in times of crisis, his charitable endeavours and a broad worldview having the power to draw people from across religions. Later tazkiras and Chishti oral tradition may have helped give rise to the charismatic image of the sheikh, but the saint was indeed a living legend. His hospice in Delhi was a continuous source of sustenance for the people there. With his death in 1325, the people lost a messiah and in the course of time, his shrine emerged as a major pilgrimage centre.

Chishti relations with the Tughluq dynasty deteriorated somewhat during the time of Nizam-ud-Din's successor, Nasir-ud-Din Chiragh-i-Dehli.[51] He managed to keep the Chishti tradition alive in Delhi during the period when Muhammad

Tughluq had turned hostile towards the sheikh, even as he insisted on the cooperation of the Sufis and ulama in strengthening his hold on the Deccan. Though the accounts concerning the shifting of the capital to Devgiri, renamed Daulatabad, are exaggerated, Sufi tradition celebrates the Chishti sheikh's insistence on remaining in his wilayat; his house is said to have been the only one where a lamp kept burning in an otherwise deserted Delhi. This earned him the epithet of Chiragh-i-Dehli, the lamp or light of Delhi. The sheikh's confidence and sense of responsibility are amply proven when one reads that he was actively involved in the enthronement of Firuz Shah Tughluq (ruled 1351–88), after Muhammad Tughluq's death while campaigning in Uchch in Sindh. These examples are often ignored in current discussions on Sufi interventions in politics.

With Chiragh-i-Dehli, the first cycle of the five 'great' Chishtis came to an end because he did not nominate any of his disciples as his chief successor in the Chishti order. A large number of Chishti Sufis, mainly the disciples of Nizam-ud-Din Auliya, had already spread all over Hindustan, Bengal and the Deccan, but their control over Delhi was weakening. Politically too, Delhi's power was waning. When in the late-fourteenth century, Central Asian empire-builder, Tamerlane or Timur, invaded and sacked Delhi (1398), the leading Chishti saint, Bandanawaz Gesudaraz, a disciple of Chiragh-i-Dehli, avoided being a victim of this calamity by leaving for the Deccan, where disciples of Nizam-ud-Din Auliya had already established themselves since the early decades of that century. Muhammad Tughluq's hostility and earlier attempts by Ala-ud-Din Khalji to relocate Muslim religious personnel had also played a role in the expansion of the Chishti network outside Delhi. The connections between the rise and decline of the Delhi Sultanate in the thirteenth and fourteenth centuries and the corresponding movements and spread of the Chishti masters in the period are too striking to be ignored.

Four major themes emerge from Chishti narratives dealing with the thirteenth and fourteenth centuries. These are:

(a) miracle or *karamat* as a source of authority; (b) relations with the Sultans and nobles; (c) using music and other cultural appropriations, with the attendant possibility of defying the orthodoxy even while remaining within the fold of Islam; and (d) attitudes towards non-Muslims and issues of conversion and Islamization.

A recurring theme in Sufi literature, both in tazkiras and malfuzat, is the authoritative position of Sufi sheikhs in the society and politics of the Delhi Sultanate. An important source of the sheikh's authority was his perceived ability to perform miracles. The Sufi sources are replete with stories of the incredible feats of saints. This is as true of Nizam-ud-Din's authoritative 'discourses' as of many other 'popular' Sufi writings from the fourteenth century. Indeed, the two main Chishti texts, *Fawa'id-ul-Fu'ad* and *Khayr-ul-Majalis*, are full of fantastic anecdotes of miracles attributed to the Sufis of the past. Nizam-ud-Din Auliya himself believed in miracles as an integral part of Sufi discipline, but he was against those who advertised their own ability to perform them. For him, it was obligatory for saints to hide their supernatural exploits and binding on prophets to display them. The sheikh classified miracles into four categories: *muajiza* (miracles of the prophet), karamat (marvels of the saints), *maunat* (paranormal feats of saintly people) and *istidraj* (occasional tricks performed by an obstinate sinner or magician). He also believed in the power of the evil eye (*nazr*) and black magic (*jadu/sehr*). He criticized the rationalist sect, Mutazila, for treating them as mere fancy ideas and not a reality. Thus, a liberal, tolerant approach towards contemporary religious traditions did not make the Chishtis 'rational' in the modern sense. Chishti tradition was a part of Sunni Islam and followed Imam Ghazali's interpretations of the shariat when attempting to wed theology with mysticism and condemning rationalists or philosophers. For this purpose, the use of political power was not abhorred.

Some scholars have suggested that the Sufis, particularly the early Chishtis, kept away from the government of their times, but a careful perusal of the sources reveals that the above formulation concerning the Chishtis is unsustainable. In theory, the Chishtis may have felt the need to keep their distance from the king and his nobles, but in practice, this was not always the case. The examples discussed earlier from the careers of leading Chishti saints reveal their proximity to political power. Differences over the question of power and patronage in their wilayat led, in some cases, to severe conflicts between the Sufis and the monarchs. Nizam-ud-Din Auliya's troubles with Qutb-ud-Din Mubarak Shah Khalji and Ghiyas-ud-Din Tughluq have been noted earlier.

Alternatively, examples of their collaboration too abound. Sufi literature particularly highlights the cordial relations between Nizam-ud-Din Auliya and Sultan Ala-ud-Din Khalji after their initial suspicions of each other's intentions were set to rest. Most of Nizam-ud-Din Auliya's closest and influential disciples held important positions in the court of the Sultans. Sufi-poet, Amir Khusrau's name comes to mind immediately, as also that of Ziya-ud-Din Barani. Thus, the relationship between the Sufis and rulers was complex and reveals that the mystics were not indifferent to the political context in which they flourished.

The Sufi sheikhs were not ascetics. They were supposed to live amongst the people and help mitigate their sufferings. For Nizam-ud-Din Auliya, *tark-i-duniya* (renunciation of the world) did not mean that one should wear a *langota* (loin-cloth) and set off for the forest.[52] As noted previously, the Sufis were expected to deploy their experience acquired through learning, meditation and travelling for educating Muslims and for bringing non-Muslims into the fold of Islam. Their claims for an authoritative position in society could run them into trouble with the official ulama, who interrogated their religious practices and resorted to violence to keep them in check. Music was one such contested practice. In the opinion of some scholars, interest in music, among the authorized forms of zikr in the Chishti tradition, distinguished it from other silsilas such as the Suhrawardis, their major rivals in the Sultanate period. It is suggested that the

Chishti practice of sama or qawwali, served a valuable practical function: it separated the Chishtis from the Suhrawardis and also opposed them to the official ulama. Thus, music became, if not the monopoly of the Chishtis, the pre-eminent symbol that crystallized their position.[53] Though the difference between the Chishti and Suhrawardi approaches to music is generally known, the Suhrawardis' attitude towards musical assemblies has not been explored properly. Several leading Suhrawardis of the Sultanate period were fond of devotional music. Hamid-ud-Din Nagauri, a Suhrawardi contemporary of Qutb-ud-Din Bakhtiyar Kaki, was one of them. Later, Ilm-ud-Din Suhrawardi defended Nizam-ud-Din Auliya during the inquest in Sultan Ghiyas-ud-Din Tughluq's court. Evidence of qawwali being held in the presence of Baha-ud-Din Zakariya, the leading Suhrawardi saint of thirteenth-century Multan, is found in authoritative early tazkiras, though his ambivalence in the matter is also noted. Further, within the Chishti order, there were differences over the use of instruments and female singers. While, Fakhr-ud-Din Zarradi permitted the use of the drum and tambourine in music assemblies, his pir, Nizam-ud-Din Auliya, did not recommend the use of instruments. Nizam-ud-Din was also against the participation of female *qawwal*s, but his disciples did employ both instruments and female singers in their music assemblies. The ambiguity is reflected in later reports, which attributed the invention of several musical instruments to Nizam-ud-Din's closest disciple and courtier, Amir Khusrau. Music, then, as a neat marker of Chishti practice as against the Suhrawardis and other Sufi orders does not hold. Similarly, the Shattaris, a branch of the Suhrawardis, were close to the Chishtis in their preference for music as a spiritual exercise.

The use of Hindi verses is also not typical only of the Chishtis. The Rishi Sufis of Kashmir too used non-Arabic vocal zikr formulae. Like the Chishtis, the Shattaris were also open to the idea of adopting spiritual practices belonging to non-Muslim mystical traditions. It has traditionally been argued that the Chishti attitude towards the doctrine of wahdat-ul-wujud was an important marker of difference between the Chishtis and Suhrawardis in the Sultanate period and between Chishtis and Naqshbandis in the Mughal era. The Naqshbandis, led by Sheikh Ahmad Sirhindi, tried to distance themselves from any conflict or contradiction between the universal Muslim belief in *tauhid*, the unity of God, and the mystical idea of wahdat-ul-wujud, which called for unity of all existence. Thus, the Naqshbandis articulated the more defensible concept of wahdat-us-shuhud for expressing their view of monism as a mystical experience. However, the more popular Chishti belief in the *wujudi* doctrine brought it very close to various streams of non-Muslim mystical traditions (such as Advaita, non-dualism), and therefore, made it more tolerant and accommodative. Irrespective of whether a Sufi was a monist or dualist, early examples of extant literature in the vernacular as well as the spread of Islam to many regions invariably involved charismatic Sufi figures.

This brings us to questions concerning the Chishti attitude towards non-Muslims, conversion, Islamization, claims of local Muslim communities converting to Islam under their influence, and long-term cultural accretion around their saints' shrines. There is a vast body of literature on these issues, both in early Sufi writings and later secondary sources, which secular historians have tended to ignore and the communalists have happily abused. Sufi literature clearly reveals how Chishtis were not averse to the idea of the conversion of non-Muslims to Islam, either directly at the hands of a leading pir or through a long process of Islamic acculturation in localities made sacred by the shrines of medieval saints. The sources record a large number of anecdotes of miraculous encounters between the Sufis and non-Muslim miracle-workers or spiritual power-holders such as yogis, sanyasis, gurus and Brahmins. Provoked by competing claims to territorial authority, these stories narrated by Nizam-ud-Din Auliya and his disciples are significant for a more informed understanding of the complex process of the diffusion of Islam in India. Even if the accounts of miracles cannot be proved rationally, in recounting them, Sufi writers and biographers seem to be celebrating the image of the saints as propagators of Islam wherever they settled down. Such reports appear in both the 'authoritative' texts and the so-called 'spurious' literature and are important for understanding the Sufi tradition in its own terms. Contrary to the modern political ideals advanced by secularists and imposed on the past, Chishtis have long celebrated the Islamizing role of their preceptors led by Khwaja Muin-ud-Din Chishti. A critical, dispassionate appreciation requires that even as exaggerated accounts of conversion are questioned, the Sufis' interest in conversion and the spread of Islam be recognized. This is not the case with much of modern historical writing.

In this context, mention can be made of the court-poet and closest disciple of Nizam-ud-Din Auliya, Amir Khusrau (d. 1325), who is greatly admired in modern secularist scholarship for his 'patriotism' and other such virtues that are expected of a good Muslim.[54] However, his court chronicles are full of hostile references to Hindus, condemning them as kafirs.[55] Khusrau stated that the Sultan was to wash the earth clean with the blood of the impure idol-worshipping Hindus, who he also referred to as the Pharaohs of infidelity. Ignoring Khusrau's reports on the countless infidels being sent to hell for the satisfaction of the Sultans, historians highlight his patriotism (if not 'nationalism', though there are indications to this effect also) by quoting his writings on the goodness of Hindustan (often confused with the whole of India) and the achievements of its people in various fields. However, it is just as possible that Khusrau's glorification of Hindustan might have been related to Muslim supremacy and the splendour of Islam.[56] The poet was appreciative of reports that said that the strong men of Hind were trodden underfoot, that they were ready to pay tribute and that Islam was triumphant in subduing idolatry. Khusrau was convinced that religious truth was to be found in Islam alone. According to Friedman, 'In this he does not differ from the consensus prevailing among the

Muslims in his time and place'.[57] Many Chishtis, indeed, believed in the superiority of Islam over other religious traditions and took considerable pains to establish that.

Another one of Nizam-ud-Din Auliya's disciples who was a courtier, Ziya-ud-Din Barani, did not differ with Khusrau on this question. It is important to note, however, that Khusrau's approach towards Hindu worship of the sun, stones and animals was different from Barani's. For the latter, all these smacked of polytheism, while Khusrau explained that these were not to be considered as similar to God, but only to be a part of His creation. Khusrau could go to the extent of saying that as a religious group, the Hindus were better than many others, including Christians.

Evidently, there is a need to de-sanitize modern histories of the Sufi tradition by taking into account all the evidence and not just a selection. Bigotry and religious conflict went hand in hand with tolerance and peaceful adaptations, depending on the circumstances. Many marks of violent or subtle influences can be noticed in music, painting, architecture, vernacular literature and the evolution of communities that incorporated beliefs and practices common to Islam as well as other religious currents. Politically, the advocacy for a clear-cut distinction between Islam and infidelity also existed, an issue we will examine in the next chapter.

3

Muslims and Kafirs in the Delhi Sultanate

This chapter attempts to examine representations of non-Muslims—often condemned as kafirs in medieval Indian Islamic literature—in court chronicles, Sufi texts and literary compositions. The divergent images of non-Muslims in the sources reflect the attitudes of various Muslim groups such as the rulers (including the *umara* [nobles]), ulama, Sufis and poets, which can be traced to the historical processes of the period. However, in this chapter, we will limit ourselves to an evaluation of the views of Khwaja Ziya-ud-Din Barani in his *Fatawa-i-Jahandari* (*c.* mid-fourteenth century).[1] Though recognizing the possibilities of analytical gains that may be derived from modern theoretical approaches to relevant problems, or to use Stuart Hall's phrase, 'conundrums of theory',[2] we will try to locate the formation of ideas about Muslims and non-Muslims in classical Islamic political thought through particular important texts. The aim is to make sense of the problems and put them in perspective, as Barani himself had adapted his ideas from the 'grand tradition' of Islam, which, in turn, was informed by the Quran, the hadis, practices of the rightly-guided caliphs and the attempts by early-Muslim jurists and political thinkers to address issues that emerged in different times and locations.

Contrary to the established position, Barani's *Fatawa-i-Jahandari* is not a typical example of the 'mirror for princes' literature. This is primarily for three reasons. First, the views expressed by Barani in the *Fatawa* are not just abstract normative ideas, even though parallels can be drawn with the works of classical Islamic political theory, some of which were known to him. The writer consciously located himself in, and compared and contrasted with, what was happening in the Delhi Sultanate. Secondly, his opinions on many issues, for instance, the status of non-Muslims in the Sultanate are found scattered all over the pages of his more famous work, the *Tarikh-i-Firuz Shahi*. It is possible that Barani himself or someone else extracted and put together his views in the form of *nasihats* (counsels) in the *Fatawa*, attributing many passages to Sultan Mahmud of Ghazna and others for greater acceptability. This is not exceptional for Barani as the extant versions of the *Tarikh-i-Firuz Shahi* also contain many passages attributed to some well-known figures. In fact, in the introduction to his *Tarikh-i-Firuz Shahi*, Barani himself writes, 'If readers peruse this compilation as a mere history, they will find recorded in it the actions of great sultans and nobles, if they search in it the rules of administration and the means of enforcing obedience, even in that respect it will not be found deficient, if they looked for warnings and admonitions to the rulers, that is also very well elucidated.'[3] Third, the tone of views expressed in the *Tarikh* is not very different from that of the *Fatawa*. Indeed, at several places, the language of the *Tarikh* is harsher than that of the *Fatawa*. All these can, perhaps, help us resolve the question as to why the *Tarikh* was frequently mentioned by early Muslim writers, whereas they are silent about the *Fatawa*. It must be clarified here that an inter-textual comparison of Barani's writings does not necessarily take away from the value of the *Tarikh* as a Persian classic.

Courtier turned historian and political theorist of the Delhi Sultanate, Ziya-ud-Din Barani belonged to a family known for its association with the Sultans of Delhi from about the latter half of the thirteenth century.[4] His maternal grandfather, Husam-ud-Din was appointed governor of Lakhnauti, a Muslim stronghold in Bengal, by Sultan Ghiyas-ud-Din Balban. His father, Muayyid-ul-Mulk, was administrator of Baran, now called Bulandshahar, in modern Uttar Pradesh in northern India, in the first year of the reign of Ala-ud-Din Khalji.[5] His paternal uncle Malik Ala-ul-Mulk was *kotwal* of Delhi and a prominent counsellor of Ala-ud-Din Khalji. With this background, Barani was able to move around Delhi's ruling circles, was known to be an entertaining conversationalist and friend of poets and courtiers, Amir Khusrau and Amir Hasan. It was probably through them that he became close to the leading Chishti Sufi of the capital, Nizam-ud-Din Auliya. Though apparently a late starter in Sultanate government service, Barani went on to be a *nadim* or boon companion of Muhammad Tughluq for nearly eighteen years.[6] Significantly, as a prince, Muhammad Tughluq had also been a disciple of Nizam-ud-Din. As mentioned in the previous chapter, according to Chishti tradition, the saint had predicted the bestowal of kingship on the prince.[7] The Sultan's reign was full of turmoil and as a close associate, Barani must have keenly observed the turn of events even though he was unable to influence the ruler much.

At the beginning of the reign of Firuz Shah Tughluq, Barani was banished from court and imprisoned in the fortress of Pahtez (Bhatnir). He was possibly associated with Khwaja Jahan Ahmad Ayaz's attempt to place a minor son of Muhammad Tughluq on the throne soon after the Sultan's death.[8] Though he was released from prison subsequently, Barani reportedly spent the rest of his life in a miserable condition. At the time of his imprisonment, he was nearly seventy years old. Yet he used the free time to emerge in a new avatar as a writer and went on to produce several books, including *Sana-i-Muhammadi* (or *Nat-i-Muhammadi*), *Salat-i-Kabir*, *Inayat Nama-i-Ilahi*, *Masir-i-Sadat*, *Tarikh-i-Firuzshahi*, *Hasratnama*, *Tarikh-i-Al-i-Barmak* or *Akhbar-i-Barmakiyan* and *Fatawa-i-Jahandari*. Some of these works have survived to this day.

Modern 'secular' historians have been very critical of Barani for his provocative views on many issues, which, according to them, smack of 'communalism'. As noted above, even in the most balanced and serious contemporary writings, Barani is condemned as a 'fanatic' or 'bigot'. The communalists, on the other hand, have tried to misuse his writings to suit their own agenda. Notwithstanding the interest in Barani's works, no matter from which perspective one is trying to read them, the author still awaits a modern biographer. The only serious attempt in this connection has been by Mohammad Habib. However, Habib's strong commitment to secularism prevented him from appreciating the career and views of this courtier and intellectual in his own context. Also, his ire against the partisan scholarship of British administrators and their projection of medieval India as a period of Muslim oppression from which British colonialism had delivered (Hindu) Indians animated Habib's formidable scholarship.[9] Accordingly, Barani's views on the ideal Muslim polity and the position of non-Muslims and people from non-aristocratic backgrounds in the Sultanate were sharply criticized by Habib. His account of Barani's life is full of disparaging remarks about the author. The attempt is not only to chastise Barani, but also to completely sanitize his understanding of Islam. Habib has, however, given sufficient illustrations from Barani's writings to prove his 'fanaticism'.

In his Introduction to *The Political Theory of the Delhi Sultanate*, which incorporates portions of the *Fatawa-i-Jahandari*, translated by Afsar Umar Salim Khan, Mohammad Habib makes it clear that he does not think highly of Barani as an author. According to him, the cynical and frustrated old man could write on the basis of his memory, translate, write a book of his own on the basis of the work of another writer, or he could put in logical order the ideas that had been developing in his mind over a period of time. Yet, Habib firmly believed Barani was not capable of undertaking any investigation or research.[10] This indeed sounds like a contradiction in terms. Clearly, Habib was trying to evaluate Barani as a researcher in a modern institution with a commitment to secularism. Also, the question of how an incompetent Barani could write two of the 'greatest works' of the Sultanate period, *Fatawa-i-Jahandari* and *Tarikh-i-Firuz Shahi*, is not adequately resolved in Habib's work. Scholars of the Persian language also claim that the language of the *Tarikh* is excellent and serves as a model of early Indo-Persian prose. Habib further notes that there may have been three reasons for this impoverished person to turn to writing: (a) to gain recognition from Firuz Shah Tughluq and his nobles; (b) to achieve salvation; and (c) for the guidance of future generations of high-born Muslims. Habib's conclusions in this connection are, again, inadequate. He writes that Barani had failed in his first mission, probably succeeded in the second, and the fact of interest in his works, six hundred years after they were written, shows that he was at least partly successful in his third objective of guiding the *ashraf* or the Muslim elite.[11]

Habib also notes that Barani was an unparalleled recorder of contemporary events, which is proved by the 'excellence' of *Tarikh-i-Firuz Shahi*. (Habib seems to ignore the fact that the *Tarikh* is a historical work and not merely a record of contemporary events.) He also says that Barani had read the history of the Arabs and knew the important events of the Prophet's and the 'rightly-guided' caliphs' times. But in Habib's opinion, '. . . of the rest of Islamic history he knew little and what he knew was all wrong'. In his introduction to *Tarikh-i-Firuz Shahi*, Barani refers to some books (characterized by Habib as 'bogus') and also to the works of the following well-known writers—Tabari, Utbi, Baihaqi, Firdausi and Minhaj-us-Siraj. In Habib's judgment, 'Barani had either never read the works of these authors in the original or else had completely forgotten them. The former alternative is more probable.' (That is, Barani was lying about having read the books of authors he has cited.) This remark is unfair as it not only casts doubts on Barani's credentials, but also devalues his writings. In contrast, the method adopted by Barani in the *Tarikh-i-Firuz Shahi* needs to be taken into account. The author himself notes that he had planned to write a general history, beginning with Adam and his two sons, but when he recalled the value of that 'marvellous' work, *Tabaqat-i-Nasiri* of Minhaj-ud-Din Siraj Juzjani, he realized that those who had read Juzjani's history would derive no advantage from reading his (Barani's) book. On the other hand, he continues, if he tried to amplify or abridge the narrative of that illustrious and venerable religious leader and scholar, it would be considered disrespectful and rash, besides creating doubts and difficulties in the minds of readers. Therefore, he decided to concentrate on the history of the later Sultans of Delhi from the point where the *Tabaqat-i-Nasiri* ended, that is, from the reign of Ghiyas-ud-Din Balban.[12]

Further, for Habib, the works referred to in the *Fatawa-i-Jahandari*, 'were either cheap and worthless fabrications, which have not survived to our days or else existed only in the imagination of our author'.[13] Habib laments that it is on the basis of his acquaintance with the bogus, fabricated literature of the Delhi Sultanate that Barani claimed to be a historian. For Habib, the *Historical Illustrations* in the *Jahandari* are sufficient proof of this and he feels that Barani's ignorance of history is appalling even with reference to the basic authorities available in the Delhi of his days. In making such a statement, Habib ignores the citations of a number of standard works, besides the Quran and the Traditions of the Prophet. Not satisfied with Barani's alleged ignorance of the history of classical Islam, Habib has added that the writer's ignorance of geography is even more shocking.[14]

Habib also questions Barani's understanding of the Sultanate's polity. According to him, '[the author's] application of the principle of contradiction to monarchy is unfortunate. After condemning monarchy as un-Islamic and sending kings to hell-fire, he goes to the opposite extreme and makes the king a partner in "the contradictory qualities of God" and declares him to be God's "deputy" and "agent". No educated contemporaries of Barani would have seriously agreed with this assertion.'[15] This remark is surprising because the concept of the Sultan as the shadow of God was already in wide currency in medieval Islamic political thought and practice. The writings of the mystically inclined theologian Imam Ghazali[16] and the Saljuqid *wazir* and noted political theorist, Nizam-ul-Mulk Tusi[17] are examples. But then, Habib is very dismissive of Nizam-ul-Mulk, who is condemned as a Sunni fanatic, again, with 'little regard for historic truths'.[18] Moreover, Barani's friend and senior colleague, Amir Khusrau called Ala-ud-Din Khalji the shadow of God on earth in his *Khazain-ul-Futuh*. In his translation of the work, Habib plays down the symbolic significance of the use of the expression by mentioning in a note that, '. . . [the] sultan was styled the "Shadow of God" (Zillullah).'[19] The fact remains that medieval Muslim rulers were viewed as shadows of God, and herein lies the root of the distinction between the modern Western and the medieval Muslim world. The secularization of the polity, or the lack of it, remains a major problem (more on this later.)

Further, as Barani represented the interests of the high-born Muslim elite,[20] he was against those who were the 'low-born'.[21] He noted that this was so because the merits and demerits of men were apportioned at the beginning of time and allotted to their souls.[22] He opposed the idea of educating the low-born and giving them important positions in the Sultanate. Barani particularly hated traders, who, for him, were lowly creatures. Habib trivializes these views by remarking that shopkeepers may 'have refused to supply him commodities on credit!'[23] Also, for Barani, piety is an attribute of the high-born. If a man is pious, there must have been some elements of aristocracy among his ancestors. However, if his low birth is proved, then his piety is mere pretence. In Habib's opinion, another expression of the same attitude is Barani's condemnation of persons who had accepted Islam through personal 'free choice'. Habib concludes that, for Barani, 'Islam, like good wine, must have matured in the muscles and tendons of a man's ancestors; to be spiritually effective, Islam must be hereditary'.[24]

Habib later writes that God had denied Barani the virtues of charity, tolerance and forgiveness; he hated, and hated intensely, and considered his hatred a virtue. Among the Muslims, his hatred was directed at philosophers, scientists, heretics and all low-born Muslims, particularly those who had risen to occupy high offices.[25] On Barani's attitude towards non-Muslims, Habib comments, 'He hated all non-Muslims and particularly the Hindus, and in order to justify "an all-out war against Hinduism", which the kings refused to undertake, he even misrepresented the doctrines of Imam Shafi'i.' (Imam Shafi'i was the founder of one of the four schools of Sunni jurisprudence.) Habib portrays Barani as an almost insane person and writes that as the author was unable 'to abuse those who had injured him personally, he found a spiritual consolation in cursing those who had done no harm'.[26]

Habib does not think that Barani's connections with some influential Sufis of Delhi was of any importance. He writes that though the author was a disciple of Nizam-ud-Din Auliya and 'claimed to be an intimate friend of Amir Khusrau and Amir Hasan, the teachings of the great sheikh and the mystic literature of the day had not touched even the periphery of his soul'. Habib concluded that Barani's conception of Islam was formal, mechanistic and earthy, that he was a complete stranger to the spiritual elements of Muslim life and that he should not be considered a worthy representative of contemporary Muslim religion and culture.[27]

Habib's position can be compared with the account of Barani's career in the essential Chishti text of the Delhi Sultanate, the *Siyar-ul-Auliya* of Amir Khwurd. Barani's profile appears amongst those of the prominent disciples of Nizam-ud-Din Auliya. The author notes that Khwaja Ziya-ud-Din Barani was unrivalled in grace, pleasing to the spiritual-minded and admired by both noblemen and common people. He is reported to have been full of wit and humour and stole the show with his soul-refreshing words at every gathering in which he was present. He is known to have had a great collection of humorous stories and anecdotes (*majma-ul-lataif wa jawama-ul-hikayat*). He also reportedly had the good fortune of being in the company of the ulama, Sufis and poets[28] because his father belonged to a noble family. Barani, says Amir Khwurd, was blessed with the discipleship of the Sultan-ul-Mashaikh (Sultan of the Sufis), Nizam-ud-Din Auliya, after which he settled down at Ghiyaspur (where the sheikh's hospice was located) and obtained a high status with the sheikh, a fact he himself noted in his *Hasratnama*.[29]

Amir Khwurd also records that owing to his elegant mind, Barani, later on, faced no competition to the post of the boon companion of Sultan Muhammad Tughluq, and went on to achieve a high status in the court as well. This was reportedly despite the apprehension that most people around him were fraudulent, deceitful and faithless. As a septuagenarian, when Barani retired from his active political career, he received an allowance from Firuz Shah Tughluq for his creature comforts and devoted himself to writing his unrivalled books, which included *Sana-i-Muhammadi*, *Salat-i-Kabir*, *Inayat Nama-i-Ilahi*, *Masir-i-Sadat* and *Tarikh-i-Firuz Shahi*.[30] It should be pointed out that Amir Khwurd did not include *Fatawa-i-Jahandari* and some other titles in his list of Barani's works. Amir Khwurd goes on to add that this saintly person (*buzurg*) spent much of his time in the company of the sultan of poets, Amir Khusrau, and the chief of scholars, Amir Hasan (who had compiled the *Fawa'id-ul-Fu'ad*, an authoritative collection of Nizam-ud-Din's malfuzat), and greatly benefited from it.[31]

Mohammad Habib translates the word 'buzurg' as 'gentleman'.[32] This is not an accurate rendering of the word as it was originally used by Amir Khwurd in his work. Amir Khwurd also used the words 'khwaja' (literally, a man of distinction, teacher, preceptor, lord, master) and 'maulana' (a Muslim religious scholar) to refer to Barani. To explain these terms a little more, a Sufi who was given permission to enroll disciples in a particular silsila was called a sheikh. As Habib himself noted, if the sheikh was a Sayyid, that is, a descendant of Prophet Muhammad, he could be referred to as khwaja.[33] The Chishtis addressed themselves as 'khwajagan' or Sufis who traced their lineage to the family of the Prophet. Further, the *Siyar-ul-Auliya* is devoted to saintly figures associated with the Chishti order and the chapter in which Barani's tazkira has been included focuses on the leading disciples of Nizam-ud-Din Auliya, of which many, including Barani, Amir Khusrau and Amir Hasan, were successful as courtiers as well.[34] Amir Khwurd further notes that in addition to the above-mentioned merits, the love for the descendants of the Prophet was firmly rooted in Barani's heart. (This statement indicates that Barani may not have been a Sayyid himself, though he mentions in the *Tarikh-i-Firuz Shahi* that his grandmother was a 'pure' Sayyid).

Eventually, Amir Khwurd writes, after a short illness, Barani departed from this world to the next like a lover of God (*mardana wa ashiqana*). At the time of his death, Barani did not own even a single coin (*dang* or *daram*). He had even given away his clothes so that his dead body was kept on a gunny-bag (*boriya*) and was covered with a piece of cloth.[35] Thus, according to Amir Khwurd, the influence on him of the company of Sultan-ul-Mashaikh Nizam-ud-Din Auliya ultimately dominated over that of kings. That he left the world in poverty is considered a Sufi ideal. He was buried in the tomb complex of Nizam-ud-Din Auliya at the foot of the grave of his noble father.[36]

Elsewhere in the *Siyar-ul-Auliya*, Amir Khwurd also refers to Maulana Ziya-ud-Din Barani's account in his *Hasratnama* of Nizam-ud-Din Auliya's reaction to the inquest at Ghiyas-ud-Din Tughluq's court over the legitimacy of the sheikh's practise of sama or music.[37] According to Amir Khwurd, Barani had noted that after returning from the Sultan's court, the sheikh had called him, along with Maulana Muhy-ud-Din Kashani and Amir Khusrau, and lamented and cursed the Hanafite ulama of Delhi for their disregard for the tradition of the Prophet.[38] It is important to note that the sheikh defended sama as acceptable in the tradition of the Prophet, a view not shared by the Hanafites who condemned music as un-Islamic. In doing this, Nizam-ud-Din followed, according to Amir Khwurd, Imam Shafi'i's interpretation, which considered music as lawful (*mubah*) even when accompanied by instruments.[39] This reference to Imam Shafi'i is important as Barani also refers to the jurist's position concerning the status of non-Muslims in Islam in the *Fatawa-i-Jahandari*. Thus, unlike the official ulama of the Delhi Sultanate who demanded the *taqlid* (blind following) of Imam Abu Hanifa's injunctions, the Chishtis and the larger circle of their followers were much more eclectic in their attitude towards the four schools of Sunni jurisprudence. In certain situations, they may even have borrowed a saying of the fourth caliph, Hazrat Ali, cousin and son-in-law of the Prophet, or from the Shi'ite Ja'fri interpretation of Islam.

Thus, the condemnation of Barani in modern scholarship as a fanatic *alim* or theologian needs to be reconsidered. His contemporaries thought of him as a close disciple of Nizam-ud-Din Auliya and this is attested by the fact of his burial in the compound of the grave of the 'great' sheikh, along with his other friends and companions, including Amir Khusrau. Sufis continued to view Barani's association with Nizam-ud-Din with respect, even veneration. Abdul Haqq Muhaddis Dehlawi even included Barani in his *Akhbar-ul-Akhyar*, considered to be the most authoritative collection of biographies of Muslim holy men in medieval India. Abdul Haqq notes that Barani, the author of *Tarikh-i-Firuz Shahi*, was a disciple of Nizam-ud-Din Auliya. He then goes on to summarize Amir Khwurd's account of Barani's attributes and career. He, however, differs a bit from Amir Khwurd and notes that Barani was buried at the foot of his mother's grave in the Nizam-ud-Din shrine complex.[40] This indicates that both his parents were buried there, further confirming the family's proximity to Nizam-ud-Din.

Abdul Haqq also quotes a lengthy account from Barani's *Hasratnama* (as recorded in the *Siyar-ul-Auliya*) to explain why Nizam-ud-Din opened the gates of discipleship to common people, unlike other sheikhs who were very particular about it.[41] Ziya-ud-Din Barani's reference occurs again in the next entry in the *Akhbar-ul-Akhyar* on Khwaja Ziya Nakhshabi. Abdul Haqq records that during Nizam-ud-Din Auliya's time, there were three persons whose name was Ziya. The first was Ziya Sanai, who was an opponent of the saint. The second was Ziya Barani, who was a disciple and faithful friend of the sheikh. The third was Ziya Nakhshabi, author of a number of works including *Silk-us-Suluk* and *Tutinama*, who was neither an antagonist nor a follower.[42] These examples mean that one must guard against the misconception that Barani was a lonely, fanatic alim and that his utterances are not significant enough for understanding the Muslim attitude towards non-Muslims in the fourteenth century. Even if Barani was exceptional in taking an extreme position, it is worthwhile to consider his ideas rather than dismiss them altogether.

Before we go any further, let us review the method adopted by Habib and Afsar Umar Salim Khan in translating the *Fatawa-i-Jahandari*. Habib writes in his introduction that the translation was done keeping in mind the following: (i) Barani's long historical illustrations, unless relevant to the main theme, 'were to be drastically summarised'; (ii) repetitions were to be ignored; (iii) expletives which Barani repeated were to be translated only once or twice, but it was indicated clearly that such abuses were habitual (one does not read any vulgar words as the narrative is completely sanitized, though some adjectives have remained despite the censoring); (iv) unnecessary adjectives were to be eliminated wherever possible; (v) Barani's confused arguments were to be restructured in a logical form; (vi) where Barani's discussion was long and tiresome, it was to be summarized within square brackets; (vii) and finally, translation was to be made as readable as possible and an attempt was made to give it 'the strength' which Barani would have certainly given to the original, had he written it eight or ten years earlier.[43] One wonders what the theorists of translation have to say about such a subversion of the text. Habib, however, claims that the project was undertaken 'while remaining sternly faithful to the original'.[44]

The end product then is not exactly a translation of the *Fatawa-i-Jahandari*, but a *Political Theory of the Delhi Sultanate* as conceived by Habib, with Barani serving as a whipping boy. The entire project at times seems bizarre because Habib highlights passages he likes, often stopping mid-narrative, deleting paragraphs and writing his own views on the subject being discussed in the text. Sometimes, Habib's initial 'H' appears at the end of a paragraph as an indication of its authorship.

To give an example of the method adopted by Habib, Barani's reference to Sultan Mahmud's two unfulfilled dreams may be mentioned here. Instead of a direct translation, Habib gives his own interpretation. According to Barani, Mahmud's first project was to capture the Abbasid city of Baghdad and rid it of rampant heresy by slaughtering the philosophers, heretics and opponents of the shariat or Muslim law. Habib intervenes here to point out that this information is not historically correct and that Baghdad was no longer a centre of innovations in the field of religion during Mahmud's time. Barani continues that the Sultan's second wish was to attack Hindustan again in order to eliminate the Hindu religion completely. Barani thought that Mahmud had a large enough army to invade Hindustan with the purpose of putting to sword some two or three lakh Brahmins, who had kept the traditions of infidelity on this vast land alive. He would then have given the rest of the Hindus the option of death or Islam, as recommended in Shafi'i Islam practised by Mahmud. Habib interrupts the narrative here to note, 'There was no point in translating and re-translating Barani's fanatical words. On the matter of the Hindus, Barani was mentally unsound.' Habib also asserts that Imam Shafi'i's views on Muslims and non-Muslims were diametrically opposed to those of Barani's. The jurist believed in the freedom of peaceful religious preaching based on the Prophet's practice following the Treaty of Hudaibiya.[45]

Clearly, given the limitations of Habib's work, there is a need to go back to the *Fatawa-i-Jahandari* again for Barani's views on kafirs/Hindus. Barani's career, in general, also needs careful study. In this regard, it might be useful to keep in mind not only the writer's familial background and the political context of the

Delhi Sultanate, but also his connection with the Sufis of Delhi. Though Habib's formulations are fraught with problems, they continue to dominate existing scholarship on Ziya-ud-Din Barani. However, there have been some attempts to evaluate him as a historian[46] and to interpret his ideas on norms of governance.[47] In this chapter, we will briefly reconsider Barani's views on non-Muslims as delineated in his *Fatawa* and compare and contrast his ideas with those of his contemporaries and also, to some extent, the classical Islamic theorists.

Addressed to the Sultans of Delhi who he called the sons of Sultan Mahmud (of Ghazna), Barani noted in the *Fatawa-i-Jahandari* that a ruler's major concern needed to be governance, a responsibility he shared with God, and which makes the monarch one to be venerated like God. For Barani, the Sultan's salvation and spiritual progress is not possible unless he takes appropriate measures that will lead to the establishment of truth and the enhancement of the status of the religion of the Prophet.[48] The sovereign is also expected to know that the dominance of truth does not mean that falsehood has been completely wiped out and that truth alone prevails in his kingdom. Barani clarifies that God Himself states that everything is created in pairs. That is, every created thing has an opposite: truth/falsehood, peace/violence, virtue/evil, piety/sin and submission/rebellion. To substantiate this further, Barani gives some other examples of dyadic creations: night/day, light/darkness, earth/sky, religiosity/heresy and theism/polytheism.[49] The above examples serve as illustrations in Barani's text that the prevalence of truth did not mean that falsehood was completely overthrown. In Barani's opinion, even if all the prophets and Muslim Sultans had worked in tandem to liquidate and eliminate falsehood, which includes infidelity (*kufr*), anarchy, sin and wickedness, so that only truth (Islam, peace, obedience and virtue) prevailed in the world, they would not have succeeded.

Barani reasoned that a world free of sinners and infidels is beyond the limits of imagination. For him, evil necessarily survives as Islam distinguishes itself from infidelity and foregrounds devotion for God in contrast to idol worship. Therefore, every distinction is identified with reference to its opposite: truth and falsehood and Islam and infidelity. Further, Barani reasons, falsehood, which denotes wickedness, infidelity, idol worship, anarchy and sin are deliberately created to make the truth intelligible.[50] Thus, for Barani, difference, though tolerated/despised, must be highlighted to establish superiority/domination. This means that domination does exist within a relationship, and dominant groups, while exercising domination, do not consume and destroy the dominated classes, for then there would be no relation of power, and, therefore, no domination.[51] Taking this argument further, difference, indifference, hostility and toleration can co-exist in a diverse, multicultural society. There may not be bloodshed all the time. The early Muslim settlers of the Delhi Sultanate seemingly deployed a number of strategies in 'image repertoire'.[52] Whereas some confrontationist ulama wanted the Hindus to choose between Islam or death, the attitudes of the Sufis, who straddled many worlds, revealed their insularity, angry silences, critical appreciations, and argumentative or combative stance, depending on the context and their temperament.[53] Barani chose to take on the 'other' by thoroughly condemning them, even as he lacked the power to check or subdue them altogether.

Barani reiterates here that the teachings of the prophets as well as the power and authority of the Muslim Sultans cannot remove evil completely, as human nature comprises contradictory features, that is, it is full of praiseworthy elements as well as meanness. For Barani, God had registered the deeds of those who were supposed to follow the path of Islam or infidelity on the day of creation itself. Thus, it is impossible to think of the complete eradication of the evil in this scheme. The real meaning of the establishment of truth is to ensure that truth overpowers falsehood, humiliates and disgraces polytheism and infidelity, and vindicates the triumph of truth in Islam.[54]

Given this argument, Barani believed that a well-meaning Sultan could use his power, authority and support of his well-wishers and followers to suppress sinners and criminals and establish the supremacy of Islam. He could ensure that the Sayyids, religious scholars, Sufis, saintly Muslims, ascetics, recluses and devotees of God would attain eminence, honour and distinction in society. Compare this with Barani's images of the 'other': ignorant, mischievous, faithless, shameless and slack when praying; they are to be downgraded, despised and humiliated. Barani further adds that under a just Sultan, holy warriors who participate in jihad would be stimulated with the desire to achieve martyrdom. The religious people and the protectors of the faith would achieve higher social status and positions, while those with bad intentions, bad faith and bad religion, founders of innovations and the enemies of faith would become contemptible, destitute and worthless. The good deeds of the faith would be established and those who have no respect for the shariat would be suppressed.[55]

Further, Barani continues, under a just Sultan, God-fearing and honest officers would be promoted, while cheats and swindlers would be dismissed. High-born people belonging to reputed families would be given positions of power and lowly creatures, ignored. Hypocrisy, jealousy, speaking evil of others and ill will towards others would be erased from the minds of the people. Mosques, schools, khanqahs and feasting places for the poor would flourish. On account of the shariat and the punishments meted out by a just Sultan, all those things that smack of injustice would be prohibited, disapproved and rejected by the people, and ultimately, the prevalence of rampant sins would be replaced with all-round respect for Islam.[56]

Barani goes on to suggest that a Sultan will not be able to establish the supremacy of Islam in Hindustan unless he makes concerted efforts to overthrow infidelity and destroy its leaders, who are called 'Brahmins'. For Barani, a Sultan must make a firm resolve to overpower, capture, enslave and degrade the infidels, and the full strength of the Sultan and the warriors of Islam should be devoted to religious campaigns and jihad. They should put their lives at stake for faith to succeed in uprooting false creeds. After that, it will seem as if false beliefs never existed because their magic or glamour would have been destroyed. On the other hand, if the Sultan, despite all the power and position that God has granted to him, is satisfied with the collection of taxes like jizya and *kharaj* from the Hindus and allows infidelity to exist and avoids taking risks to destroy it, then there will hardly be any difference between the Sultans of Islam and the chiefs of the infidels. This is because even the kafir rulers who shared the false religion of the Hindus collected taxes and filled up their treasuries. In fact, Barani says, they collected a hundred times more taxes.[57] However, Barani must also have been aware of the fact that practical considerations prevented the collection of jizya on a regular basis. The concept seemingly lost its specific legal sense during the Sultanate period and was imposed as a general tax or tribute.[58]

Further, Barani wondered, if the Sultans, despite their royal power and authority were content with letting infidelity continue in return for the payment of jizya and kharaj, then how could the tradition of the Prophet be implemented?[59] Barani reiterated that the purpose behind Allah's dispatching one lakh twenty-four thousand prophets was to eliminate infidelity, and as Muhammad was the seal or the last of the prophets, destroying infidelity simply through the teachings of the prophets was no longer possible. The only way infidels and polytheists could be overthrown and disgraced, and the supremacy of Islam established and heavenly blessings procured, was if the Sultan deployed all his might with the necessary preparations.[60]

It is inaccurate to say that Barani's views were exceptional. His contemporary and near contemporary authors have also offered similar formulations. Indeed, classical Islam had already formulated what the status of the ahl-i-kitab or the zimmis[61] would be in an Islamic dominion. Zimmis are different from both the Muslim and the kafir. Originally, only Jews and Christians were included in this category, but subsequently, it became necessary to consider Zoroastrians, followers of a number of minor faiths in Central Asia, as well as the Hindus as zimmis. The inhabitants of India were treated as zimmis from early on, though classical Quranic exegesis did not regard them as ahl-i-kitab or People of the Book. This expansion of the concept to include Hindus entailed a compromise with idolatry that was not accepted by all the schools of Islamic jurisprudence (mazahib). The Shafi'i and Hanbali jurists (*fuqaha*) counted only Jews, Christians and Zoroastrians as zimmis. On the other hand, the Malikites and the Hanafites included all non-Muslims (even idolaters) who were not Arabs or apostates (*murtad*) in the zimmi category. The preponderant Hanafite position of the ulama enabled medieval Indian rulers to legally justify a tolerant policy or attitude towards the Hindus. Significantly, the decision to categorize Indian (Hindu) idolaters as zimmis is attributed to Muhammad bin Qasim, the early-eighth-century Arab conqueror of Sindh, who had reportedly stated that the idol temples of the Hindus were similar to the churches of the Christians, synagogues of the Jews and fire temples of the Zoroastrians. Despite occasional demands for strict regulations, the status of the Hindus as zimmis was never questioned in a serious way.[62] Yet, the 'virtual consensus' on the legal standing of the Hindus did not preclude the emergence of great variations in Muslim attitudes towards them in a more general sense. These attitudes ranged from 'utmost hostility to almost total acceptance of Hindu religious beliefs'.[63] During war time, Hindus were to be dismissed to hell as kafirs; during peace, one could as well learn commitment and devotion to God from them. Both these positions can be found in several of Amir Khusrau's writings.

Taking a hostile position, Barani suggested that the Sultans needed to first strengthen their administration and then, with high resolve, risk their power, prestige and dignity to elevate Islamic customs and make the religion of truth prevail over falsehood. However, Barani warns that kings should understand the true meaning of why they need to establish truth in order to dedicate their lives to the struggle to achieve it, to consider it their most important objective, and finally, to be fully prepared to sacrifice their own and their supporters' lives to achieve the aims of the prophets, caliphs, friends of God, truthful men and earlier monarchs. For their struggles and sacrifices, Barani says, the rulers will get prestige in this world, which will last till the Day of Judgment. Subsequently, in heaven, their status will be at par with that of the prophets and saintly Muslims, and they will receive God's blessings.[64] Barani further exhorts the rulers: 'If you want not to be ashamed before God and the Prophet and your record of life is full of virtuous deeds, then you should use your royal power to uproot the infidels, polytheists and heretics, and humiliate them.'[65]

According to Barani, a majority of religious scholars and intellectuals of both early and later times were convinced that the Sultans enjoyed enough power to ensure the following: true religion overrunning false creeds, the word of God being respected, weakening the customs and traditions of infidelity and polytheism, and favouring and honouring Muslims. The rulers could make sure that the infidels and the irreligious were impoverished and disgraced. The rules and orders of illegal kingdoms and opposing believers could be removed, the laws of the shariat implemented, and the enemies of God and the Prophet condemned, banished, repudiated and terrorized.[66]

Sharing similar sentiments much later, Sheikh Ahmad Sirhindi also suggested that the honour of Islam required the humiliation of infidels, who were to be oppressed, treated like dogs and mercilessly forced to pay jizya. With utter disregard for Hindu sensitivities, Sirhindi emphasized that a very effective way of establishing the supremacy of Islam was the slaughter of cows, which was 'one of the most glorious commandments of Islam in India'.[67] Sounds like a 'pre-fascist' agenda? The fact remains that the Sultans of Delhi like Shams-ud-Din Iltutmish and Jalal-ud-Din Khalji did not 'give' kafirs the option of Islam or death. It is likely that they were not even in a position to prevent the Hindus of the capital from publicly professing their faith and taking out religious processions. The frustrations of Jalal-ud-Din Khalji are noted in the *Tarikh-i-Firuz Shahi* by Barani himself. It could also be that Barani was attributing this lapse to Jalal-ud-Din to prove his argument on the failure or inability of the Sultans to crush the infidels.

Barani lamented that despite seven generations of Muslim power and rule in this land, 'truth' could not be established here, the supremacy of the word of God was not possible and true religion was not able to keep people of bad faith in check because the kings of Islam were allowing the customs of infidelity to flourish in their capital and other cities. According to Barani, idols were allegedly worshipped openly and people were following traditions of infidelity with greater insistence than before. The kafirs, he says, engaged, openly and without fear, in teaching false creeds. They decorated their idols, beat drums, and sang and danced while celebrating their festivals. Further, he says, after paying a few tankas as jizya, they continued with the practice and teaching of the instructions of their 'books of falsehood'. In such a situation, Barani says, it was impossible to effectively implement the traditions of Islam, to establish piety and prevent evil.[68]

Barani was convinced that the Sultans did not possess the desire and passion to overthrow the kafirs, idol worshippers and polytheists. On the contrary, he says, because the heathens paid kharaj and were treated as zimmis, they were honoured, distinguished, favoured and even achieved eminence. For Barani, the Sultans bestowed gifts of drums, standards, jewels, gold-embroidered robes, armoured horses, governorship and high ranks and positions on them. They not only allowed idol worshippers to flourish in their capital (the grandeur of which was a model for other Muslim cities), but were also apparently pleased to see that the infidels, polytheists, idolaters and cow-dung worshippers constructed palace-like houses, wore brocade and rode Arab horses caparisoned with gold and silver ornaments. Further, according to Barani, the kafirs had much power and strength, led luxurious lives, employed Muslims in their service and made them run in front of their horses. Finally, he says, in the capital of Islam, which was the source of Islam's prestige, the Hindu chiefs were respectfully addressed using their hereditary titles like Rai, Rana, Thakur, Saha, Mehta and Pundit[69]—that is, they ranged from influential zamindars to successful traders and venerated scholars. It is clear from Barani's lamentations that the condition of non-Muslims during the Sultanate period fit the descriptions of neither the Hindu right nor certain Muslim groups.

In condemning the 'wretched cow-dung worshipping' Hindus, who enjoyed power and prestige in the Sultanate, Barani was evidently invoking the doctrinaires' suggestions on the question of the position of zimmis in an Islamic state. In classical Islamic thought, zimmis and Muslims are not to be treated equally. Apart from the jizya to be paid in a submissive manner, a zimmi is not allowed to marry a Muslim woman, though a Muslim man may marry a zimmi woman. Similarly, a zimmi cannot own a Muslim slave, although the converse is permitted. Also, according to doctrines going back to the Ummayad caliph, Umar bin Abdul Aziz, zimmis were supposed to wear distinguishing garments, the original intention of which was reportedly to prevent administrative errors, but which gradually came to be regarded as a sign of humiliation. Such restrictions on dress were accompanied by complementary restrictions such as the prohibition of fine cloth, noble steeds and uncut forelocks.[70]

Authors like Ziya-ud-Din Barani and later, Mulla Abdul Qadir Badauni, wanted such rules to be implemented by the Sultans. Badauni, who wrote a counter-narrative to Akbar's 'inclusive' programme of 'sulh-i-kul' or 'peace with all' in the latter half of the sixteenth century,[71] referred to the regulations imposed on zimmis by his previous master, Husain Khan Tukariya. As the governor of Lahore during Akbar's reign, Husain Khan had ordered all Hindus to stitch a patch of cloth of a different colour near the bottom of their sleeves. This earned him the sobriquet 'Tukariya', derived from the word for a piece of cloth, *tukra*. Badauni also uses the Arabic word for tukra, *ghiyar*,[72] which means a part of the dress or uniform that distinguishes soldiers or sects of people, as well as a strip of yellow cloth worn by Jews in Persia.[73]

This served as a distinguishing badge to identify a *ghair* (different) person.[74] According to Badauni, Husain Khan had also ordered that the kafirs should not ride on saddles, but on pack saddles, claiming his injunction to be a requirement of Muslim law.[75]

It is known that Islam tolerates zimmis in general, subject to them following some restrictions—it is forbidden to insult Islam and to seek to convert a Muslim. Both the preacher and the apostate can receive death penalties for breaking these restrictions. Though existing places of worship are to be protected, the construction of new religious buildings is forbidden and, in some cases, the reconstruction of old buildings fallen into decay is opposed by the rigorists. There were also various limitations to expressions of worship, such as a ban on processions and the use of bells, though these were not strictly implemented in early Islam. All these factors held true for the Delhi Sultanate. However, in the Mamluk state, which existed at the same time as the Delhi Sultanate, due to various pressures, including the Crusades, Mongol invasions and campaigns by Muslim religious leaders like Ibn Taimiyya, restrictions on zimmis were implemented with varying degrees of success. Thus, zimmis in the Mamluk state were required to wear distinguishing dress, were only allowed to ride on donkeys and could not possess houses built on higher levels than those occupied by Muslims.[76] (In the Muslim context, this meant that the mosque building needed to be the highest one in a neighbourhood.) This may perhaps explain the nondescript nature of Hindu places of worship in medieval north India, as compared to the grandeur of mosques, tombs and palaces of the Muslims.

The above reference to Ibn Taimiyya also is not without value. A messenger of the Egyptian religious reformer had visited the court of Muhammad Tughluq and it is likely that Barani may have met him. In any case, the similarity in the attitude towards non-Muslims once again shows that Barani was not an isolated figure thinking aloud for the cause of Islam at the end of his life. He must have developed his ideas over a long period of time, reading books, and also through his interactions with contemporary intellectuals, writers and religious leaders. Barani's insistence on the recruitment of responsible *muhtasib* (censor officials) also reminds one of classical theorists' suggestions in this regard. The censor official was not only to be entrusted with the maintenance of order in the streets and markets, but was also expected to supervise the maintenance of controlling measures on zimmis.[77]

The Sunnite doctrinal position, though not necessarily conforming to one school of jurisprudence, is also reflected in Barani's instructions on the need for the governance of Muslims based on the teachings of the Prophet. Barani wrote that if the Sultans did not desire to protect the faith and establish the pious laws of the Prophet, then the Muslims themselves would have the freedom to indulge in impious and sinful trades and professions. Wine shops, brothels and gambling dens, Barani feared, would open on every street. There would be no restrictions on music parties and the Sultans would be satisfied merely with the taxes on them. The result would be that sinners and upholders of vice and immorality would flourish without fear and the Sultan, whose responsibility was to ensure that pious activities flourish and evil is crushed, would be doing the contrary. Barani again wonders how in such a condition the banner of Islam can flutter.[78]

Barani insisted that the world was full of wicked people who could be kept in control only through the power and authority of the king and not through the teachings of the Prophet. The rightly-guided caliphs could rule for some time according to the Traditions of the Prophet, but Barani also noted how three out of four of them were killed by their Muslim opponents, that too soon after the death of the Prophet, whose style of governance was a miracle in itself. For Barani, if a contemporary Sultan tried to follow the Traditions of the Prophet, his kingship would collapse then and there. It is only through the terror of the king's power that Barani felt people could be kept in check and prevented from oppressing one another—a view that had already been expressed by theorists like Ghazali and Tusi. Barani also said no Muslim, from as early as two hundred years after the death of the Prophet, has been righteous enough to be ruled by the early caliphs, Abu Bakr and Umar.[79] Barani, therefore, proposed that secular/extra-religious state laws, called zawabit, needed to be evolved. Zawabit could derive and adapt rules of governance from diverse traditions, including pre-Islamic Sassanid Persia, with utmost respect for the shariat.[80] Barani's reference to the corruption of Islam is significant as his preceptor Nizam-ud-Din Auliya also lamented the deterioration of Islam since the time of the rightly-guided caliphs of seventh-century Arabia. Like Barani, Nizam-ud-Din too denounced the lack of moral integrity amongst Muslims of his time.[81]

For Barani, the control of society required a strong rule of arm. If the Sultans continued to allow the philosophers and other enemies of the faith to exist, they would be emboldened to preach their books openly. Barani pointed out that philosophers called the Greek sciences (which were critical of the teachings of ancient and the last of the prophets) *ilm-i-maqulat* (rational sciences) and the science of the shariat, *ilm-i-manqulat* (traditional knowledge). Further, he states, they declared that the world was eternal and did not believe in the Day of Judgment, hell and heaven, and questioned the limits of God's knowledge. According to Barani, the heretics not only preached their doctrines, but also refuted the fundamentals of Islam in their argumentative tracts. If such people were allowed to live in the Sultan's capital with dignity and honour, spread their doctrines, privilege rationalistic over traditional knowledge, then, Barani feared, true religion would not be able to emerge victorious over false creeds.[82] It is not a coincidence that Nizam-ud-Din Auliya was extremely critical of the rationalistic views of the Mutazila.[83] The latter had already been crushed, but their books and ideas were still in circulation, and, therefore, a source of anxiety to the torchbearers of Sunni Islam. The above issues recur in the history of Islam in India and we shall discuss them again later.

It must be mentioned here that a number of Barani's contemporaries also praised the Sultans' efforts to dispatch infidels to hell. Indeed, the court chronicles record a series of violent conflicts between the Muslims (led by the Turks, Afghans and the Mughals) and non-Muslim chieftains like the Rajputs. These conflicts, mainly for political power and prestige, which have been projected in the sources as jihads with ghazis (victorious soldiers) and shahids (martyrs), actually involved large-scale loot and plunder, including the destruction of temples, in the hope of gaining rich rewards both in this world and the 'hereafter'. The claims of the demolition of temples might have been greatly exaggerated,[84] but the rhetoric of Persian accounts cannot be dismissed altogether. If one grants that the reports are not relevant for understanding the contexts in which they were written, then, at least, they point to the 'personal' views, temperament or interests of the authors concerned; but these authors were no ordinary people and do attract attention. The case of Barani's friend and fellow courtier, Amir Khusrau, has already been mentioned earlier.

Modern scholars of medieval Indian history have not addressed these issues adequately. Most influential, pluralist and left-oriented scholars deny the existence of any religious struggles between Hindus and Muslims prior to British rule. For them, Hindu–Muslim identities are modern constructions that did not exist in pre-colonial or early-modern India. However, alongside, there has existed a 'separatist' Muslim scholarship with its rigid assumption that Hindus and Muslims are two different 'nations', and that their separate histories may be traced back to Muhammad bin Qasim's conquest of Sindh. Not surprisingly, there also exists another stream of scholarship with an overt pro-Hindu tinge. The basic premise in the literature produced by this group is that medieval India under Islamic rule, characterized by the large-scale destruction of temples and the constant humiliation of Hindus, was a dark phase in the otherwise glorious history of Hindu civilization. Dubious as the above propositions are, it goes on to conclude that many of the 'evils' facing Hindu society today are a legacy of Muslim rule. Obviously, historians have approached the theme from diverse vantage points, but our reading of some of the sources suggests that the views summarized above need to be considerably revised.[85]

It has to be reiterated that contrary to the claims of certain sections of historical scholarship, religious contestations were not unheard of in medieval India. Such contestations did not necessarily lead to widespread violence in all cases. The resistance and protests, even calls for the need to deploy reason in communal relations, can be viewed as attempts to maintain religious, cultural and literary purity. The sixteenth-century Marathi Bhakti poet, Eknath's presentation of a hard-hitting argument between a Hindu and a Muslim in his drama-poem, *Hindu-Turk Samvad*, may be mentioned here. The aggressive Muslim protagonist is made to realize that both Hindus and Muslims were created by God. Their 'goal is one', though 'the ways of worship are different'. Eknath's Hindu character also castigates the Muslim, who is supposed to grab a Hindu and convert him to Islam: 'Did God make a mistake in making a Hindu? Is your wisdom greater than His?' The practices and rituals of the Sufi shrines are also questioned: 'You tell us we worship stones. Why do you place blocks of stone over the dead? . . . You cover the stone with flowers and silk cloth; you burn incense before it!' More trenchant is the criticism of the popular veneration or 'worship of a *haji* of stone (Ka'ba in Mecca)'. The drama ends on a consensus: 'The argument was about oneness. The argument became agreement'.[86] It is important to note that the consensus does not dissolve the question of identity. It only shows the author's concerns to illustrate the commonality of certain beliefs and rituals, and resist the conversion of Hindus to Islam.

If the juristically-inclined ulama wanted an all-out war against the kafirs, Muslim attitudes towards the latter were tempered by the more politically correct position taken by a large number of Sufis. Many Sufis who mingled freely with people adhering to diverse formal/informal religious traditions considered it unadvisable to use political power for spreading Islam. Some of them refrained from converting people without a proper 'introduction' to Islam through personal interaction over a long period of time. The most powerful and articulate argument on this issue came from the influential Chishti saint and Barani's pir, Nizam-ud-Din Auliya, who asserted that no amount of force could change the hearts of kafirs or Hindus. (Significantly, the words 'Hindu' and *qaum* [community] were already in currency in the early decades of the fourteenth century, though the connotations of these terms might have been different from how they are understood today.) The saint felt that the Hindus needed to spend time in the company of good Muslims to be transformed into good Muslims themselves.[87] Conversion, then, becomes a matter of formality. Thus, it is through long-term association with Sufi centres like hospices and shrines that many individuals and groups of people embraced Islam.

Though colonial enumeration did play a role in sharpening categories such as Muslim and Hindu, this does not mean that these categories did not exist at all in medieval times. To deny this is to ignore the views of medieval Muslim intellectuals like Ziya-ud-Din Barani, who clearly identified himself with one political and, shall we say, cultural group. Barani's writings show the contestations that were involved in what constituted a community or umma of Islam in relation to kafirs. It is also clear that the self-righteous, privileged groups amongst Muslims wanted to utilize all the tools of dominance to subdue those who belonged to lower groups in a socially stratified and sectarian conflict-ridden society. Barani wanted the kafirs to be sent to hell, even as he condemned converted Indian Muslims in the Delhi Sultanate as Islam's internal 'others'. We shall carry our discussion forward in the next two chapters on what was considered Islamic and non-Islamic in Mughal India.

4

Islam and Heresies in Mughal India

This chapter will address the question of what constituted heresies under Islam in late-sixteenth-century Hindustan, especially with reference to the debates in the ibadat-khana (literally, house of worship) of the Mughal emperor Akbar, during the tumultuous period of 1575–80. The extended discussions in the court and private chambers of the emperor and their implications for policy will also be taken into account. For this, we will focus on the period of Akbar's reign as described in Abdul Qadir Badauni's controversial text, the *Muntakhab-ut-Tawarikh*,[1] which provides a counter-narrative to the much-celebrated official account of Abul Fazl in *Akbarnama* and *Ain-i-Akbari*.[2] This is important because in much of the scholarship, Abul Fazl's account is privileged; indeed, even paraphrased. By contrast, Badauni's views are often dismissed as the outpourings of a reactionary *mulla*.[3] The intention here is not only to give Badauni a fair representation, but also to compare and contrast the diverse positions taken by interested parties in the debates on the merits and virtues of defending traditional Islam, and advancing a rational or philosophical stance in dealing with theological questions vis-à-vis contemporary problems.

Though the intellectual commitments of medieval writers and scholars were important, we will see to what extent personal rivalries and competition for positions in the Mughal nobility and for gaining the emperor's favour were camouflaged as ideological struggles. So, much of the discussion here will deal with Badauni's writings on the years AH 983–87 (1575–80).

The Mughal scholar's descriptions of and charges against the official ulama, Sufis, liberal intellectuals and others who were engaged in debates supporting one position or the other are scathing. He was particularly hostile towards Abul Fazl, who seemingly represented the liberal face of Islam. However, he did not ignore the alleged impiety of the two leading official ulama of the time, Sheikh Abdun Nabi and Makhdum-ul-Mulk Abdullah Sultanpuri. Clearly, much was at stake for Badauni himself, which we will identify in our discussion below.

Badauni postpones recounting details about the ibadat-khana,[4] to discuss Abul Fazl, who went to Akbar's court for the second time in the month of Zil Qad AH 982 (1574–75). Badauni says that styled as Allami, Abul Fazl was supposed to be a man who could set the world on fire; who lighted the lamp of reason and was determined to oppose all the sects of Islam.[5] He presented the emperor with a commentary on a set of Quranic verses, *ayat-ul-kursi*,[6] which contained a good many of the subtleties of the Quran. Badauni notes that though the commentary was probably written by Abul Fazl's father, Sheikh Mubarak Nagauri, it was his son who was praised for it. Akbar liked the tract and according to Badauni, judged Abul Fazl to be a man capable of teaching the mullas, who had begun behaving like Pharaohs (*mullayan firaon sifat*), a lesson. Though Badauni condemned the ulama as the 'Pharaohs', he also sincerely noted a conflict of interests: Akbar's expectations from Abul Fazl were opposed to the confidence he had reposed in Badauni.[7] Despite the arrogance of the official ulama and lack of integrity amongst them, Badauni still took the traditional line on respect for the laws and institutions of Islam, unlike Abul Fazl.

According to Badauni, Abul Fazl's charges against the Islamic orthodoxy can be understood in the context of the harassment his family had to endure at their hands: at the time, it was easy to suppress those who tried to introduce innovations in religious matters. Learned men in Akbar's court such as Abdun Nabi and Makhdum-ul-Mulk represented to the emperor that Abul Fazl's father, Sheikh Mubarak pretended to be a *mahdi* (a guide who is the forerunner of the messiah) and belonged to a group of innovators (*ahl-i bidat*), the Mahdawis. Sheikh Mubarak was thus considered to have not only damned himself, but also to have led others to commit heresy. Having obtained a permission of sorts to 'remove' him, they ordered for him to be brought before the emperor. On discovering, however, that the sheikh had fled with his two sons, Abul Fazl and Faizi, they had the pulpit of his mosque demolished. The sheikh, in turn, approached Salim Chishti, who was then at the height of his glory, and requested him to intercede on their behalf.[8] However, contrary to their expectations, Sheikh Salim only arranged for some money and told him to escape to Gujarat. So, Sheikh Mubarak applied to Akbar's foster brother, Mirza Aziz Koka, who brought the sheikh's learning and piety (*mullai wa darweshi*) and the excellence (*fazilat*) of his sons to the emperor's attention. Aziz Koka also apparently added that Mubarak had never received a revenue-free land grant (*inam*), and that he could not understand why the sheikh was being persecuted.[9]

Convinced, Akbar revoked the order for executing Sheikh Mubarak and soon matters took a more favourable turn. In Badauni's opinion, when the faithless flatterer beyond all bounds, Abul Fazl, gained favour with the emperor, he used every opportunity to revile his antagonists. Consequently, misery and misfortune broke upon the ulama, who had persecuted the family. Eventually, Abul Fazl, who was continually studying the emperor's whims, became the cause of the ruin of all the Muslim men of religion, whose grants were cut.[10] Further, Badauni says, during disputes, when the edicts of any *mujtahid* (a recognized authority on Muslim law) were quoted, Abul Fazl would arrogantly dismiss them as the arguments of a sweetmeat seller (*halwai*), cobbler (*kafash-doz*) or tanner (*charam-gar*).[11]

In his account of the following year, AH 983 (1575–6), Badauni notes that the emperor appointed him imam of his mosque, as well as *mansabdar* (nobleman), in command of twenty horses. Apart from leading the prayers, namaz, on one day every week, Badauni was also directed to undertake the branding of imperial horses—a job he disliked as he was not sanctioned any travel expenses. To start with, Badauni notes, Abul Fazl too was treated in the same way and began his career at a *mansab* (rank) of twenty horses. Badauni accuses Abul Fazl of working so strenuously at the *dagh-o-mahalli* business (a reference to the corruption in the nobility regarding the number of horses to be maintained), that he managed, with his intelligence (*ziraki*) and time-serving qualities (*zamana-sazi*), to rise to a mansab of two thousand horses, a rank equivalent of wazir (minister). By contrast, an inexperienced simpleton (*be-tajurbagi wa sadah-lauhi*) such as Badauni himself remained stuck at his lowly mansab of twenty horses. He lamented that he could neither make any progress in Mughal service nor withdraw altogether.[12]

Badauni continues to recount the tale of his own sad plight and notes that in the month of Shawwal AH 983 (1575–76), he was denied leave, though the emperor excused him from the inspection of horses. Additionally, an unfriendly *sadr* (a high ecclesiastical official under Akbar), Sheikh Abdun Nabi, allotted Badauni a mere thousand *bigha*s of land (about five-eighths of an acre) as *madad-i-ma'ash* (revenue-free land grant). When Badauni complained that with such a small grant, he could not always afford to be in attendance, the emperor replied that he would also grant him subsidies and presents during the marches.[13] The sadr, Abdun Nabi, also added that no person of Badauni's qualification and rank had received such a large grant. Finally, Badauni complains that the promise of presents was largely illusive.[14]

In the same year (AH 983 [1575–76]), the construction of the buildings of the ibadat-khana was completed. According to Badauni, for many years, the emperor had gained remarkable and decisive victories, and the empire had grown in extent;

everything had turned out well and there was no opponent left. That was when Akbar came in contact with the Sufis (*fuqra wa mujawiran*) associated with the shrine of Muin-ud-Din Chishti and began spending time discussing the sources of Islamic tradition, including the Words of Allah and those of the Prophet, Sufism, philosophy and jurisprudence. Badauni says that the king spent whole nights meditating and chanting the name of God for his heart was full of reverence for Him; he thanked God for his success and spent many mornings alone in prayer.[15]

Badauni recounts that at this time, Akbar also heard of other influential political figures such as Sulaiman Kararani, governor of Bengal, and Mirza Sulaiman of Badakhshan, who closely followed the precepts of Islam and spent time with ulama and Sufis. Inspired, Akbar had the cell of Sheikh Abdullah Niyazi Sarhindi—a former disciple of Sheikh Islam Chishti, who had later joined the Mahdawis[16]—repaired, and also built a spacious hall around it. He named the cell, ibadat-khana (prayer hall), which was, remarks Badauni, gradually transformed into an *iyadat-khana* or a place for visiting the sick.[17] In the Persian script, the difference between 'ibadat' (prayer) and 'iyadat' (visiting the sick) is just an additional *nuqta* or point; though Badauni was trying to be subtle, it is clear what his opinion was of the participants of the debates in that hall pulling each other down over a point or two.

On Thursday evenings and after the Friday congregational prayers, Akbar held meetings on a diverse range of topics in this building, where sheikhs, ulama, pious men and a few of his own companions and attendants were invited.[18] To start with, ill-feeling arose over the seats and order of precedence; so *amir*s, or nobles, were asked to sit on the eastern side, sayyids on the west, the ulama to the south and the sheikhs on the north.[19] The emperor sat with these groups and engaged in scholarly discussions. Badauni mentions that a large quantity of perfume was used here and a huge amount of money was distributed as rewards of merit and ability amongst the worthy participants, some of whom had obtained entry through the favour of courtiers. Also, many fine books, which had belonged to Itimad Khan Gujarati and had been acquired during the conquest of Gujarat, were placed in the imperial library. These were subsequently distributed amongst the learned (*ulama wa fuzala*), including Badauni.[20]

Badauni relates an incident, when one night, the outraged ulama became very noisy, which led to much confusion. The emperor got very angry with their rude behaviour and said to Badauni, 'In the future, report any of the ulama who talk nonsense (*sukhan na-maqul*) or cannot behave properly, and we shall make him leave the hall.' Badauni then whispered to Asaf Khan, 'If I carried out this order, most of them would have to leave.' Badauni notes that Akbar was highly pleased with his comment and mentioned this remark to those sitting near him.[21]

According to Badauni, the emperor used to summon Makhdum-ul-Mulk to these gatherings only to annoy or hurt him, and would set him up to argue against scholars like Haji Ibrahim or Abul Fazl, the new entrant and leader of the 'new' religion (*mazhab-i nau*). Akbar purposely interrupted the Maulana often and at the slightest hint from him, his companions would also intervene. The Maulana had apparently issued a fatwa that *hajj* was not only no longer obligatory, but also hurtful. When asked to explain the rationale for such an extraordinary directive, the Maulana remarked that the two roads to Mecca, through Persia and Gujarat, were impractical. This was because people travelling by land, that is, through Iran, had to suffer the injustices of the Shi'ite Safavids (*qizilbash*), while those travelling by sea were exposed to indignities by the Portuguese (*firangi*), whose travel documents (*ahd-nama*) had pictures of Mary and Jesus on them. To make use of the latter alternative meant supporting idolatry (*but-prasti*). Hence, the Maulana reasoned, both options were closed.[22]

Further, Badauni says that according to another report, Makhdum-ul-Mulk evaded paying his taxes (zakat). He did this by transferring all his property towards the end of each year to his wife and then taking it back before the year had passed. Thus, the surplus wealth could not be counted as being either in his or his wife's possession for the whole year and, therefore, could technically not be taxed. Several other stories also circulated about his contemptible conduct. For Badauni, most of his vices were actually practised against Muslim holy men and other deserving people, which came to light one by one, thus verifying the warning in the Quran: 'There is a day when secrets shall be disclosed'.[23] Sufficiently outraged, Akbar concluded that the Maulana had to be sent to Mecca and though he refuted these allegations, he was forcibly dispatched for hajj.[24]

At a time when the fortunes of Makhdum-ul-Mulk Abdullah Sultanpuri were fast waning, those of another ecclesiastical official, Sheikh Abdun Nabi, were ascending. Badauni writes that on account of his great reverence and respect for Abdun Nabi, Akbar would often visit his house to hear lectures on the Traditions of the Prophet (hadis). He also made the eldest prince attend the sheikh's school to study the hadis.[25] Adbun Nabi, in turn, twisted a particular hadis in an erroneous manner to claim that, 'The prudent course is to hold an evil opinion of others.' Many years later, Mirza Aziz Koka reminded Akbar of this fact and since the emperor had already lost interest in him and other mullas, Badauni says that action against him was just a matter of time.[26]

In Badauni's account of the same year, AH 983 (1575–76), he mentions that Akbar gave orders that revenue-free land grantees, *aimma,* were to bring the farman in which grants, subsistence allowances and pensions were described to the sadr, Abdun Nabi, for inspection and verification. A large number of 'worthy' people from the extreme east of India to as far west as Bhakkar were forced to visit the court. Those who knew the amirs closely were protected and could manage to get their farmans renewed. Those without proper connections had to bribe Abdun Nabi's staff to push their case. Thus, Badauni notes, unless people had strong recommendations or resorted to bribery, they were utterly ruined, while some even perished.[27]

Though Akbar heard of these reports, no one dared speak of them openly. Also, according to Badauni, when a haughty

Abdun Nabi took his official place, and influential amirs introduced learned or pious men to him, he behaved impolitely with them. For example, it was after much persuasion that he granted a teacher of the *Hidayah* (or 'Guidance', a book on Muslim law) and other standard texts, one hundred bighas or so, thus taking away from the man the land he earlier had in possession. On the other hand, wretched men and even Hindus, Badauni alleged, were granted land for the first time.[28]

In Badauni's opinion, it was not only learned Muslim men whose ranks fell, but even some great amirs, who had to endure humiliation. However, they eventually took their revenge:

> *rusatai agar shawad qazi*
> *hukmhai kunad ke bakushand*
> [When a rustic becomes a judge
> He issues such orders that they kill him.][29]

Badauni claims that never in the time of any emperor had such absolute power been enjoyed by a sadr.[30] In a measure, the author was evidently expressing his own discomfort with Abdun Nabi's arbitrary style of working.

Badauni writes that Akbar's questioning of the integrity of his officials entrusted with religious matters was, to start with, posed in intellectual or theological terms. He writes of a question that the emperor asked, which would go on to alter the power relations between the state and the ulama. Akbar's question was: 'How many freeborn women may a man legally marry by *nikah* (*chand zan asil ra ba-nikah awardan durust bashad*)?' When the jurists answered that four women was the limit fixed by the Prophet, Akbar remarked that in his youth, he had not considered the question and had married as many women as it pleased him, both free-born (*azad*) and slaves (*banda*). He now wanted to know what remedy (*ilaj*) the law had provided in his case. The king argued that Abdun Nabi had once told him that one of the mujtahids said that as many as nine wives were allowed for Muslims. To this, some of the jurists replied that some mujtahids had even said that eighteen were allowed, the result of a literal translation of the verse of the Quran[31]: 'Marry whatever women you like, two and two, and three and three, and four and four' (2+2+3+3+4+4=18. The mujtahid who counted nine, interpreted it as 2+3+4=9. The usual interpretation is 'two or three or four').[32] When Akbar confronted Abdun Nabi with this argument, he replied that he had merely wanted to point out that a difference of opinion existed amongst the jurists and that he had not given any fatwa to legalize irregular marriage proceedings. Badauni says this annoyed the emperor, who said, 'The sheikh told me at that time a very different thing from what he tells me now.' Akbar apparently never forgave Abdun Nabi for misleading him on a theological point of considerable importance.[33]

Following Akbar's question, after much discussion, the ulama, who consulted every Tradition on the subject decreed: first, that by *mutah* (short-term marriage contract) not by nikah, it was permissible (mubah) for a man to marry any number of women he pleased; and, second, that mutah was allowed as legal (*jayez*) by Imam Malik. Badauni adds that someone reported that the Shias loved their children born in mutah wedlock more than those born of nikah, contrary to the Sunnis, a point that made the discussion rather lively.[34] To further complicate the matter, Naqib Khan produced a copy of the *Muwatta* of Imam Malik and pointed to a hadis, which the Imam had cited as proof against the legality of mutah marriages. Khan thus asserted that Imam Malik's name was being wrongly used to support the practice of mutah.[35] From Badauni's description of this discussion, it becomes clear that Akbar's officials were either utterly ignorant of standard juridical positions or were just being wicked.

As the issue remained unresolved, Qazi Yaqub, Abul Fazl, Haji Ibrahim and a few other scholars were invited to meet the emperor. Abul Fazl, who had been selected as the opponent, began the discussion by citing several hadis on mutah marriages (which, in Badauni's view, were compiled by his father, Sheikh

Mubarak). Badauni was also invited to speak on the subject and he notes that the conclusion to be drawn from so many contradictory Traditions and interpretations is this: Imam Malik and the Shias are unanimous in accepting mutah as permissible; Imam Shafi'i and the great Imam, Abu Hanifa, treated mutah as unlawful (*haram*). However, if at any time a qazi of the Maliki school decided that mutah was legal, it would be binding on everyone, including Shafi'is and Hanafis; any other opinion on the subject, for the writer, was idle talk. Badauni claimed that Akbar liked this explanation immensely, even as Qazi Yaqub muttered something unintelligible to defend himself.[36]

Badauni further states that using this opportunity, he reminded Yaqub that when a matter is unresolved, it is generally in the power of a qazi to judge. Qazi Yaqub was thus cornered by both the liberals and the conservatives. Disappointed with the outcome of this discussion, Akbar then reportedly ordered Yaqub's sacking and the appointment of Husain Arab Maliki as the qazi adjudicating the matter concerning his numerous wives. This was immediately implemented and Qazi Husain, who followed the Maliki school, promptly issued a decree legalizing mutah marriages.[37]

The veteran ulama were the losers in this episode and, according to Badauni, from this moment on, their power began to wane. Soon Maulana Jalal-ud-Din of Multan, a learned man whose grant had been transferred earlier, was ordered to move from Agra to Fatehpur Sikri, and was appointed the qazi of the realm. Yaqub was sent to Gaur, Bengal, as a district qazi. From then onward, the road of opposition to religious orthodoxy and difference of opinion with the ulama lay open, culminating in Akbar's appropriation of the position of mujtahid,[38] which we will read about later.

On another occasion, Abdun Nabi and Makhdum-ul-Mulk were ordered to examine the jizya amount to be levied on Hindus (*hinduan*). Accordingly, farmans were issued, but Badauni comments this order disappeared as quickly as a reflection on water (*an hukm chun naqsh bar-ab zawad*).[39] In yet another instance of the ulama losing power, the emperor inquired how people would react if the phrase '*Allah-o-Akbar*' was engraved on his seal and coins. Most said that they would like it, but Haji Ibrahim Sarhindi objected and said that the phrase had an ambiguous meaning (that is, it could be read either as 'God is great' or 'Akbar is God'). He suggested that the emperor substitute it with the unambiguous phrase from the Quran, '*lazikrullahi akbaru*' ('To commemorate God is the greatest thing'). But the emperor was not convinced by his argument and wondered, 'How could it be so reasonable that his meaning should be so distorted and claims of divinity (*khudai*) attributed to him?'[40] In other words, Akbar protested that it was unfair to attribute to him any divinity—a claim which he himself had no intention of making—though he did accept that the invocation of the phrase, 'Allah-o-Akbar', was confusing enough. It is important to note here that 'Allah' and 'Akbar' were getting mixed up at a time when the emperor was questioning almost all the established beliefs of traditional Sunnite Islam.

Continuing with his account of the year AH 983 (1575–6), Badauni also refers to the death/murder of Sayyid Muhammad Mir Adl, committed at Haji Ibrahim's behest, for his opposition to a fatwa issued by the latter that made it legal for men to wear red and saffron clothes.[41] Badauni then mentions the appearance in court of three brothers from Jilan—Hakim Abul Fateh, Hakim Humayun (who later changed his name to Humayun Quli and lastly to Hakim Human), and the poet Nur-ud-Din Qarari. The eldest brother, Abul Fateh, reportedly became a favourite of the emperor in a short time due to his winning manners. He flattered him openly, adapted himself to every change in the religious ideas of the monarch, even guessed them in advance, and, consequently, became a most intimate friend of the ruler.[42]

It is in this year that Badauni writes of the arrival from Persia of Mulla Muhammad of Yazd, who had taken the name Yazidi. (This name linked him phonetically to Yazid, son of Amir Mawiya, the founder of the Umayyad Caliphate with its base in late-seventh-century Damascus. This was a contradiction in terms as Yazid is condemned in the Shi'ite tradition and the mulla was perceived to be a Shi'ite fanatic!) He apparently reviled the *sahaba* (companions of the Prophet), told strange stories about them and even tried hard to convert Akbar to Shi'ite Islam (*padshah ra khwast ke ba-janib tashi kushad*). However, Badauni says that he was soon left behind by Bir Bar (Birbal),[43] [who Badauni refers to as 'that bastard' (*haram-zada*)], and later, by Abul Fazl and Hakim Abul Fateh. In Badauni's view, these men successfully turned the king away from Islam (*az din munharaf sakhtand*) and led him to reject revelation (*wahi*), prophet-hood (*nabuwwat*), miracles (karamat) of the Prophet and of the saints, and even the law itself. Badauni noted that he could no longer bear their company.[44]

Meanwhile, Badauni writes that Akbar had not yet given up on Islam completely as he ordered Qazi Jalal-ud-Din and several ulama to write a commentary on the Quran, which led to great tensions among them. In this context, Badauni also calls Deb Chand, the raja of Manjhola, a *maskhara* (fool or jester) because the raja had once made Akbar's court laugh by saying that Allah had great respect for cows (*gao*) as the first chapter of the Quran was named after that animal.[45] The raja had apparently meant to say that both the Quran and the Vedas revered the cow.

In this period, Akbar also had the early history of Islam read out to him and, according to Badauni, began to disrespect the companions of the Prophet. Soon, observances such as the five prayers and fasting, and belief in everything connected with the Prophet began to be questioned, and man's reason (*aql*), not tradition (*naql*), was acknowledged as the only basis of religion. Portuguese priests (*firangiyan*) also attended Akbar's court frequently and Badauni says that the emperor seemed interested in their beliefs, which were supposedly based upon reason (*iteqadiyat aqli*).[46] (This means that the circle of discussants in the ibadat-khana was growing. It was not only the entrenched orthodoxy and new ulama or scholars who were attending these gatherings; other interested parties such as non-Muslim religious leaders, gurus and *padri*s were also participating in the discussions and attracting Akbar's attention.)

Badauni records that Sheikh Badr-ud-Din, the son of Sheikh Islam Chishti who had joined the Mahdawis, too was invited by the king. Having given up attending on princes, he had become his father's successor and spent all his time in prayer. As a result, he no longer observed the norms of courtly conduct and committed many breaches of etiquette. Other misfortunes that followed apparently made him leave the court in sheer disappointment and despair. He left for Ajmer and from there for Gujarat, where he boarded a ship for Mecca. He eventually died there, or as Badauni put it, obtained spiritual union with God.[47]

In his account of the year AH 983 (1575–76), Badauni also mentions the arrival of a learned Brahmin from Deccan, who had converted to Islam, Sheikh Bhawan. Incidentally, it was in this year that the emperor asked Badauni to translate the *Bed Atharban* (*Atharva Veda*) into Persian. Badauni notes that several religious precepts of this book resembled the laws of Islam. He found many passages difficult to understand when translating this text and he says that Sheikh Bhawan could not interpret them either. So, the king reportedly ordered Faizi and then Haji Ibrahim Sarhindi to translate it. The latter accepted the responsibility, but in Badauni's opinion, could not do it in a satisfactory manner.

Badauni notes that one of the precepts of the *Atharva Veda* said that no man would be saved unless he read a certain passage, which contained repeated references to the Arabic letter '*laam*', which resembled the *kalima*, the Muslim profession of faith that reads '*la ilaha illallah*' ('There is no God except Allah'). Besides, Badauni found from the *Atharva Veda* that a Hindu, under certain circumstances, was allowed to eat beef (*gosht-i gao*) and bury, not cremate, the dead. Using Badauni's insights, Sheikh Bhawan reportedly defeated other Brahmins in arguments and also confessed that these points had, in fact, led him to embrace Islam.[48] In later years, Akbar 'forced' Badauni to undertake the translations of such classical Indic texts as the *Ramayana* and *Mahabharata*. Badauni says that he reluctantly worked with the help of Brahmin interpreters as well as other collaborators, and that the emperor appreciated his competence, but was always sceptical of the scholar inserting his own prejudices and assumptions about the Hindu belief systems into the translations.[49]

Badauni also mentions that Akbar sustained his faith in the shrine of Muin-ud-Din Chishti during this period of religious disputations and visited Ajmer on 17 Zil Qad AH 983 (1575–76),[50] in the first half of the month of Muharram AH 984 (1576–77), in the month of Rajab AH 985 (1577–78), when he also introduced Man Singh to the shrine,[51] during the annual *urs*, the death anniversary of the Khwaja,[52] and again, in the following year on the sixth day of the month of Rajab AH 986 (1578–79).[53] Early in the year AH 986 (1578–79), Badauni reports that the emperor visited the tomb of Sheikh Farid-ud-Din Ganj-i-Shakar at Pak Pattan.[54] All these visits occurred amidst campaigns in western India. Though Akbar did not visit the Ajmer shrine after 1579, it will be inaccurate to say that he turned away from the Chishti fraternity in the wake of his disgust with Muslim religious personnel and break with Islam in general.[55] Amidst all the anxieties—competitive religiosity and violence over which form of religion should dominate, the questioning of the worth of the emperor's faith in the mausoleum of Muin-ud-Din Chishti in the year AH 987 (1579–80)—Akbar sent Prince Daniyal, Sheikh Faizi, who was his teacher, Sheikh Jamal Bakhtiyar and a number of courtiers to Ajmer with a donation of 25,000 rupees to the *faqirs* of that shrine.[56]

Back in Fatehpur, in AH 986 (1578–79), when he was still frequenting the Ajmer shrine, the king spent a lot of time in the ibadat-khana with learned men and sheikhs. On Friday nights especially, he reportedly engaged in discussions on questions of religion (*tahqiq masail-i din*). As a witness of these discussions, Badauni records that the learned men lambasted each other with mutual contradiction and opposition, and the antagonism reached such a pitch that they began accusing one another of heresies and stupidity (*takfir wa tazlil*). Badauni says that the disputes used to go beyond the usual differences of Sunnis and

Shias, Hanafis and Shafi'is, and jurists and philosophers (*faqih wa hakim*)—they attacked the very basis of belief.[57]

An indication of personal rivalry and mutual hatred affecting even those from the same intellectual background was Makhdum-ul-Mulk Abdullah Sultanpuri coming out openly against Sheikh Abdun Nabi. Makhdum-ul-Mulk wrote a pamphlet in which he accused the latter of having unjustly killed Khizr Khan Sarwani, who was suspected of blaspheming the Prophet (*sabb-i nabi*) and Mir Habsh, who was suspected of being a Shia (*rafzi*). Attributing other sins and inabilities to Abdun Nabi, Makhdum-ul-Mulk also claimed that it was not right to participate in prayers led by him. In response, Abdun Nabi dismissed Makhdum-ul-Mulk as a fool and heretic (*tajhil wa tazlil*). Thus, the mullas were divided and, according to Badauni, behaved like the Jews and Egyptians in hating each other.[58] Clearly, Badauni himself was not siding with either of the mullas and it is important to recognize this distinction and not dismiss Badauni's account as uncritically advocating the cause of the official ulama, which is how his work is generally represented in conventional histories of the secularists.

The philosophers and the rationalists, whom Badauni characterizes as persons of novel and whimsical opinions, took advantage of the bickering amongst the theologians. Badauni alleges that typical of their pernicious ideas and vain doubts, they openly recommended wrong (*batil*) as right (*haqq*) and vice versa.[59] The emperor—who, in Badauni's opinion, possessed an excellent disposition (*jauhri nafis*) and was an earnest searcher of truth (*talib-i haqq*), but a mere novice in matters of religion and used to the company of infidels and base persons (*ba-kufrah wa arzal*)—was perplexed as doubt upon doubt was heaped on him till he lost all traces of Islam and his every belief was turned upside down.[60]

Though Badauni was clearly exaggerating, his writing alludes to many potential reasons that gave rise to the chaotic situation during 1575–80. He narrates that learned men and sages of various religions and sects visited the court and were honoured with private conversations with the emperor. They reportedly discussed profound points of science, subtleties of revelation, curiosities of history and wonders of tradition. The monarch picked anything that pleased him and chose from anyone, except the hitherto influential Sunnite Islam, and anything that was against his disposition and ran counter to his wishes, was rejected. Badauni further notes that the king had appropriated ideas from various religions and sectarian beliefs, and by a peculiar inquisitiveness and a talent for selection, had also made his own all that could be found in books.[61]

In Badauni's opinion, given these influences, Akbar concluded that wise men and ascetics with abilities to perform miracles could be found in all religions. Therefore, according to Badauni, Akbar thought, how could it be right to consider the truth/right (haqq) as confined to one religion (*din*), that is, Islam, which had only recently made its appearance and had not yet survived a thousand years? In fact, he questioned the very basis of the claim of the supremacy of Islam over other religious traditions.[62]

Thus, Badauni records, even shamans and Brahmins gained the honour of private interviews and association with the emperor. He also says that these religious men were in every way superior in reputation to all learned men for their treatises on morals and the physical and religious sciences, as well as for their level of religious ecstasy and spiritual progress towards human perfection. It is important to note here that unlike the secularist rendering of Badauni as one who uncritically advocated the 'Muslim cause', the scholar does not blindly condemn the shamans and Brahmins as infidels and, in fact, goes on to add that they presented arguments based on reason and traditional testimony for the truth of their own and the fallacy of Muslim beliefs. Badauni also says that they presented their doctrine with such firmness and assurance that they affirmed mere imaginings as though they were self-evident facts, which the doubts of the sceptics could not shake.[63] However, Badauni lamented that

Akbar not only denied the notions of resurrection and day of judgment, of which the Prophet was the repository, but also made his courtiers listen to his tirades against Muslim beliefs and urged them to follow his path.[64]

Badauni gives a few examples of the nature of personal interactions between Akbar and Hindu men of religion in his writings: a Brahmin named Purukhottam (Purushottam), who had written a commentary on the *Khirad-Afza*, the Persian translation by Badauni of the Sanskrit classic, *Vatrisha Simhasana* (*Sinhasan Batisi*), had private interviews with the emperor and was asked to invent Sanskrit names for all things in existence. Another Brahmin, named Devi, who worked with Badauni on the *Mahabharata* translation project, was hoisted up along the wall of the fort on a *charpai* or cot till he reached a balcony where the emperor had made his bed chamber.[65] (Clearly, Akbar was also attempting to create a spectacle around his philosophical inquiries.) Whilst thus suspended, the Brahmin instructed the king on the secrets and myths of Hinduism (*asrar wa afasanaha-i hindi*), and the manner of worshipping idols, the fire, the sun and stars, as well as the chief deities of the unbelievers (*asatin-i kufra*) such as Brahma, Mahadev, Vishnu, Krishna and Ram.[66] Here Badauni inserts his own position on the matter—he notes that the existence of these gods is a supposition and their non-existence is a certainty, though some of them are looked upon as gods (*ilahi*) and others as angels (*malaika*).[67]

Badauni further says that Akbar, on realizing how much the people of the country he ruled valued their religious beliefs, began to look upon them with affection. He reportedly became firmly convinced of the doctrine of the transmigration of souls (*mazhab-i tanasukhiyat*) and consequently, insincere flatterers composed treatises to establish indisputable arguments in favour of the doctrine, while the emperor instituted research into the religions of the unbelievers of Hindustan (*kuffar-i hind*; 'kuffar' being the plural of kafir), who possessed a number of sacred books, but could not be considered ahl-i-kitab (People of the Book).[68]

Akbar also invited Sufis such as Sheikh Taj-ud-Din, son of Sheikh Zakariya of Ajodhan, who adhered to the doctrine of wahdat-ul-wujud (unity of existence) for discussions. Addressed as *Taj-ul-Arifin* (Crown of the Sufis), Taj-ud-Din was considered second only to Sheikh Ibn-i-Arabi in mysticism and theology, and had written a comprehensive commentary on the *Nuzhat-ul-Arwah*. The Sheikh was also lifted up along the wall of the fort in a blanket and the emperor reportedly listened to his discourse on Sufism the whole night (which Badauni condemns as Sufic obscenities and follies).[69] Seemingly, Badauni subscribed to the older form of traditional Indian Sufism that centred on the shrines of the major figures of the earlier generation, and was ill at ease with the more recent fashion of theoretical expositions.[70]

Badauni notes that Sheikh Taj-ud-Din, who was not bound by the injunctions of the shariat, introduced arguments concerning wahdat-ul-wujud, a topic that Badauni thought only idle Sufis discussed, which eventually led to heresy (*ba-ibahat wa ilhad*). The Sheikh also introduced the emperor to the question of the faith of the Pharaohs ('the curse of God be on him'), which is mentioned in Ibn-i-Arabi's *Fusus-ul-Hikam*. Thus, Badauni alleged, the Sheikh became one of the chief causes of the weakening of the emperor's faith in the commands of Islam.[71] Here, Badauni seems to have gone further from his charges on Makhdum-ul-Mulk, Sheikh Abdun Nabi and other 'official' ulama and Sufis, who, because of their alleged lack of integrity, drove the emperor away from Islam to explore the genuineness of other holy men. He was unable to make sense of the new trends in Islamic mystical philosophy.

Badauni also accuses Sheikh Taj-ud-Din both of doubting that infidels would be punished in hell-fires for eternity and of introducing many changes in the text of the Quran and hadis. The expression '*insan-i-kamil*', the Perfect Man, was used by him (Taj-ud-Din) to refer to the caliph of the age (Akbar), in the sense of the holiest man and, according to Badauni, meant interpreting most things in a manner not wholly sensible (*la-aql*) and even utterly nonsensical (*khurafat*). Taj-ud-Din advocated sijda (prostration) before the emperor, also called *zaminbos* (kissing the ground) and hailed reverence for the king as an absolute religious command (*farz-i-ayn*). He also reportedly described the face of the emperor as *ka'ba-i-muradat* (sanctum of desires) and *qibla-i-hajat* (goal of necessities). To support his arguments, he cited some traditions and the practice of the disciples of some of the Sufi sheikhs. Thus, Badauni notes, after some time, the titles 'The Only One', 'The Absolute', 'The Perfect Man' became commonly applicable to the just and magnificent emperor.[72] Significantly, Badauni continued to have a high regard for Akbar despite his drifting away from traditional Sunnite Islam under the influence of the latest philosophical interpretations of Islamic traditions.

Badauni also states that he greatly regreted that the differences among the ulama—from whom one would pronounce something as unlawful and another, by some process of argument, would characterize the very same thing as lawful (*yaki faili ra haram mi-guft wa digari ba-haila haman ra halal mi-sakht*)—had been a cause of the emperor's loss of belief. Since he looked on each alim of his age as superior in dignity and worth to Imam Ghazali and Imam Razi, and since he knew the worthlessness of those of his own time, he inferred the unknown from the known and rejected also their predecessors (*qayas ghayb bar shahid kardah salf ra niz munkar shudand*).[73] What Badauni meant to say was that Akbar initially considered his official ulama to be as good as the great scholars of classical Islam. However, after knowing them to be silly in conduct and wanting in knowledge, he not only condemned the ulama of his time, but also lost respect for those of earlier generations.

To add to the emperor's confusion, according to Badauni, learned priests from Europe (*afranja*), called padri—with a religious head called *papa* (Pope), who was allegedly able to change religious ordinances as he deemed advisable for the moment and to whose authority kings submitted—brought the Gospel to court and presented proof of the existence of the

Trinity. In Badauni's opinion, the emperor firmly believed in the truth of Christianity (*nusraniyat*). (This, however, does not match the Jesuits' reports from Akbar's court.) Thus, he notes, Akbar ordered Prince Murad to take a few lessons from the Christian priests and assigned Abul Fazl the task of translating the Gospel into Persian. In doing so, Badauni says, instead of the traditional Islamic introductory invocation '*Bismillah-irrahman-irrahim*' ('In the name of the gracious and merciful God'), '*Ai nami way Gesu Christu*' ('O thou, whose name is Jesus Christ') was used. Also, Abul Fazl's brother, Sheikh Faizi apparently added the hemistich, '*Subhanaka la siwaka ya hu*' ('Praise be to Thee, there is none like Thee, O He').[74] Sufficiently outraged, Badauni further accused the padris—those 'wretched' men—of ascribing the attributes of the accursed Antichrist (*malaun dajjal*) to Prophet Muhammad.[75]

Badauni's charge about Akbar converting to Christianity is certainly an exaggeration because the Jesuit priests writing at the same time expressed their frustration over their inability to formally convert Akbar to Christianity.[76] This was also the time, AH 986 (1578–79), when the emperor began adopting many Hindu practices, both in private and public life. Badauni alleges that the 'accursed' Birbal tried to persuade the emperor that since the sun gives light to all, ripens all grain, fruits and products of the earth, and supports the life of mankind, that luminary should be the object of worship and veneration. Birbal, Badauni says, also argued that while praying, one's face should be turned towards the rising and not towards the setting sun; thus, towards the east and not the west, the direction of Mecca, towards which Muslims turn to perform their namaz. Birbal also allegedly recommended that the people should venerate fire, water, stones, trees, and all natural objects, even cows and their dung. Further, he reportedly advised the emperor to start wearing the sectarian mark on his forehead (*qashqa*) and the sacred thread (*zunnar*). Badauni adds that several courtiers confirmed that the sun was the greater light of the world, benefactor of its inhabitants and patron of kings.[77]

Badauni concluded that Birbal's influence led to Akbar worshipping the sun on the *nauroz-i-jalali* and beginning a festival to celebrate the date of his accession to the throne. The author also says that Akbar began wearing clothes of the colour that accorded with the regent-planet of the day, and began to chant prayers, which Hindus taught him, at midnight and early dawn for the purpose of subduing the sun to his wishes. Further, he prohibited the slaughter of cows because Hindus devoutly worshipped them and considered their dung pure. (Instead of cows, Badauni laments, he sacrificed fine men.) Besides, it was also reasoned in Akbar's court that the physicians had identified beef as difficult to digest and the cause of several kinds of disease.[78] (The condemnation of red meat, then, has an older genealogy.)

And if heretical philosophers and scientists, innovative Sufis, quarrelsome ulama, ambitious padris and opportunist Hindu gurus were not enough, Badauni noted how fire-worshippers came from Nausari in Gujarat. They proclaimed the religion of Zardust as the true one and declared that reverence to fire was a superior form of worship. The fire-worshippers also attracted the emperor's attention and taught him their ordinances, rites and ceremonies. As a result, according to Badauni, Akbar put Abul Fazl in charge of the sacred fire, following the kings of Persia, in whose temples a perpetual fire reputedly blazed. Abul Fazl was to ensure that it was never extinguished, for it was one of the signs of God.[79]

Further, Badauni reports, Akbar had from early youth, in compliance with his wives' wishes, the daughters of Rajput chiefs (*dukhtaran-i rajaha-i hind*), conducted *hom*, a ceremony derived from sun-worship. To mark the beginning of the twenty-fifth year of his accession, the emperor prostrated publicly both before the sun (*aftab*) and the fire (*atish*), and in the evening, the nobles were expected to stand up respectfully when the lamps and candles were lit.[80]

Badauni reiterates that the emperor treated as manifest and decisive every precept that was presented by the leaders of other religions, which were, in turn, often in contradistinction to Islam. He says that Akbar began condemning all the doctrines of Islam as senseless (*na-maqul*), its founders as nothing but poor Arabs, a set of scoundrels and highway robbers, and its followers as accursed (*malaun*). For Badauni, this affair was carried to such an extent that the emperor no longer considered proofs necessary for abolishing the precepts of Islam.[81]

Badauni recalls that in the early days of these discussions on religion, he had an argument with Abul Fazl in the privy audience-chamber at Fatehpur. The argument ended with Badauni asking Abul Fazl, 'For which of these notorious heresies have you the greatest inclination?' Abul Fazl, who had grudges against the whole set of scholars and intellectuals at the court, replied, 'I wish to wander for some days in the valley of heresy for the fun of it' (*mi-khwaham ke rozi chand dar wadi-i alhad sairi ba-kunam ba-mutaiba*).[82]

According to Badauni, Abul Fazl went on to boldly engage in disputes with such imbecile old men as the sadr, the qazi, Hakim-ul-Mulk and Makhdum-ul-Mulk, and did not have the slightest hesitation in putting them to shame—something that pleased the emperor. Badauni, however, questions Abul Fazl's integrity and characterizes him as an opportunist. The opponents, apparently looking out for a compromise, privately sent a message to Abul Fazl, asking him why was he always coming in their way. Abul Fazl apparently responded that he was just making hay when the sun was shining in his favour, as the emperor was not going to live forever and could also possibly change his opinion about him.[83]

Badauni further observes that Abul Fazl was able to defeat all his antagonists in a short time by dint of his own exertions, his father's assistance, the patronage of the caliph of the age, that is, Akbar, and by the favour of fortune. Not one of the people of Islam, except Hakim Abul Fateh and Mulla Muhammad Yazdi could keep pace with Abul Fazl in any of the discussions.[84]

Evidently unable to understand the spectacular rise of Abul Fazl as Akbar's favourite intellectual, Badauni notes that Abul Fazl's affairs resembled that of the poet Hairati of Samarqand. He writes that annoyed by the 'cool and sober' people of Transoxania, Hairati had joined the 'old foxes' of Shi'ite Persia and chose the pathless road (*rah-i be-rah*). The identical responses of Hairati and Abul Fazl to harassment by their contemporaries reminded Badauni of the proverb, 'Prefer hell to disgrace' (*akhtarat al-nar ala al-ar*).[85]

Writing about himself, Badauni says that when the enterprises and propositions (*maqasid wa matalib*) of the rivals overtook what he could do, he retired to private life, thus falling into disfavour and becoming estranged from the emperor (*hama ashnai ba beganagi kushid*). Still, Badauni visited the court and prostrated before the emperor intermittently.[86]

In his account of the year AH 986 (1578–9), Badauni returns to the activities of Sheikh Abdun Nabi and Makhdum-ul-Mulk. For Badauni, their having fallen out with one another had been the cause of people distrusting religion and deviating from it (*mujib inharaf az din qawim shudah budand*). Akbar had them both sent to Mecca with the official caravan led by Mir Hajj. By the next year AH 987 (1579–80), they had completed the hajj and returned to the fold of Islam.[87] Badauni laments that official hajj delegations were subsequently discontinued by Akbar and he also complains that he could never be a part of the contingent because Abdun Nabi, who used to finalize the list, was ill-disposed towards him.[88]

Badauni writes that having lost trust in his officials who looked after ecclesiastical matters, Akbar wanted to unite in his person the spiritual and secular headship. Also, as he had heard that the Prophet, the rightly guided caliphs and some of the most powerful kings, such as Amir Timur and Mirza Ulugh Beg had themselves read the khutba, he resolved to do the same. Badauni feels that though the apparent motive was to imitate their example, in reality, this move allowed Akbar to appear in public as the mujtahid of his age.[89] So, on the first Friday of Jumada-ul-Awwal (the fifth month of the Hijri calendar) of the year AH 987 (1578–79), Akbar began to read the khutba in the Jama Masjid of Fatehpur, which he had built near the palace. However, Badauni says that the emperor stammered and trembled, and though assisted by others, could scarcely read the three verses of a poem that Sheikh Faizi had composed for the occasion. Quickly getting down from the pulpit, he handed over the duties to Imam Hafiz Muhammad Amin, the court *khatib*.[90]

Badauni quotes these verses composed by Faizi, which Akbar had wanted to recite from the pulpit:[91]

> *khudawandi ke ma ra khusrawi dad*
> (The Lord, who gave to us sovereignty)
> *dil dana wa bazuwi qawi dad*
> (Who gave us a wise heart and a strong hand)
> *ba-adl wa dad ma ra rahnamun kard*
> (Who guided us in equity and justice)
> *bajaz adl az khayal sabirun kard*
> (And drove from our hearts all save equity)
> *bud-o-sifash za-hadd faham bartar*
> (His description is beyond imagination)
> *ta'la shanahu allah-o-akbar*
> (Exalted is His Majesty, Allahu Akbar!)

The content and form of this composition is entirely different from the standard khutbas read out in Sunnite mosques. These khutbas are meant to connect Muslims and their leaders all the way back to Prophet Muhammad through invocations of well-known spiritual and political genealogies. At the time, however, Badauni records, many precepts of Islam were being questioned. Wretched Hindus and indigenized Muslims (*musalmanan hindu-mizaj*), he claims, reviled the Prophet, while the villainously irreligious ulama pronounced Akbar to be infallible in their works. Content with just mentioning the unity of God, the ulama reportedly wrote down the various titles of the emperor and lacked the courage to mention the Prophet's name. For Badauni, this was a matter of general disgrace (*badnami-i am*), depravity and disturbance (*fasad-o-fitna*). Besides, as Badauni mentions, 'base' and 'low' men (*arzal-o-sifla*), professed to be the disciples (murid) of the emperor, their motivation for this being hope and fear, rather than the search for truth.[92]

When discussing the much-talked about mahzar (manifesto) of 1579, Badauni notes the contents of this document that was signed by Makhdum-ul-Mulk Abdullah Sultanpuri, Sadr-us-Sudur Sheikh Abdun Nabi, Qazi-ul-Quzzat Qazi Jalal-ud-Din of Multan, Sadr-i-Jahan, the Mufti of the empire, Sheikh Mubarak Nagauri, Abul Fazl's father and a leading scholar of the time, and Ghazi Khan of Badakhshan, who was unrivalled in the rational sciences (ilm-i-maqulat). The issue the document raised was the settling of the question of the absolute superiority of the *imam-i-adil* (the just leader) over the mujtahid (the jurist, who is recognized as the ultimate authority on Islamic law). In so doing, they also set right some disputed points, so that one could no longer refuse obedience either to religious (*sharai*) or political (*mulki*) edicts.[93] The document raised questions such as: For whom was the title mujtahid and the word ijtihad (legal or theological decision) applicable? Was the duty of the imam-i-adil, who was adept in politics and held a higher rank than the mujtahid, to rule on, according to the requirements of the time (*maslihat-i waqt*), all legal questions on which there existed a difference of opinion? In spite of these contentious questions, all those belonging to the Islamic orthodoxy signed the document, whether willingly or otherwise.[94] This is the text of the document provided by Badauni:

> Whereas Hindustan has now become the centre of security and peace, and the land of justice and beneficence, a large number of people, especially learned men and lawyers, have immigrated and chosen this country for their home. Now,

we the principal *ulama*, who are not only well-versed in several departments of Law and in the principles of jurisprudence, and well acquainted with the edicts which rest on reason or testimony, but are also known for our piety and honest intentions, have duly considered the deep meaning, first, of the verse of the Quran [IV, 62]: Obey God, and obey the Prophet, and those who have authority among you, and, secondly, of the authentic Tradition . . . Surely the man who is dearest to God on the day of judgment is the *imam-i-adil*; whosoever obeys the *amir*, obeys Thee, and, thirdly, of several other proofs based on reasoning or testimony; and we have agreed that the rank of *sultan-i-adil* (the just ruler) is higher in the eyes of God than the rank of a *mujtahid*. Further, we declare that the king of Islam, *amir* of the faithful, shadow of God in the world, Abul Fath Jalal-ud-Din Muhammad Akbar Padshah Ghazi (whose kingdom [may] God perpetuate!) is a most just, a most wise, and a most God-fearing king. Should therefore in future a religious question come up, regarding which the opinions of the *mujtahids* are at variance, and His Majesty in his penetrating understanding and clear wisdom be inclined to adopt, for people's benefit, and as a political expedient, any of the conflicting opinions, which exist on that point, and issue a decree to that effect, we do hereby agree that such a decree shall be binding on all of us.

Further, we declare that, should His Majesty think fit to issue a new order, we and the people shall likewise be bound by it, provided always that such order be not only in accordance with some verse of the Quran, but also of real benefit to the world; and further, that any opposition on the part of his subjects to such an order passed by His Majesty shall involve damnation in the world to come, and loss of property and religious privileges in this.

The above lines, written with honest intentions, for the glory of God, and the propagation of Islam, is signed by us, the principal *ulama* and lawyers, in the month of Rajab of the year 987 [1579–80].[95]

Five major issues emerge in the above document. First, Akbar is accorded the status of imam-i-adil and *sultan-i-adil*, which are positions comparable to that of the caliph. Second, this position is placed above that of the mujtahids, or interpreters of the shariat. Third, in case there is a difference of opinion amongst the mujtahids, Akbar's recommendation resolving the issue would be binding on all. Fourth, Akbar could issue orders in conformity to the Quran. Finally, it was aimed at establishing the glory of God (*hasat-ullah*) and the propagation of Islam (*izharul ajra haququl islam*).

It is possible that through this mahzar, Akbar was trying to project his image as the caliph of the age by challenging the supremacy of his contemporary Ottoman Sultan, whose name was read in the khutba even in the mosques of Mecca and Medina. Nurul Hasan has argued that theoretically, the position of the Ottomans was in no way better than that of Akbar and, according to the accepted legal practice of Sunnite Islam, Akbar's aspirations for the caliphate could be considered legitimate.[96] This was the time when four great powers—Mughals, Safavids, Uzbegs and Ottomans—were battling for supremacy in the Muslim world.[97]

Within the Mughal empire, the document also possibly aimed at checking the influence of some powerful theologians, who were perceived to be irresponsible in their dealings. Badauni himself recorded many examples of the arbitrariness of Abdun Nabi and Abdullah Sultanpuri, as has been mentioned earlier. Badauni also observed that soon after the emperor had obtained this legal document, the path for a new religious interpretation was opened (*rah-i ijtihad maftuh gasht*) and the superiority of the intellect of the emperor was established (*aqliyat imam mutahaqqiq shud*).[98]

Badauni mentions Akbar's continued belief in the shrine of Muin-ud-Din Chishti, to where the emperor reportedly made his fourteenth pilgrimage during Rajab–Shaban AH 987 (1579–80).

To Badauni, this presents a contradiction as the ruler still reposed such a faith in the khwaja of Ajmer, even as he was perceived to have rejected the very foundation of the faith.[99]

Also, Badauni reports that the emperor was determined to publicly use the formula, 'There is no god but God, and Akbar is God's representative or caliph' (*la-ilaha illallah akbar khalifat-ullah*). This was met with disapproval and the emperor restricted the use of this formula to a few of his adherents. Badauni describes the year of this event, AH 987 (1579–80), with the words, '*fitnahai ummat*' (disturbances in the community). The emperor reportedly tried his best to convert Qutb-ud-Din Muhammad Khan and Shahbaz Khan, but they staunchly objected. The former was even accused of being a secret agent of the Ottoman Sultan for stating that Akbar's innovations could be viewed as scandalous by the kings of the West. He was asked to migrate to Rum, Turkey or beyond. According to Badauni, when Birbal [whom he condemns as the dog from hell (*sag jahannami*) and on a previous occasion, as a bastard] intervened and attacked the faith, the conversation became all the more unpleasant. Shahbaz Khan condemned Birbal as a *kafir malaun* (wretched infidel). Akbar, who was known for his weakness for the jester, was incensed by this and remarked how he wished the face of the antagonist was beaten with a slipper full of filth.[100] It may be mentioned here that existing literature on religious leaders who tried to convert Akbar to their respective faiths ignores how the ruler himself put pressure on his nobles and officials to convert to the 'imperial ideology'. Those who resisted had to suffer in different ways.

The year AH 987 (1579–80) also saw Qazi Ali of Baghdad being appointed, in spite of Sheikh Abdun Nabi still being around, to look into the administration of revenue-free land grants. According to Badauni, the large-scale acquisition of land by Akbar's state left precious little with the holders of land grants. In his exaggerated concern for the condition of revenue-free land grant holders, Badauni, who himself was at the receiving end of this drastic move, noted that schools and mosques were abandoned, great numbers had to leave their native country and their children, who remained there, in course of time, got a reputation for mean conduct (*ba-paji-giri*).[101] Badauni complained of his own difficulties in retaining his one thousand bighas of subsistence land, that neither Qazi Ali nor Abdun Nabi supported his case, and that his landholding was severely curtailed after much argument. He writes that this was punishment for not consenting to be branded as a disciple of the emperor, who, according to the author, frequently alluded to it.[102] Some courtiers also put great pressure on him to diligently attend court sessions and he again fell into the snare.[103] By contrast, at this time, Abul Fazl's career graph continued to rise. The emperor was apparently very severe towards Hakim-ul-Mulk on account of his opposition to Abul Fazl, whom Akbar affectionately, but erroneously called 'Fazlah' ('*fazl*' means 'excellence', but '*fazlah*' is 'refuse' or 'leavings'). Abul Fazl's adversary was dispatched to Mecca,[104] which had by then acquired quite a reputation as the place for banishing any dissenters or trouble-makers.

Badauni also notes that in this year (AH 987/1579–80), the *tamgha* (inland toll tax) and the jizya, which, according to him, brought in several crores of *dams* were abolished, and farmans to this effect were sent all over the empire.[105] The value of the amount collected in jizya seems to be an exaggeration, for Badauni himself indicated elsewhere in his text that the order in this regard was hardly implemented.

Badauni also mentions some opposition to the policies of Akbar from sections of the ulama during this year, which was backed by a fatwa issued by Mulla Muhammad Yazdi, who had been appointed the *qazi-ul-quzzat* (chief qazi or judge) of Jaunpur. Those who had been unsettled by curtailments in their land grants and other measures had fought desperate battles, but had been suppressed in different ways. Some were transferred to distant territories, others were brutally drowned in the Yamuna, and yet others were imprisoned in Rantambhore fort and left to die. As mentioned above, anyone, whether a mulla or a liberal scholar, who was either opposed to Akbar's innovations or disputed with Abul Fazl was severely punished.[106] Accordingly, the punishments meted out to Mulla Muhammad Yazdi (drowned in the river) and Haji Ibrahim (whose body was left to rot inside the Rantambhore fort) reveal the limits of the much-celebrated tolerance of the emperor and his guides or philosophers. Disagreements with the likes of Abul Fazl, Shah Fatehullah and Hakim Abul Fateh could also possibly be tolerated only up to a degree, but of this latter set, Abul Fazl was clearly privileged and protected.

Against this, Badauni laments the plight of Muslim holy men. He complains that any piece of orthodox learning which a man acquired became his bane and the cause of his degradation. Akbar not only inquired into their land grants and pensions, but anyone known to have pupils or organized assemblies for dervish dancing or who indulged in any form of perceived 'false worship', was condemned as running a shop or *dukan* (that is, making his religion a trade). Such people were either imprisoned or dismissed to the inhospitable frontiers of Bengal or Bhakkar.[107]

Badauni comments that pirs and sheikhs who had reached old age were better off. He complains that on account of the farmans, Sufis, who gave themselves to dancing and ecstasies, were questioned by Hindu officials, and on account of their despicable state, they forgot their religious ecstasy, '*az bad-hali hal framosh kardand*' (notice the pun on the two meanings of the term *hal*: state and ecstasy, that is, because of their bad condition, hal, they forgot how to achieve hal, ecstasy). Badauni's own position in this matter reveals that his stand was closer to that of the traditional ulama. So, he writes, in truth, he felt that the wretched assemblies and absurd ceremonies of the worthless hypocritical Sufis were worthy of perishing.[108] Indeed, compared to the terrible fate of the disenchanted liberals, the anxieties of conservatives and their harassment appear to be less harsh and more rhetorical.

Badauni also accuses some hypocritical Sufis, who were summoned by the emperor, of flattery and open blasphemy to protect themselves.[109] It must be noted that the author has throughout his narrative, at least, for the period of 'religious struggles', maintained that the lack of integrity amongst the ulama and Sufis of the time had led to the rejection of an entire tradition of Islam. To illustrate his observations, Badauni presents a few examples, including one where he refers to a sheikh who told the emperor that a certain lady of the harem would give birth to a son; but as it so happened that a daughter was born and his prophecy fell rather flat.[110] Desperate to get a son, Akbar may not have liked it at all.

Further, according to Badauni, low and mean men, who pretended to be learned, but who in reality were fools, presented evidence, that the emperor was the *sahib-i-zaman*, who would remove all differences of opinion among the seventy-two sects of Islam as well as between the two communities (*millat*) of Muslims and Hindus.[111] Clearly, a massive struggle was going on to reconcile religious and communal differences, as well as to emphasize the domination of one over the other. The ruler's role here was extremely important; the social and religious diversities demanded an equitable distance from the interested parties or competing groups.

Badauni, however, concluded that the innovative propositions of the so-called philosophers, heretical Shi'ites and other men of religion who lacked moral integrity made the emperor more inclined to claim the dignity of a prophet for himself, and even something more, perhaps, divinity itself.[112] Such a portrayal of the emperor has persisted in traditional Muslim circles, though historians have argued that Akbar's exertions were aimed at the welfare of all his subjects and not of Muslims alone.[113] Though Akbar's attempts were informed by a commitment to a rational or inclusive framework of governance, the entrenched forms of Sunnite Islam and their interest in politics were not crushed altogether. At least, the Islamic orthodoxy continued to assert itself, which was manifested in many ways, including the struggles of Sheikh Ahmad Sirhindi and also in a more general attempt to emphasize the need to go back to the Quran and hadis, as we shall see in the next chapter.

Akbar himself pandered to the whims of the Islamic orthodoxy when his son, Salim (Jahangir), rebelled in the last years of his reign. By that time, perceptions about Akbar in theological circles had already changed. It was recognized at the time of his death in 1605 that 'despite all his "innovations", he remained a Muslim king'.[114] One of the victims of the power struggle between the father and son was Abul Fazl, who was brutally murdered by Bir Singh Bundela at Salim's behest.[115] Though the gruesome assassination of Akbar's friend and philosopher is not linked to the struggles in the Mughal court over Islam and heresies, for someone like Badauni, Abul Fazl died the way he lived—as they say, his end was despicable. The irony is that this happened to someone who had more respect for infidels than a conservative baying for their blood.

However, Abul Fazl was killed for his politics and not for unbelief. It is important to avoid simple explanations to be able to comprehend the complexities of medieval politics. As we saw earlier, Badauni was not one to support all strands of even Sunnite Islam; he was no simple mulla and his support for traditional form of Islamic mysticism was also conditional. The alleged lack of integrity of intellectuals, whether conservative or liberal, was viewed as a serious problem by Badauni, who himself was extremely apologetic about being an incurable 'sinner'. Amongst a host of worldly attractions, the yearning for homosexual love was Badauni's major weakness, as we shall further see in chapter six. The existence of weaknesses and worldly attractions, however, did not mean that the practices of Islam were to be abandoned altogether. Neither Badauni nor Akbar attempted to do so, though Akbar's questioning of traditional Islamic beliefs and his patronage of holy men of different sects created some consternation among religious leaders, whether mullas, gurus or padris, each of whom claimed to represent the 'truth'—something which could not be rationally argued and established, which is what Akbar expected.

This problem remained unresolved and continued to affect politics and society in later times. Though Badauni had to conceal his work to avoid the wrath of the Mughals, he most probably lived till the year 1615, halfway through the reign of Jahangir (ruled 1605–27).[116] This was the period when issues addressed by Badauni were being raised by Muslim intellectuals such as the Naqshbandi leading light, Sheikh Ahmad Sirhindi, and Qadiri scholar, Sheikh Abdul Haqq Muhaddis Dehlawi, with even greater vigour and from different vantage points. Abdul Haqq's emphasis on following the path of Islam by turning back to the Quran and hadis will be discussed in the next chapter.

5

Recommending Right and Forbidding Wrong

In this chapter, I will present debates that raged in the late sixteenth and early seventeenth centuries on what actually constituted Islamic norms in the light of the Quran and the Traditions of the Prophet (hadis), and will also discuss how these norms were sought to be established in a Muslim society. In particular, I will focus on the Quranic instruction, '*amr bil ma'ruf wa nahi anal munkar*', which advises Muslims to recommend what is considered to be just and right in Islam to others and to forbid what is perceived as false or wrong. This injunction has given a license to many reformist zealots to take upon themselves the responsibility to correct things from their own perspective or understanding of Islam, even though Muslim jurists have proposed a set of conditions and regulations for implementing the guidelines. We will study in some detail the forms and degrees of perceived deviance, as well as actions that qualify a person as a renegade.

The focus of this chapter will mainly be on a normative text, the *Adab-us-Salihin*,[1] of Sheikh Abdul Haqq Muhaddis Dehlawi (1551–1642),[2] a well-known scholar of the Traditions of the Prophet and author of nearly one hundred books in Arabic and Persian on Islam. His collection of the biographies of Sufis, *Akhbar-ul-Akhyar*, which has been referred to in earlier chapters, is a particularly useful work for the study of Sufism in medieval India. Abdul Haqq also wrote a biography of the Prophet,

Madarij-i-Nubuwwat, and a general history of India, *Tarikh-i-Haqqi*.[3] He travelled to Mecca and Medina in 1587 and stayed there for more than two years, during which he studied the hadis and *tasawwuf* (Islamic mysticism) under Abdul Wahhab Muttaqi, a renowned scholar of Indian origin. After returning to Delhi, he combined his study of the hadis with his exposure to the Qadiri order of Sufism to train many generations of students and disciples. Through his long life of ninety-four years, Abdul Haqq lived through the reigns of three Mughal emperors, from Akbar to Shah Jahan, and participated in debates on Islam and unbelief in Mughal India from the late sixteenth to the early seventeenth century.[4]

Taking a conservative position, Abdul Haqq cut off his relations with Abul Fazl's brother, intellectual and poet, Faizi, for deviating from the traditional path of Islam. Despite this, Faizi continued to have a lot of respect for Abdul Haqq and kept requesting him for comments on his writings.[5] However, unlike Badauni, who was a contemporary of Abdul Haqq and also communicated with him, the latter's riposte was sophisticated, indirect and scholarly.[6] Badauni mentioned in his writings that Abdul Haqq spent some time at Fatehpur Sikri before leaving for Hijaz. His companions during the period of his stay there included Faizi, Nizam-ud-Din Ahmad Bakhshi (a leading official in Akbar's army and author of the well-known general history of India, *Tabaqat-i-Akbari*) and Badauni himself. Later, Nizam-ud-Din Ahmad reportedly facilitated Abdul Haqq's travel from Gujarat to Hijaz.[7]

Abdul Haqq also engaged in discussions with Sheikh Ahmad Sirhindi, the Naqshbandi Sufi reformist leader, who is celebrated in the Sunni Muslim intellectual tradition for his struggle for the cause of Islam in medieval India.[8] Sirhindi is generally held responsible for the shift from the policy of religious tolerance initiated by Akbar, to the narrower outlook of Jahangir and Shah Jahan, which culminated in Aurangzeb's shariat-driven governance framework. While these formulations do need reconsideration,[9] our concern here is Abdul Haqq's treatment of the binary Islam and deviance, and his ideas on how to ensure that Islam prevails.

Thus, we are dealing here with a debate that recurs in Muslim societies. This is further reflected by the fact that Abdul Haqq drew from the writings of Imam Ghazali (d. 1111), a major Sunni Islamic revivalist of the Abbasid Caliphate. The Mughal scholar used two well-known books by Ghazali—the Arabic *Ihya Ulum al-Din* (*Bringing the Religious Sciences to Life*) and the Persian *Kimiya-i-Sadat* (*The Alchemy of Happiness*). The second work is mainly a translation of the former and includes Ghazali's take on what constitutes permissible akhlaq for this-worldly concerns and, more importantly, recommends adab in the light of religion.[10] (We will discuss Ghazali's campaign for establishing Sunni Islam as a major force backed by the caliphate in the concluding chapter of this book.) Here, we are concerned with the norms or adab for forbidding wrong and recommending right in Islam, which were adapted by Abdul Haqq from Ghazali's exposition on the subject.[11] Other works on adab by Abdul Haqq include the *Adab-ul-Libas* (on the appropriate style for clothing in Sunnite Islam; this issue keeps recurring and was raised in Akbar's time) and the *Adab al-Mutaliqa wa al-Munazira* (on the proper norms of conduct during discussions and disputations, possibly necessitated by Mughal officials creating a pandemonium in Akbar's ibadat-khana).[12]

Given the continuous disputes over what is recommended in normative Islam and what is abhorred, the connections between Islam in medieval India and the Middle East need careful reconsideration. It would be worthwhile to analyse which Middle Eastern religious traditions continue to be meaningful or adapted in the Subcontinent, whether during medieval or modern times. In this chapter, as mentioned earlier, we will focus on the Quranic instruction to prevent falsehood and establish the truth. The focus on this instruction mirrors Barani's advice to the Sultans of Delhi. However, unlike Barani's politically motivated pronouncements to chastise the infidels, the concerns in Imam Ghazali and Abdul Haqq's work are of a juridical and cultural nature and aim at reforming Muslims from within, both to make them better Muslims and to differentiate them from others (though the political ramifications of the project cannot be ignored altogether).

Thus, Abdul Haqq discusses those verses of the Quran that refer to the responsibility of Muslims to ensure that the straight path of righteousness is followed, virtue and piety are advocated and evil and sin prevented. This responsibility is to be borne for the community of Islam (umma). However, this divine command is not considered obligatory on all Muslims and can be an additional task, which can be performed by a few Muslims on behalf of the larger community. Thus, in the vocabulary of the jurists, recommending right and forbidding wrong is not a *farz-i-ayn* (principal duty), but a *farz-i-kifaya* (supplementary obligation).[13] Significantly, this major distinction is often ignored in practice, especially when individuals take immediate and direct action to stop, what is in their opinion, inequity, vice or falsehood. Also, though the Quran makes these responsibilities imperative only for guiding the umma of Islam, enthusiasts prefer that even non-Muslims be bound by this framework.

This attempt to bring non-Muslims within the purview of the 'amr bil ma'ruf wa nahi anal munkar' injunction is not supported by a hadis, which is referred to by Abdul Haqq. According to the hadis, the Prophet once told a group of his followers to dread the time when their women would disobey their commands, their children deviate from the way of truth and righteousness and they themselves would give up the path of jihad or struggle against their own lust and desire.[14] Then, responding to a companion's query on whether such a transformation in the community was imminent, the Prophet warned that worse could follow. He explained that there could soon be a time when his followers would cease to differentiate between truth and falsehood. According to the Messenger of God, in the following phase of decline and deterioration, his followers would not only engage in unlawful activities, but also, in complete violation of the ideals of Islam, propagate it.[15] In such a situation, the Quranic injunction would be completely overturned: right conduct would be censored and wrong preached. This would happen in three phases: first, sin would become rampant; second, evil would be confused with virtue and vice-versa; and third, vice would be promulgated and piety suppressed. Given this possibility, according to the Prophet, the community needs to guard itself against gradual degeneration; hence the Quran recommends the need to be vigilant against lapses in right conduct within the community.

Another hadis refers to Allah's curse on someone who happens to be present where injustice and tyranny is widespread and who does not condemn or prevent the disorder. Juristically, however, there are two possibilities in such a situation. First, it is possible to escape the charge of indifference by ascribing to the path of the ascetic. Therefore, it is recommended that one should not stay at such a place deliberately or without purpose. That is, one must avoid seeing evil if one cannot stop it. Second, if someone knows that Allah's commands are not being followed at a particular place and yet goes there intentionally, then the charge of being a party to the evil can be levelled against such a person. In other words, in the first case, one might be excused for helplessness and withdrawal despite full knowledge of violence and inequity, while in the second case, that is, being inactive or a passive witness to oppression can invite reproach or punishment.[16] Following the first suggestion that it is unlawful to enter a place of oppression and sin and be present where sin is being committed, a group of early ascetics of Islam withdrew from the world so that they did not witness evil deeds in markets, festivals and assemblies, where they would not be able to check it.[17]

Further, in response to a question on whether impious villages and towns where pious and saintly Muslims lived were also ruined, the Prophet answered in the affirmative and explained that even though the saintly Muslims were not sinners, they remained silent in the face of sins committed by people around them. According to the hadis, the Prophet said that this would lead to Allah's curse and the destruction of the entire locality, which would consume the virtuous and silent observers as well.[18] This Tradition, once again, calls for action in favour of piety and prevention of vice. However, as we shall see below, there are certain conditions for action and specific people are to be entrusted to take charge of the situation.

Another Tradition of the Prophet records a wrathful Allah's order to an angel for the destruction of a place, literally asking for the place to be overturned on the heads of the people who inhabit it. Even though the angel reported that there was a person in the area who had never disregarded His commands, Allah insisted that the faithful was also to be consumed by the destruction. For, even if the person concerned had refrained from committing any sin, he was not at all affected by the transgressions of the people in his neighbourhood.[19] Indifference to the violations of the commands of God is a violation in itself. According to another report, Allah was bent on punishing a whole town, which was also inhabited by as many as eighteen thousand saintly Muslims whose deeds were comparable to those of the prophets. Yet, they were to be punished precisely because they had abandoned the command for 'amr bil ma'ruf wa nahi anal munkar' and lived in a world of their own, a world otherwise full of sinners.[20]

A number of other Traditions also refer to the generous rewards promised by Allah for recommending and ensuring that the straight path is followed by people. The rewards include hundreds of *houris* or virgins waiting to serve the righteous believer who strives for the cause of Allah and who would be placed in the upper echelons of heaven. The righteous believers would be counted amongst the best of the martyrs, such as the Prophet's uncle, Hamza, and Ali's brother, Jafar, if they are killed by a tyrant ruler for advocating the virtuous path of Allah.[21]

The utterances ascribed to the companions of the Prophet further point to the value of 'amr bil ma'ruf wa nahi anal munkar'. According to an anecdote, Huzaifa ibn Aliman was once asked who are the dead amongst the living. He replied that a person who was witness to sin, but who does not utilize his hand, tongue or heart to disavow it is the dead amongst the living. That is, it is necessary for a person to first of all use his hand to set things right; a heavy hand is recommended when effective. Secondly, if the person concerned does not command enough force to suppress the sinners, then a condemnation, loud and clear, is advised. Thirdly, if neither direct action (using hand) nor condemnation (verbal outrage) is possible, then, at least, the wrongdoings should be silently criticized (keeping it as a secret matter of heart). If none of the three strategies can be resorted to and immorality remains unchallenged, then it can be assumed that the conscience of the people concerned are dead, which means that they themselves are as good as deceased.[22] In line with the Traditions, the Prophet's companion, Huzaifa, dreaded the time when people would prefer to lament the death of a donkey rather than express concern for a Muslim who recommends Allah's path and prevents deviation.[23] Further, a report attributed to the second rightly-guided caliph, Umar, suggests that not repudiating a sin from the heart even silently is an indication of the extent to which a person's heart or soul is corrupted, or put literally, so blind that it is unable to discriminate between good and bad.[24] Similarly, another account in the Book of Moses further strengthens the argument in favour of recommending Allah's path.[25]

Thus, the Quran, hadis, anecdotes pertaining to the companions of the Prophet and, in one case, even a longstanding Semitic tradition have called for action in matters related to 'amr bil ma'ruf wa nahi anal munkar', if a person is capable of doing that. Since taking the law into one's hands might be counter-productive, it is advised that deviation from the way of God should be condemned, which, in turn is tantamount to inviting trouble and harm. Therefore, the best strategy is to identify immorality as such and refrain from practising it. Also, if one capable person takes the initiative in challenging what is identified as an offence in the eyes of Allah, then the obligation for the required intervention is not binding on the rest of the community.[26]

Who are the people who are capable of intervening in matters between Allah and his servants or followers?

There are certain conditions for appointing a muhtasib, or the official or person in charge of endorsing the *right* behaviour and disallowing *wrong* conduct. To start with, the individual concerned must be known for his fine qualities and uprightness (*mukallaf*) as an intelligent adult male, that is, he should be *aqil* and *baligh*. Thus, people who might lack credibility such as an insane person or a minor boy are not expected to take the initiative for *ihtisab*, or forbidding disorderly activities in the community. This is because a lunatic lacks rational sense, aptitude and integrity, while a minor lad does not have experience and any credible sense of judgment. In other words, commending right and disapproving wrong is not obligatory (*wajib*) for a mad person or a young male; ordinary people, slaves and women are also considered unfit as they are assumed to lack the required level of intelligence, strength and ability.[27]

Nevertheless, it is valid (*jaiz*) for a teenager to take action if he can, for the law only requires a discerning mind, aql and *tamiz*. This is applicable especially to someone who is an adolescent, still developing the qualities of a mature mind. Such a person may be able to reject impiety and prevent unlawful activities by, for instance, vandalizing a wine shop, overturning a container of alcohol or by destroying equipment for entertainment such as musical instruments. It must be noted here that indulgence in both wine and music is condemned by most schools of Islamic jurisprudence, though there are certain qualifications regarding the kinds of music which are allowed.[28] Juristically, no one can stop a young man from taking the law into his own hands in such matters, even when he has no political support. The legitimacy for his deeds comes from the fact that they are perceived to be a kind of prayer (*ibadat*) that leads to rewards or *sawab*; ihtisab is considered to be a form of worship or service to Allah. For this reason, even a commoner or a slave, even though both of them might be lacking in political power, is permitted to disarm a polytheist, ransack his belongings and even kill him. In certain conditions, for both an adult and a minor, irrespective of whether they enjoy political power, restraining a sinner is equal to suppressing an infidel.[29]

How does one explain this reversal of order in terms of political authority? Would not individuals taking the law into their hands lead to anarchy? For this reason, Ghazali condemned any situation where an ignorant mob defied political authority. Ghazali also abhorred the idea of a territory without legitimate political authority, no matter how despotic the ruler.[30] The king, after all, represented the sovereignty of God. Possibly, the moral rights of righteous Muslims could be emphasized in times of political upheavals or in contexts where the ruler is incapable of implementing the laws of Islam. So, whether a Muslim, young or old, can legitimately take action, violent or peaceful, in matters relating to the shariat hinges on the given political situation. A belligerent assault might be permitted in certain political contexts, especially in situations where established rules for governance have collapsed or have been suspended and there is no justice in society (*adl-wa-insaf*).[31]

Returning to the discussion on the ideal conditions for ihtisab, apart from being aqil and baligh, the muhtasib should also be a believer, for ihtisab is a contribution to the cause of Allah and a non-believer is not expected to have any interest in the matter. Thus a kafir or an idolater cannot be a muhtasib. Further, though the stipulation prescribes a good and believing Muslim for the position or role of a muhtasib, even a Muslim sinner, whose integrity is otherwise questionable on account of his neglect of decorum, behaviour and appearance, can preach righteousness to others. This is because, irrespective of the fact that a person does not practise what he preaches, his utterances in support of the Truth are a form of prayer and, therefore, acceptable to Allah.[32] Ghazali insisted that though God does not like people who do not practise what they preach, it is lawful for a great sinner to enjoin good and forbid evil.[33] The discourse of the sinner would then be qualified with the caveat that his audience should listen to what he says in the light of the shariat, even if he himself is incapable of adhering to the law in his own practice.

In this context, it is important to refer to a Tradition, where the Prophet advises his companions to command people to do only what is lawful, even though they themselves may not be strictly following all the laws. Similarly, the companions are asked to prohibit what is unlawful in the eyes of Allah, even if they themselves may not be refraining from all such activities themselves.[34] Since there are a number of ways in which ihtisab can be conducted, as we shall further see, it is permitted for a sinner to use his strength or power to set things right using a heavy hand (this refers to the first option mentioned above, the others being through speech and by appealing to one's conscience), instead of sermonizing or counselling. Further, it is clarified, even if a sinner is capable of giving a scholarly oration and, therefore, does not need to resort to violent means of ihtisab, he should do it at a place where he is not known. It is reasoned that if he goes around preaching in an area where he is already known as an impudent and worthless fellow, there will be little credibility attached to his words. However, as a matter of strategy, in known contexts, a reprobate is advised to use his image of a tyrant to subdue people into submission to God's will. In the opinion of some Muslim political theorists, such people are, indeed, required for areas where only severe violence will eventually yield fruitful results, though this position deviates from certain verses of the Quran which question the integrity of people who go around preaching religion to others.[35]

This explains why political theorists such as Ghazali, who worked within the framework of adab or theologically informed political theory, supported the powers of Muslim Sultans and recommended the inclusion of their names in khutbas (sermons preached during the Friday congregational prayers), even though some of the Sultans were completely irreligious in their demeanour. The Sultans, in turn, invoked the rhetoric of Islamic laws both for appeasing orthodox Muslim groups such as the ulama, as well as for providing legitimacy to their claims as 'shadows of God' (zillullah). Many of them even appointed a muhtasib (in this case, a censor official) to ensure that the stipulations of the shariat were strictly followed in their kingdoms. In general, however, little was done to actually implement the regulations. Active interest in enforcing the shariat was, in reality, the exception rather than the rule. Though such enforcement could make life difficult for the infidels and other sets of 'sinners', the invocation of shariat often had some nuisance value for the population during political regimes that identified themselves as Islamic. Also, the preachers often lacked the requisite moral integrity and this weakened their case. As mentioned earlier, it was for this reason that the Quran and some prophetic reports advised believers to search their own souls before criticizing or counselling others.[36]

Further, medieval Indian Muslim monarchs had realized early in their experience of rule in the Subcontinent that a vast majority of the non-Muslim population could not be governed using a narrow interpretation of the shariat, even if Islamic institutes or law were not be abandoned altogether.[37] The regulations were modified to suit the circumstances. The muhtasibs, then, served as the superintendents of police, examined weights, measures and provisions, and also worked towards preventing gambling, drinking, etc. The duties of the muhtasibs resemble those of the modern police and were aimed at suppressing crime and ensuring law and order. They were not in reality expected to serve as the soldiers of Allah who prevented evil in society. Therefore, what we are discussing in this chapter is the recommended ideal and not actually what happened during the medieval Muslim regimes of the Subcontinent. Yet, it is important to keep in mind that there was enough pressure on Muslim rulers to enforce Islamic guidelines and the tension between the ideal and actual practice has always been a major concern in Muslim societies.

Continuing the discussion on the requirements for ihtisab, Abdul Haqq has drawn attention to the fact that apart from being an intelligent adult and believer (aqil, baligh and Muslim), the preacher is also expected to be a practising Muslim. Any lack of integrity on the part of the muhtasib would mean that he will not be taken seriously, as the required moral weight for his promulgation of the laws of Allah would be missing. Therefore, a qualified, but non-practising Muslim alim is condemned as a potential inhabitant of hell because the dubious nature of such a person makes a mockery of the whole project of Islam. His case would provide legitimacy to the counter-argument that if such and such activities were unlawful, the alim himself should not be indulging in them. A Muslim sinner's preaching is considered as absurd as a kafir showing the way to a Muslim in matters of law. Even as a kafir could not be allowed to judge a case involving a believer, the situation worsens if the alim, whose words should otherwise carry some authority, happens to be a sinner.[38]

Now, assuming that all the required conditions for being a muhtasib are met, that is, a person is aqil, baligh and a pious Muslim, then the question of the circumstances under which action may be considered obligatory arises. The measures taken can be in the form of (i) direct intervention to set things right; (ii) verbal protest; or (iii) recognition of the evil in one's own personal opinion. If the first two options are not feasible, then tolerance or patience (*sabr*) is the most recommended strategy, as ihtisab should not lead to *fitna* (disorder) in society. In case the muhtasib is capable of repressing wrongdoing, it is valid for him to take the necessary action; if not, his inquisitions might be unprofitable or useless, and, therefore, in certain cases, even unlawful (haram).

Thus, even though it is recommended that a glass of wine or a musical instrument can be destroyed, if possible, such a step is to be avoided if there is a danger of an equally strong reaction. This means that though facing hardships for the sake of Allah is considered to be a virtuous act and a drastic action is permitted despite the risk involved, generally, discretion is perceived to be a better option. For instance, in a case where a tyrant ruler is sitting with a cup of wine in one hand and a sword in another, the advice is to avoid proclaiming the truth at that moment, for if the monarch is accosted, he would retaliate by killing the muhtasib. Since the latter would have been aware of the possible repercussion when he took action, there is no or little ground for ihtisab here. Any overzealous enthusiasm on the part of an advocate of Allah in a situation like the one mentioned above will essentially be a haram or forbidden act.[39]

Related to this is the question of prioritizing. All the muhtasib's energies and attention may be spent in crushing a big sin, even as smaller ones are permitted for the time being. In either case, calm reflection and fair judgment are required.[40] Indiscriminate action cannot govern matters relating to the shariat for unless it is certain that the ihtisab will be fruitful, the temporary suspension of Allah's command is the most advisable strategy. In other words, a well-intentioned individual must not consider actions that are *makruh* or disapproved, but not unlawful, that loathsome in an extraordinary situation. His legitimate *matlub* (desires or pursuits) can force him to abandon 'amr bil mar'uf wa nahi anal munkar' for a while, though purists argue that a sincere struggle for the cause of Allah even in extreme adversity is a commendable act. In all cases, a fatwa (religious decree) from one's own heart or a continuous soul-searching can help guard against the danger of the exigencies of the time becoming a permanent affair. The bottom line is that the distinction between the merits of *mar'uf* (uprightness or obedience to God) and the perversity of *munkar* (things that are unlawful or hateful in the eyes of God and man) might get blurred from time to time, but it should not be erased altogether.[41]

There is a dispute between jurists about the level at which the permission of a Muslim ruler, caliph or Sultan/*badshah*, is required for ihtisab, and whether only a person who is appointed by the ruler to the position of the muhtasib should have the right to interrogate people or advise them on the do's and don'ts of Islam. Abdul Haqq has argued that the authorization from the Imam or the ruler is not a precondition for ihtisab at all levels.

For him, the first level is to just draw an individual's attention to matters concerning digressions from the faith. The second level of action involves exhortation through public preaching of Islam. At the third level, when a polite approach is not working, sterner tactics are recommended, which might require harsher language. Here, sinners or deviants can be scolded and told that they are ill-mannered and foolish. The fourth kind of ihtisab demands force and violence to stop evil and chastise the sinners. These four types of interventions, according to Abdul Haqq, do not need state or political mediation. It is only in the fifth category of ihtisab that the presence and role of the Imam (spiritual and/or political leader of the community) acquires importance. In this case, sinners who do not refrain from breaching the laws of Islam in spite of warnings, can be arrested and jailed or subjected to severe thrashing. Thus, it is only in the fifth stage that some sustained violence or third degree methods can be deployed as punishment, and for that, the state, represented by the police or army, is required to be involved.[42]

In Ghazali's language, the five stages are (i) giving simple advice; (ii) sermon with sweet words; (iii) abuse and harsh treatment; (iv) forcible prevention from doing a sinful act, such as throwing wine out of its container, snatching away a silken dress and returning stolen articles to their rightful owner; and (v) assault, beatings and threats to prevent someone from committing a sinful act. Except in the fifth instance, a man is not required to obtain permission from the authorities to take such initiatives.[43]

As we noted earlier, whereas the presence of the state is not a precondition for the first three cases, the fourth involves the capacity of the righteous individual to resort to violence—an act that makes the presence of the state redundant. This last issue has been a major problem that remains unresolved in Muslim societies, even as the role of the state is not entirely denied in the fifth condition. In this case, Abdul Haqq's example[44] about the difference of opinion between rulers (umara and Sultans) and the ulama or saintly, pious Muslims gains importance. This example discusses the issue of whether the latter have the right to call for a judicial inquest, independent of political authorization. When questioned by the ruler as to who had appointed them as muhtasibs or guardians of the faith, the pietistic ulama retorted that the same one who had made him a badshah, had made them muhtasibs—possibly meaning Allah. Thus, the monarch, who claimed to be a representative of God, was silenced. This example of the inability of Muslim sovereign powers to come out of the shadow of God shows a major limitation that existed through the middle ages. Clearly, the political transformation of the kind witnessed in Christian Europe, where religion was separated from politics and relegated to the private domain of an individual, did not take place in the Muslim world.[45] An unflinching commitment to the cause of Allah remains a defining feature of Muslim public life—the promotion of virtue and prevention of vice thus becomes a major project.

Further clarifying the point about the recommended form of ihtisab in specific contexts, Ghazali has suggested that in case one must enjoin the ruler to goodness and forbid evil, only the first two of the five modes mentioned above can be adopted—other methods of harsh treatment, abuse, assault and fight must be avoided. In other words, rulers should only be advised in polite language, despite the full knowledge of their evil actions because applying other modes in their case would create disturbances and loss of peace and tranquillity, which is unlawful.[46] However, anecdotes about learned men from early Islam who enjoined good and forbade evil reveal that they cared little for the power of the ruler and depended entirely on the belief that God would grant them the benefit of martyrdom for their actions.[47] Ghazali's narration of such anecdotes has led an Orientalist to erroneously believe that the Muslim political theorist considered it 'virtuous to rebuke rulers harshly for their misdeeds' and 'was strongly in favour of this'.[48]

Additionally, as Ghazali has shown, Muslim jurists have identified a whole range of delinquencies: (i) major sins for which there are prescribed punishments in the Quran, the prevention of which is obligatory; (ii) sins which are committed continuously—such as wine-drinking, wearing silk clothes, using cups of gold and silver—and need to be prevented compulsorily; and (iii) sins which can be committed in the future.[49] However, there are certain conditions governing any action taken for the prevention of these sins. One important condition is that the violation of the shariat should be publicly known and there should be a prima facie case for immediate action. The muhtasibs are not expected to work as a vigilante group, secretly uncovering vices and attempting to prevent offences yet to be committed. Prying into what both Allah and the men involved have thought fit to conceal is a forbidden act. This does not mean that sins committed in private are acceptable to Allah, but interrogators are not expected to take action on mere suspicion. The muhtasibs are required to intervene only when there is an open defiance of the shariat and its widespread violations.

Thus, Abdul Haqq noted, if a person commits a sin within the four walls of his house and has locked himself in, the muhtasib has no right to enter his house to inquire into the matter. However, in a situation where the impact of the offence is clearly affecting the public, as in the case of loud music or the raucous utterances of drunkards, then intervention is considered necessary. In this context, once confirmed, a musical instrument can be seized and destroyed. Further, if a person carries a bottle of wine under his arm or hides it under his clothes, then exposing him is invalid even when the person concerned is a known offender. This is because he may be given the benefit of doubt, for even a crook could be carrying a bottle of vinegar and not alcohol as suspected. Disciplinary action in such a case needs to be suspended till it becomes evident to the general public through the spread of odour that the bottle contains alcohol. It is only when the nuisance created by the person concerned becomes public knowledge that action against him is legitimate. In such a case, the bottle may be snatched and broken. Thus, both the cases—of smell emanating from a bottle of alcohol and the detection of a musical instrument—fall within the purview of 'open secrets' for which the muhtasib does not have to go beyond his brief to uncover them. The two cases then call for questioning and punishment.[50]

However, as Abdul Haqq has suggested, it is important to reiterate that till such a time as when an alleged disobedience of Allah's command remains the private affair of an individual, instead of ihtisab, concealment of the blemish of a fellow Muslim is the primary responsibility of another Muslim. A proactive approach to exposing the shortcomings of people and taking them to task is discouraged by the Quran, while covering the defects of a Muslim is considered noteworthy in the eyes of God.[51] This is obviously contrary to the enthusiasm shown by some Islamist groups in contemporary Muslim societies. Harassment and intimidation by the moral police can be entirely indiscriminate and is, therefore, a departure from the recognized sources of Islamic law. Even in the case of an offence committed in public, the legitimacy of the culprit's punishment hinges on reliable evidence and witnesses. At least two just and pious Muslims must testify in support of the ihtisab; alternatively, one just and equitable Muslim and two slaves can swear as witnesses, where the evidence provided by the second set of witnesses carries less weight.[52]

Further, if an accused points to differences of opinion amongst jurists of the four schools of Sunni jurisprudence (Hanafi, Shafi'i, Maliki and Hanbali) on the legality of a particular action, the definitive positions of the respective schools have to be respected. Abdul Haqq has given the following example: if a person defends his consumption of crabs, frogs and other such creatures as legal according to the Shafi'i school that he follows, then the Hanafite muhtasib has no right to prevent him from doing so. Since the differences amongst jurists are largely matters of opinion, the fatwas of the respective schools have to be tolerated, even respected. In such cases, the ihtisab is deemed illegal, as it is considered possible that the imams or the founders of the schools of jurisprudence might have erred in judgment on points where the sources of Muslim law did not provide clear guidance. Therefore, in order that their intentions are not doubted, all schools need to be respected. On the contrary, in the case of Shias and Mutazilas with whom the Sunnis have fundamental differences and who are supposed to be following falsehood, interrogation and punishment are considered lawful.[53] In the latter case, however, sinfulness and heresies need to be stopped through counselling and violent methods of war and strife are to be avoided.[54]

In all cases, a deviant Muslim should be given the benefit of doubt, for it is possible that his defiance of Allah's authority is due to ignorance rather than deliberate rebellion. It is argued that polite intervention will work in reforming an ignorant sinner, whereas his harassment, especially public humiliation, can prove counter-productive.[55] The Chishtis of the Sultanate period, for example, privileged a repentant (*taib*) over a pious person (*muttaqi*) because the former was considered to have seen and done all before finally returning to the path of Allah, while the latter had no idea of the pleasure involved in sinning and was therefore not sacrificing anything for Allah's sake.[56] The jurists, however, felt that if the sinner's insolence is deliberate and polite suggestions to desist from defying God's command do not work, then varying degrees of force can be deployed to ensure that the sinner understands the wisdom of following the path of Islam.[57] In cases requiring corporal punishment, hands and legs can be targeted while thrashing the sinner and it should be kept in mind that the weaker parts of the body are not hurt to the extent that he becomes fatally injured.[58] Killing a fellow Muslim is an extreme crime. If it is not confirmed that the deceased was involved in the gravest of sins (*gunah-i-kabira*) and yet remained unrepentant, he can earn the status of a shahid, martyr.

This brings us back to the discussions on the norms of conduct for the muhtasib. The muhtasib must have three qualities—knowledge of Islam, piety and affability. The knowledge of religious decrees is essential for identifying cases for interrogation, defining the requisite level of intervention and recommending punishment. The piety and chastity of the muhtasib adds to his credibility and, thus, provides legitimacy to his actions. Being a pious person himself, the muhtasib, it is assumed, will be careful not to cross the limits imposed on him. He is expected to guard against self-righteousness caused by the power of knowledge and excessive self-confidence because of being a devout Muslim. The muhtasib is expected to be affable in his dealings with the sinners for wise counselling requires polite exhortation and sermons, whereas a short-tempered and haughty person might lose his balance in meting out justice in the name of Allah. Together, the three attributes provide the required authority to the muhtasib to fulfil his responsibility of ensuring 'amr bil mar'uf wa nahi anal munkar'.[59]

Without going into further details of specific cases requiring intervention and degrees of punishment, it may be noted that the duties and responsibilities of the advocates of Allah demand the utmost care. Whereas derelictions, whether deliberate or otherwise, are condemned, the excesses of incompetent enthusiasts of Islam are also discouraged, for if not properly handled, they can lead to the discrediting of divine commands, thereby providing further grounds for transgressions.

Many historical situations have witnessed deviations both from the straight path of Islam and ways and means to ensure adherence. Islam in Indian history and society is no exception to this. For the theorists, as Abdul Haqq points out, particularly outrageous is the possibility of a rapist preaching to a woman, shortly after assaulting her, the virtues of modesty and the need to cover her body in front of a stranger.[60] As the devout like to put it: *wallah a'lam* or Allah knows best! Passing the responsibility on to Allah can also be a strategy to cover one's failures in following the recommended path of Islam. The official ulama attached to the court of medieval Muslim rulers took upon themselves the responsibility of checking any deviations from the recommended path.

It may be worthwhile to recapitulate here the social and political role of the ulama in medieval India, keeping in mind that that there is no 'church' in Islam and no centralized organization of priests, such as for instance, in Christianity. There was, of course, the *khilafat*, which purportedly combined both religious and political authority, but which, by the end of the twelfth century itself, was reduced to having only a symbolic importance, devoid of power to establish its will.

The ulama's primary aim is to ensure strict adherence to the shariat, both by ordinary Muslims in their day to day life and by rulers in matters of governance. In medieval India, after completing traditional Islamic education in a madrasa (religious seminary) or under a recognized theologian, a qualified alim could serve as a teacher, imam (leader of prayer) of a mosque, qazi (judge), juriconsult, mufti (one who issues fatwas or religious decrees), reformer or advisor to the state. The ulama thus had several roles and functions in medieval India. Also, since the shariat, as defined by the theologians, does not distinguish between the religious and secular, the ulama also had a role to play in public affairs.

The Islamic orthodoxy in India generally comprised Sunni ulama who followed the Hanafite interpretation of shariat, and therefore most *maulvis* tended to follow the Hanafi *fiqh* (jurisprudence). As mentioned previously, there are four schools of jurisprudence (referred to as mazahib) in Sunni Islam: Hanafi, Hanbali, Maliki and Shafi'i (named after the founders of these schools). There is a separate system of jurisprudence for Shi'ite Islam called the Ja'fri school. This occurred because the standard, orthodox interpretations of Islam were established within the first few centuries of Islam during the Abbasid Caliphate, amidst a lot of contestations over the correct reading of the sources. The ulama belonging to each of these schools expected from Muslims a blind conformity to the tenets of Islam as interpreted by their great masters or imams. Imam Abu Hanifa's followers were influential in Central Asia, from where Hanafi Islam came to the northern parts of the Subcontinent. In southern Indian coastal regions, such as Malabar, where Islam came directly from Arabia, the Shafi'i interpretation of Sunni Islam was 'imported'.

In medieval India, the ulama's relationship with the ruler and his court tended to be one of dependence. This was because most of the institutions involved in the education and employment of ulama were directly or indirectly controlled by the state. The centres of learning, *maktab*s and madrasas, were largely founded by the ruling elite and funded through charities and grants given by the state. Secondly, a qualified alim's main hope of employment was to get a job within the administration as a qazi or mufti. Even if he wanted to become the imam of a mosque or teacher (*mudarri*s) in a madrasa, both the mosque and the madrasa were dependent on the generosity of the ruler. By and large, therefore, theologians acted as paid servants of the state. As a result, they were generally expected to interpret Islam to suit the politics of rulers.

While there were variations in the attitudes of rulers towards the orthodox ulama, the medieval state did not allow theologians to dictate policy, and one may recall here Ala-ud-Din Khalji's statements on political pragmatics and Ziya-ud-Din Barani's complaints about the neglect of the interests of Muslims. Sultan Ala-ud-Din is supposed to have declared that he did not care for the commands of the shariat and would rather act according to requirements of the time. This is further testified by Barani, who lamented that rulers did not bother to implement the shariat, nor was it feasible to do so in the Indian context. Instead, he writes in his controversial *Fatawa-i-Jahandari* that rulers had evolved an almost secular state law, called zawabit, or regulations, as has been discussed in chapter three. Protestations by rulers of veneration for the shariat were however not uncommon. This was mainly to placate the ulama for such purposes as obtaining legitimacy for their rule. Historically, even supposedly pious rulers like Firuz Shah Tughluq and Aurangzeb used religion for political purposes. They employed the ulama in their administration to act as judges and religious advisors, and also to make their Muslim subjects believe that they were running an Islamic state. Thus, un-Islamic states were projected as

Islamic through the khutbas or religious sermons proclaimed during congregational prayers in mosques that celebrated the contributions of the rulers to the cause of Islam. The same need for legitimacy led the Delhi Sultans to seek robes and titles from the caliphs, wherever they could be located, especially in the aftermath of the sacking of Baghdad by the Mongols.

Due to their dependence on the state and their commitment to an older interpretation of Islam (Hanafi, in this case), the ulama produced little by way of independent, original religious thought or philosophy. Another reason for this is that Indian Islam was dependent on scholars from other parts of the Muslim world, mainly those coming from Central Asia, for guidance and inspiration. Many foreign theologians came to the Subcontinent during the medieval period seeking employment and this prevented an independent local tradition of scholarship from developing. The emphasis remained on blind conformity to the established opinion, to the extent that no alim of the stature of Imam Ghazali ever emerged in India.

Ghazali, who was trained in the Sufi tradition of the late eleventh–early twelfth century Abbasid Caliphate, emerged as a major theologian and defended traditionally accepted Sunni Islam against the rationalists/philosophers and defeated the latter, insofar as ensuring that rulers were compelled to follow the rigid position taken by the ulama. His books were in circulation in medieval India and some of them were also paraphrased because of the demand for normative religious literature, as in the case of *Adab-us-Salihin*, which is discussed in this chapter.[61] In the history of the first century of the Delhi Sultanate, references to a number of religious thinkers do appear: Kamal-ud-Din Zahid, Ziya-ud-Din Sunami, Badr-ud-Din Ghaznavi, Ala-ud-Din Usuli, etc. These thinkers were opposed to the official ulama, because for them, the latter served not God but the state. They were opposed to the state because its structure and policy were perceived to be a negation of the shariat. The interpretation of the shariat, then, has been a matter of contestation. The mainstream Sunnite 'official' ulama called for following a particular interpretation of Islam, a rather literal reading of the sources of Muslim law, mainly the Quran and hadis. They insisted that doors of ijtihad or fresh interpretation were closed and that there were enough examples in available interpretations to guide Muslims for all time to come. Thus, established interpretation, in this case of Hanafi Islam, was safeguarded and its commands were expected to be followed blindly.

Contrary to the narrow framework and fanaticism of theologians, philosophers of the first few centuries of Islam came up with their own readings of the shariat. Their version of Islam, particularly of the political ideals sanctioned in it, was much more inclusive and derived from diverse ancient sources. Ideas borrowed from a variety of traditions were blended together and presented in Islamic idioms in such a way that they could not be easily identified as something outside the pale of Islam. The ulama sodality, however, ensured that such borrowing or appropriation was allowed only up to an extent. In general, a strict vigil was maintained to ensure that deviations from the standard early interpretations were within limits, even as concessions were sometimes made for extraordinary situations in certain contexts. In the struggle to use political power to ensure that particular interpretations of Islam dominated Muslim polities and societies, the conformist ulama succeeded over rationalist philosophers, as we shall see later in this book. The success of theologians, however, did not mean that the everyday life of common Muslims in medieval India was all about virtue and piety. Sinners always did transgress the limits imposed by the shariat. In the next chapter, we will study the wide possibilities of sinning and the pleasures offered by deviance in medieval India.

Yet, the theologically inspired political interventions put serious limitations on norms of governance and on the power and authority of medieval Muslim rulers. The Quran and hadis defined the terms of reference not only for the private lives of the people, but also gave direction to medieval politics, which remained hostage to men of religion with all their pretensions to piety and righteousness. I conclude this chapter with Ghazali's suggestion that knowledge, patience and kindness are necessary in the matter of recommending right and forbidding wrong. For this, he quoted the Prophet of Islam, who said: 'He who is not patient in enjoining good and forbidding evil and has got no understanding of what is wrong and what is right should not take upon himself the task of amr bil ma'ruf wa nahi anal munkar'.[62]

6

Violating Norms of Conduct

Moving on from our discussion on the recommended norms of conduct, akhlaq/adab, in Sunnite Islam, forms of Islamic religiosity, pretensions of the orthodoxy to piety and devotionalism and contestations between rulers, ulama, and Sufis over what was identified as Islamic or non-Islamic, we will now explore the actual possibilities of defying these parameters of moral conduct. For this, we will focus on the works of Mir Muhammad Jafar Zatalli as literary articulations of 'improper' acts in Mughal India.[1] Jafar Zatalli, who lived in the second half of the seventeenth and the first decade of the eighteenth century, is often dismissed or ignored by modern scholars for his alleged vulgarity. Nevertheless, he enjoys the distinction of being the first major Urdu literary figure who attempted to redraw the boundaries of what was considered permissible in literature. Belonging to a Sayyid family of Narnaul, now in Haryana in northern India, Jafar Zatalli addressed issues of morality, particularly among the Mughal elite, including the princes and nobles. His writings have often been overlooked as mere *laffazi* or facile eloquence of little value. He even represented himself as a *zatalli* or idle talker, as we can see from his *takhallus* or nom de plume. Yet, no historian of Urdu language and literature can afford to ignore Zatalli and his work.[2] Jamil Jalibi, a leading scholar of the history of Urdu literature, has noted that Zatalli has generally been ignored as a jester who wrote nonsensical verse, and a proper evaluation of his work from the historical, cultural and linguistic perspectives has not been attempted. Jalibi himself locates the themes of Jafar's corpus in what was perceived as the moral decline and hypocrisies of late Mughal India. Instead of joining the dominant trend or withdrawing like a Sufi, Zatalli opted for critiquing the prevailing attitudes through satire, as we shall see below.[3]

Contrary to the indifferent attitude of the historians of medieval India towards him, it is important to note that Zatalli heralded a linguistic turn of sorts by publicly exposing the rampant duplicities of Mughal society through his satire and poetry of protest, which were in a no holds barred language—an idiom that was hitherto restricted to the oral domain. He wrote of love and sex in a way that no one had done before him in Mughal India. His oeuvre also pre-dated the poetry of love and/or self-flagellation over unfulfilled desire, *ghazal*, which subsequently emerged as the dominant form in the next generation,[4] though satire in Urdu also grew into an important trope for resistance and protest in north India in the first half of the eighteenth century.

Zatalli, however, wrote during a period when the poets were still mixing Persian and Urdu expressions in their compositions. Their language was called *rekhta*—gibberish or mixed language. The eighteenth-century sophistication of Urdu language had not yet come about and an accomplished *ustad* (master) like Siraj-ud-Din Ali Khan-i-Arzu (1687–1756) was yet to emerge. Khan-i-Arzu corrected and polished the language of many Urdu poets who flocked to Delhi, and some of them went on to be counted amongst the all time greats—Mir Taqi Mir, Muhammad Rafi Sauda and Khwaja Mir Dard come to mind immediately.[5] Later, Khan-i-Arzu and many of his pupils left Delhi for greener pastures in the wake of the turmoil at the Mughal court, which will be detailed later in this chapter. To his credit, although the learned scholar died in Lucknow, his body was transported to Delhi and buried there in accordance with his last wishes.

The larger processes in the history of Urdu literature also need to be kept in mind here. The latter half of the seventeenth century witnessed the growth of Urdu language and literature in Delhi, though Persian continued to dominate politically, culturally and intellectually. The subsequent arrival of Wali Dakani in north India and the impact of his works in Deccani Urdu are often referred to in the context of the growth of Urdu.[6] More importantly, political and social changes were transforming the linguistic sphere as well, a process that received a significant boost in the eighteenth century.[7] As mentioned earlier, Jafar Zatalli's compositions, both prose and poetry, are amongst the earliest examples of rekhta or early Urdu. Even as he used established Persian literary conventions, he often departed from tradition to showcase his mastery of Urdu.[8] Therefore, in many instances, his work reads like a mixed language. Sometimes, a couplet in Persian is followed by another in Urdu. In yet another case, one line of a couplet is in Persian, and the next in Urdu. Also, Persian and Urdu expressions are sometimes used in the same line, providing a spectacular example of literary and cultural appropriation.

Though Zatalli excelled in such bilingualism or in preparing a '*lisani khichri*'[9] (linguistic hotchpotch), this form has, in fact, a longer history that goes back to the Sufi fraternities of the Delhi Sultanate. Seen in this context, these works reveal the engagement between the Perso-Arabic form and lexicon, and Indic syntax and diction.[10] Yet, extant examples are few and far between as they were circulated orally for a period before being written down and are limited in terms of the range of genres. As mentioned earlier, though the Urdu that has come down to modern times took its mature shape only in the early eighteenth century during the period of Mughal decline, Zatalli's Urdu prose and poetry serve as interesting early examples of literary exercises in this language, executed with considerable finesse. His juxtaposition of a large vocabulary of Indic words, phrases and proverbs with Persian expressions shows the ease and flair with which he was able to transcend the barriers of language and culture.

Jafar Zatalli compiled his compositions from across a variety of literary genres in his *Kulliyat* (collected works), *Zatal-nama*, during the latter half of Aurangzeb's reign, that is, the last quarter of the seventeenth century. It is possible that Zatalli put together his *Kulliyat* some time between the twenty-ninth and thirty-ninth years of Aurangzeb's reign, that is, between 1687 and 1697.[11] A large number of manuscripts of Zatalli's work have survived, including a text from 1791–92. Notwithstanding modern historians' reluctance to engage with Zatalli's work, the popularity of the text in Urdu circles, though somewhat restrained and surreptitious, can also be ascertained from the fact that at least half a dozen printed editions have appeared in the 150 years from 1855 to 2003. For our purpose here, we will use the latest edition of *Kulliyat*, prepared by Rashid Hasan Khan, who has also written a detailed and important evaluation of the ten manuscripts and four previous editions.[12]

It is possible that Zatalli's work was subsequently edited and updated by the poet himself or by some later poets and writers. Rashid Hasan Khan has identified certain verses and prose compositions that are attributed to Jafar Zatalli in the text, but which seem to have been composed by some other writer(s) with lesser abilities. Khan has selected and included the potential later additions—both of doubtful authenticity and or those that seem to be outright false attributions—in separate appendices at the end of the *Kulliyat* edited by him.[13] Even if some portions of the work were possibly falsely ascribed to Zatalli, it is significant that the themes covered by the poet as well as his language and form were of interest to the Urdu-reading public. In addition, he was clearly imitated by his contemporaries and certainly by later poets, including several well-known literary figures from the first half of the eighteenth century. However, none can surpass Zatalli in crudeness and in his carefree knitting together of phrases from backgrounds as diverse as theological and virtuous Arabic, polished and deceptive Persian, and rustic and direct Hindustani. Many examples of such usage will be noted below in the samples of his compositions.

It is important to keep in mind that Jafar Zatalli was not an ordinary, frustrated public intellectual of the bazaar with nothing else to do. Nor was he a regular hoodlum loafing around the streets and passing comments on pedestrians. Also, his writing is not that of an ordinary soldier who maintained a diary in crude language.[14] In the opinion of an early biographer, but for his nasty cracks, his literary abilities were of the level of a malik-us-shuara (poet-laureate).[15] From time to time, he was employed in the service of some influential Mughal princes. For instance, he was for some time in the army of Aurangzeb's son, Kam Bakhsh, which was engaged in Mughal campaigns in the Deccan. Known for his not care a damn approach to life and work, Zatalli wrote a vulgar satire on his own generous employer, Kam Bakhsh, as well. The poet accused the prince of screwing a pet goat he loved. The satire begins with the couplet where Kam Bakhsh is charged of attacking the little opening (*ghachchi*) of the goat with so much force that it gets damaged (*pakhsh*) and is transformed into a gaping hole (*pichchi*):[16]

zahe shah-e wala guhar kam bakhsh
ke ghachchi buz kard pichchi wa pakhsh
(Well done! Jewel of the prince, Kam Baksh
The little opening of the goat is ruptured into a gaping hole.)

Note the poet's deployment of phrases in the *radif* (last words of the couplet), which highlight the contradictory qualities of the prince: bakhsh (generosity and forgiveness) counterpoised with pakhsh (beastly suppression and disfigurement). Further down in the verses, Zatalli becomes more explicit and declares that the prince's repeated penetration ('*ghusera ghuseri*', shoving and thrusting) causes the goat (called Manohar) to begin silently moaning in pain ('*ghusera ghuseri ke mi-kard shah/manohar pari khufiya mi-kard aah*).[17]

Understandably aghast with Zatalli's charge of bestiality, imagined or real, Kam Bakhsh, who reportedly had a lot of affection for the untamed poet, sacked him from service. The resultant poverty, as the poet writes in his verses, reminded him of the comfortable life he led under the patronage of the prince—all the delicacies (*faluda, firni, shirni*) he savoured, the comfortable bed he slept in and the time he spent in the company of women (*faluda wa firni che shud, pan bhatta wa shirni che shud / aan bistar wa balein kidhar, ke jafar ab kaisi bani*).[18] Following his sacking, Zatalli was forced to leave Deccan and, mercifully, Kam Bakhsh spared his life. He wrote that God saved his head, despite the fact that he antagonized the ruler (*ba badshah tayin bayr ki, sar par khuda ne khayr ki*).[19] Zatalli writes he regretted his utter lack of tact in provoking the prince, though he had done it for the fun of it. He says he realized that it was too late to undo the damage and lampoons himself in the poem '*hasb-e haal-e khwud gufta*' by asking in the radif, '*jafar ab kaisi bani*' or 'Jafar, how does it feel like now'.[20]

Banished from the Deccan, the poet chose to stay in Delhi and was engaged, for a period, in the service of Aurangzeb's second son, Prince Muhammad Muazzam, who succeeded his father to the Mughal throne and was subsequently known as Bahadur Shah I. It is possible that Zatalli ended up antagonizing his patron once again by writing a scandalous spoof called *Gand marawwa nama,* or *Gandu-nama* ('An Account of a Catamite'),[21] though it is not clear whether he wrote this before or after his dismissal from Bahadur Shah's service. One couplet of this satire was too explicit to leave any doubt about the character of the king:[22]

badshahi hai bahadur shah ki
ban banakar gand marawwa kheliye

Literally, this couplet translates as, this is the kingdom of Bahadur Shah, make yourself up for the fun of anus-sex. The religious condemnation of homosexual love apart, Muslim societies make a distinction between the 'subject' and an 'object' of male homosexual love, demeaning 'passivity' in men and making the 'exchange' pederastic, that is, hierarchical, non-mutual and controlling. The relationship then has a victorious 'male' and victimized 'female'. Following this binary, a *launde-baz* (pederast; literally, boy-player; sodomite) is not as emphatic a term of abuse as gandu (catamite; literally, anus-defined; coward).[23] Thus, to address Aurangzeb's son and successor as a gandu is the worst kind of abuse that only a Zatalli would dare to hurl.[24] More so, because the Mughals were supposed to be mature men, not going around removing their trousers for men or boys as they had harems comprising women of all kinds, available for meek subjection and for bearing sons.[25]

Since no detailed and authoritative biography of Zatalli has survived, it is difficult to ascertain the exact chronology of his career. Therefore, samples of his exploits and rewards, on the one hand, and punishments, on the other, can be given here only to highlight the extent of his literary transgressions, which eventually turned out to be a fatally flawed course of action in the prudish society of the time. It is important to remember that Zatalli was violating norms at two levels: first, he deviated from the norms of the literary culture of Mughal India in the latter half of the seventeenth century, especially compared to the sophisticated writings of figures like the Persian poet, Mirza Bedil, who did not utter a word in public not allowed by the norms of comportment, adab; second, Zatalli not only wrote in a language and form not acceptable in 'high' Mughal literary culture, but also committed transgressions by writing about what were construed as misdemeanours on the part of Mughal princes and nobles. While his literary transgressions ensured for a time that Zatalli was not taken seriously by literary purists, especially when Urdu literature was coming to be identified as a form of adab itself, his consistent pointing to the violations of Mughal norms by the upholders led to serious consequences.

Zatalli was killed following the emperor Farrukh-Siyar's order in 1713, ostensibly for commenting on the ruler's brutal method of eliminating rivals and opponents by strangling them to death using a leather belt (*tasma*), that is, instead of lashing or beating, which was the usual practice to chastise criminals and sinners; the whip was generally used for throttling the offenders till they died.[26] According to some reports, the nobleman Nawab Zulfiqar Khan Bahadur and his father were asphyxiated with a leather belt. Zatalli was also strangled in the same way for pointing out this innovation in a verse (*badshah-e tasma kush farrukh-siyar* or 'Farrukh-Siyar, the king who kills by the leather-belt'). It is possible that the ruler was affronted not so much for being condemned as a '*tasma-kush*', but for the poet's mocking his unjust rule. As one early biographer of Zatalli recorded, '*mizaj-i padshah barham gasht, ishan ra ba-jannat farastad*' ('The emperor was outraged; he, the poet, was dispatched to heaven!').[27] The wordsmiths derived the date of his death from the hemistich:

'haveli' chhod, yu bola zatalli
'andheri gor mein latkan lage paag'

Computing the numerical equivalent of the second line (*andheri gor mein latkan lage paag* or 'the legs were hanging in the dark grave') as well as leaving out the numbers derived from the word *haveli* (mansion; *haveli chhod*: a mansion which was to be vacated), the year of Zatalli's execution is poetically arrived at AH 1125 (1713).[28] Incidentally, the second line was providentially composed by Zatalli himself in his poem, *Budhapa-nama*, where he laments his deteriorating condition in old age.[29]

Since one of his couplets refers to his age as sixty years, Zatalli was possibly born during the reign of the Mughal emperor Shah Jahan and was a close witness to the reign of Aurangzeb, for whom he shows a deep personal respect. Therefore, speaking in the language of conventional history, Zatalli's writings are an important contemporary historical source for Aurangzeb's reign, and, as we shall see later in this chapter, he has praised the rule of the emperor.

Many of his satires, letters and a number of other compositions in a variety of genres, reveal Mughal culture as one that provided significant space for deviance from recommended norms of conduct that derived either from shariat-driven adab or from the elitist sophistication of Persianate society. (It may be pointed out that the term 'Persianate' is being used here and throughout this book in the sense of a society that is influenced by what is identified as Persian language and culture, but which is not necessarily one that directly originates from Persia or Iran. Similarly, the term 'Islamicate' is deployed to represent a set of ideas, beliefs or practices broadly identified with Muslim culture and civilization, but which does not blindly conform to any strand of Islamic theology with a constricted framework.) As James Grehan has written with reference to the norms of conduct for public officials in seventeenth- and eighteenth-century Damascus, ideally, a good Muslim was expected to carry himself with an air of serenity, dignity and patience. Laughing and jesting were out of the question. Gossip, lies, insults and all kinds of unbridled speech were considered abhorrent and dishonourable; so too were displays of anger, haughtiness and bravado. Pious men, whether ulama or Sufis, were supposed to always be in command of both body and soul, accomplished in what is referred to as 'arts of impression management'. The ideal man of learning was to be adept at sprinkling various pleasantries in his everyday speech along with appropriate citations from the Quran and other scriptural sources.[30]

In contrast, Zatalli was direct, impolite and frivolous. However, it is important to remember that he was careful enough to not antagonize any guardians of Islam who could retaliate with charges of heresies. He also did not mock the Prophet and his companions—symbols of virtue and infallibility—as we shall see later. Only some rulers managed to go as far, especially those who were able to subdue the ulama and Sufis under their authority, sometimes by generous grants and sometimes by force. The main targets of Zatalli's attack, in turn, were the rulers, mainly Mughal princes and nobles, as well as a number of elite women whose escapades were public knowledge. The transgressions of his subjects were well known to people in chowks, bazaars and army camps in Delhi and other major Mughal locations, but Zatalli was courageous enough to put them in writing and invite trouble for himself. As he wrote in his outrageous *Gandu-nama*:[31]

hukm-e qazi, muhtasib za'il shuda
dil badhakar gand marawwa kheliye

pir se aur baap se, ustad se
chhup-chhupakar gand marawwa kheliye

In the first couplet, the poet exposes the extent of sexual transgressions (in this case, '*gand marawwa*' or 'anus-sex') that occurred despite the presence of the qazis (Muslim judges) and muhtasibs (censor officials), whose powers were in decline (*za'il shuda*). In the second one, he points out how this was done, playfully, away from the gaze of (*chhup-chhupakar*) the father (*baap*), teacher (ustad) or the religious guide (pir). The poet also refers to the locations for and postures of homosexual intercourse—*ban banakar* (after a make-up), *dil badha-kar* (with an open heart), *bagh ja-kar* (in the garden), *dhol baja-kar* (over the trumpet), *darmiyan-i-khas-o-aam* (amidst the elite or the commoner), *paan chaba-kar* (while chewing *paan*), *ghar bula-kar* (through invitation at home), *chit laga-kar* (while lying on the back), and *taang utha-kar* (by raising the legs), to name a few.[32]

In this context, it must be noted that in his *Najat-ur-Rashid*, Abdul Qadir Badauni, whose critique of heresies in Islam has been discussed earlier in this book,[33] has quoted the Quran (al-Araf, verse 81) where it is stated that those who go to men instead of women for sexual purposes cross the limits of decency. Therefore, Badauni felt relieved when he was punished for his crime of homosexual love in this world itself. He was subjected to nine sword-wounds by the family of the 'beloved' youth with whom he was caught in a compromising position in a bush. This punishment was in keeping with the Quran (An-Nur, verse 2), which states that any man or woman who is characterless and indulges in what are identified as immoral acts should be administered one hundred lashes.[34] So, what we are dealing with here is apparently a longstanding concern in medieval Muslim societies and even in modern times, if oral reports that occasionally spill out of the closed and segregated seminaries are any indication.

Before proceeding with this discussion, however, it must be clarified that homosexuality is a matter of choice or preference and does not necessarily stem from situations of sexual segregation and nor should it be viewed as a general decline in moral standards. An investigation into this matter involving low-grade theologians and their pupils, and cases of sodomy and non-consensual love, is out of the purview of this work and such reports should be taken as aberrations unless proved by conclusive evidence as an established practice. Discussions on homosexuality and religion also tend to be riddled with sensitive issues. In fact, the most vehement opposition to homosexuality might come from religious leaders of different hues.

In general, however, what a study of Zatalli's work shows is that same-sex love was not unheard of despite the lashes or sword-wounds, as in the case of the punishment meted out to Badauni. The scholar, it would seem, was a habitual 'offender', despite the fact that he was otherwise considered one of the conscience-keepers of Islam in an age of unbelief or heresy under Akbar. Lest scholars and activists dealing with contemporary politics of sexualities have problems with some of the above formulations, it may be clarified that the intention here is not to privilege any normative form over the 'alternative', heterosexuality over homosexuality, or the moral over the titillating. Much of the emotional debates in the literature on sexuality are with reference to modern or contemporary issues and contexts, and needless to say, interested parties are extremely touchy about the issues.[35]

There are not many good studies on seventeenth-century Mughal India that foreground alternative sexualities and displace heteronormity as the supreme form of sexual behaviour. Instead, it would appear that a conservative sexual morality condemned as misdemeanour forms and expressions of desire that were perceived as unnatural, unprocreative, or effeminate; gandu was one such derogatory characterization. Increasingly asserting themselves in modern times are a variety of categories such as queer, lesbian, gay, bisexual, transgender, third gender, transsexual, and transvestite, as well as sexual relationships like adult and consensual, pre-marital, extra-marital, non-marital, group/orgy, promiscuous, paid-for and spouse-swapping sex.[36] In the language of the theologians and the moral brigade, most of these forms of sexual behaviour and conduct are fit to be suppressed till nothing remains of them. Also, while the moralist position on lesbians and homosexual men is discriminatory, it remains ambiguous on the sorry figures of the impotent as well as the neutered, that is, the castrated eunuchs, or *mukhanna*s, who guarded harems.

Returning to Zatalli, it is entirely possible that he was externalizing his frustrations over his miserable financial condition in the service of Bahadur Shah I, as he complained in another poem, *Qinat-nama*, 'A Report on Contentment', where he mentions the name of the ruler. He mockingly deploys the phrase '*ghanimat ast*' in the radif of this poem to highlight his poverty and claimed that whatever little he received can be considered a boon or blessing (*ghanimat*). He concludes the poem by recommending contentment (*qinat*) and submission to the will of God (sabr).[37] It is also possible that the poet was reflecting as much on his own despicable state as on the deteriorating grandeur of sections of Mughal nobility. This theme recurs in the satirical Urdu poetry of the early eighteenth century, as in that of Sauda; in the same vein, Zatalli suggests that if you do not get a horse of good quality, having a mule (*khachchar*) or donkey (*gadheri*) from Palam (near Delhi) should be satisfying enough.[38] Further, when he was punished for taunting Kam

Bakhsh, he realized the hazardous terrain he was traversing and wanted to stay away from censuring others:

dil ko thikane lao ab, kar sabr mat pachhtao ab
har giz mago bar-e digar, ke jafar ab kaisi bani!

In the above couplet, the call for self-restraint (sabr), exhortation for discretion (*har giz mago bar-e digar*, 'never utter a word about others') and suggestions to keep one's emotions in check or come to your senses (*dil ko thikana lao ab*) are backed by the observation that there was no point in regretting after the harm was done with the reminder, *ke jafar ab kaisi bani*, 'how does it feel to be punished for your follies'. However, the warning is just a trope in his sense of poetic justice, for the poet would resume targeting people with his acerbic compositions soon enough. In particular, he attacked their sexual licentiousness, mainly fascination for homosexual love, and the alleged unrestrained libido of their womenfolk, both in *purdah* and out of it.

Thus, Zatalli assailed, apart from Kam Bakhsh and Bahadur Shah I, Khan-i-Jahan, Sabha Chand, Fateh Ali Khan, Mirza Zulfiqar Beg (the kotwal of Delhi), Mirza Khudayar Beg and Muhammad Yar Beg, among others. For instance, he warned Sabha Chand, using the Indic epithet 'ji' after his name (that is, Sabha Chandji) to follow his wise counsel (*nasihat*) and spend time in remembering God (Ram) and chanting his name (*hamari nasihat rakho gosh bich/japo ram mala, raho hosh bich*).[39] The poet also threatened Sabha Chand of dire consequences for his craftiness (*chatur-chiti*). Accusing him of being a back-biter, Zatalli warned that he was capable of jumping on his back and subduing his buttock (*chughal ki uchhal gand pharun pachhar*).[40]

The well-known women he targeted included Ismatun Nisa Begam (maternal grand-daughter of Mughal noble, Mamur Khan) and the wives of Sabha Chand. The latter's two wives have been portrayed as *makkara* (cheats), *badkara* (sinful, sexually immoral), *ayyara* (cunning) and *chhinal* (whores), not to mention a host of other invectives. The alleged delinquency of Sabha Chand's wives is discussed in Zatalli's tirade against him. The gendered nature of assaults can certainly destroy a man's reputation and honour in many social and political contexts, as was the case in Mughal India. Though there might have been other reasons, Sabha Chand was ostensibly abused not only for being aware of what was going on in his family, but also for taking advantage of the exploits of his womenfolk to advance his own interests. Thus, he was projected as a *bhadwa* (pimp or cuckold) and *chandal* (low-caste wretch).[41] Also, even though Zatalli has given many examples of sexual licentiousness of various kinds, sometimes with approval and sometimes in rabid opposition, his diatribe against female sexuality is, in a measure, typical of the assumptions of a male-dominated society—always scrutinizing and controlling female behaviour which may not conform to the required standards of subordination.[42] In fact, imputations about a woman's sexual morality could be freely deployed even in arguments or disputes which were not about women and sex at all.[43] Characteristically then, Zatalli claimed, in another composition that highlights a traditional saying, that the penis can never subdue the vagina, despite all the controlling powers of society (*suni baat mayen pir fartut se/ke lauda na jita kabhi chut se*).[44] (Polite company calls for purity of tongue and to block out offensive speech, a normative text would recommend plugging your ears with your fingers.[45])

On account of the abusive language used by Zatalli in many of his poems and other writings, scholars who sing paeans about the sophistication and sobriety of Mughal culture tend to dismiss the poet as a writer of obscenity who should better be ignored. However, it is important to remember that not all of Zatalli's writing represented a vulgar expression of an uncultured and frustrated man unable to fit into an urbane, Mughal scheme of things. As shown above, Zatalli was associated with many princes and nobles of his time. Moreover, making fun of others was serious business, even as the poet also castigated himself for his own failures and lack of prudence. In doing so, however, he was basically commenting on the culture of his time. Jafar's non-conformist utterances exposed the tantalizing difference between the acceptable standards of moral conduct and contemporary social realities, religion and deviance, and importantly, piety and sin.

To clarify, terms such as religion, heresy, piety, sin and transgressions are being used in this chapter and elsewhere in this book in the sense in which they are done in the established tradition of scholarship on medieval Islam, much of which will be unintelligible to those who have been trained to think only in terms of Christianity and Western modernity, which is a major limitation of modern Western education. The problem becomes particularly acute when influential modern Western theories are imposed on the very different empirical or historical context of medieval Muslim societies. There is a veritable epistemological disconnect that causes many misunderstandings regarding Islam and Muslim traditions, which is one of the outstanding problems in the relationship between Islam and the West, but this should not prevent us from pursuing our own inquiry.

To return to Zatalli, since he had lived through roughly the entire reign of Aurangzeb, his compositions are a reflection of the society and culture of the period of pre-modern/pre-colonial, Mughal India, as has been pointed out earlier. He was also a witness to the political flux that eventually shook the Mughal empire under Aurangzeb's successors in the early eighteenth century. The events in the last years of Aurangzeb's rule were a portent of the hara-kiri about to happen soon after his death. The rumours about the wide gap between accepted norms and the moral conduct of his sons and nobles made them lose the legitimacy to rule the huge empire they had inherited. They were also accused of being so incompetent as to be unable to govern the empire efficiently. Thus, Zatalli's comments are not out of place—he was a close witness to the unfolding saga of the decaying Mughal army, camps and forts.

The fratricidal warfare following Aurangzeb's death further weakened the Mughal imperial household and the grandeur and awe was also eventually lost with the emergence of successor states and independent principalities. Though historians have advanced a number of reasons such as agrarian crisis, backwardness of the Mughal army, and, more importantly, the religious policy of Aurangzeb for the decline and fall of the Mughal empire, Jafar Zatalli had considerable respect for Aurangzeb and the Mughal dominion, if not for the imperial household. The emperor not only escaped the poet's lethal attacks, but was actually, for a change, a subject of Zatalli's praise, which was a rare honour. In his eulogy (*Dar tarif Aurangzeb*), the poet extolled the extraordinary bravery and steadfastness of Aurangzeb, which created a flutter (*khalbali*) in the Deccan (*zahe dhak-e aurangshah-e bali/dar aqlim-e dakkhan pari khalbali*).[46]

Another couplet projected Aurangzeb as an exceptional warrior who could stand on the battlefield like an unmoveable mountain (*mahasur, joddha, bali be-badal/chu al-burz qaim, chu parbat atal*).[47] Notice the use of aggressive phrases from the language of warfare of the Indic tradition here. The emperor is referred to as a great warrior-hero, using the following Sanskrit/Hindi synonyms: *bali*, *mahasur*, *juddha*, *atal*, *hanumant* and *balbir*. In contrast, his rivals in Deccan such as Sikandar Hasan, ruler of Bijapur, Abul Hasan Tana-Shah, ruler of Golconda and Shivaji's son, Sambhaji, among others, are belittled as insignificant creatures. Zatalli reserved his worst comments for Sambhaji's agent, Pratap, whom he addressed with the rhetorical remark, *che jhant ast partab ibn-ul-hammar*, which refers to Pratap as an ass or son of a donkey and dismisses him as male pubic hair. Further, in the concluding part of his eulogy, the poet extolled Aurangzeb's virtues such as *wafa* (faithfulness), *haya* (modesty, shame) *baqa* (everlasting), *ghina* (wealthy), *marawwat* (kindness), *fatuwat* (generosity) and *daya* (mercy).[48] The poet eventually declared that in all his experience of travels and pilgrimages (*tirath*, including a visit to Dwarka), he never met a more merciful person (*dayawant*) than Aurangzeb (*phira mayen bahut tirath aur dwarka / na dekha dayawant tujh saarka*).[49]

In sharp contrast to the generous tribute paid to Aurangzeb, Zatalli attacked the incompetence and hypocrisies of his sons, which, according to him, not only complicated the proper and efficient management of the Deccan campaigns, but also spoiled the whole project (*hama kar-o-baar-e pidar bhand kard*).[50] In particular, the poet pointed out their relentless propensity towards sex and wrote that chatting and fantasizing about the wet vagina or anus were a round-the-clock obsession for them (*rahe raat din gaand ke zikr mein/ba lahu luab chut ki fikr mein*).[51]

In another set of compositions, *Akhbarat-e siyaha-e darbar-e mualla*, written on the lines of a daily record of imperial orders, Zatalli also pointed out how the emperor's long stay in the Deccan, for roughly the whole of the second half of his reign, weakened the Mughal administration in north India.[52] Yet, Zatalli maintained his respect for Aurangzeb and wrote a *marsiya* or elegy on his death.[53] Referring to the terrible struggles between the sons of Aurangzeb for the Mughal throne and revealing the anxieties caused by the political crisis, Zatalli concluded his elegy by warning himself of the consequences of his remarks in the changed scenario: *baya, jafar, sukhan ra mukhtasar kun/ze daur-e mukhtalif dar dil hazar kun* (literally, come on, Jafar, cut short your utterances; the time has changed, keep it to your heart).[54]

Zatalli's celebration of the reign of Aurangzeb is in line with the later image of the ruler in traditional Muslim circles—an efficient and pious badshah, who led a simple life. This portrayal is different from the charges of fanaticism and bigotry attributed to Aurangzeb that occurs in sections of later scholarship. This also does not require any apology and nor does it involve any embarrassment that one notices in another set of writings on the emperor. Drawing on a previous attempt to use some modern Urdu scholarship on Aurangzeb and medieval India generally,[55] unlike the uncomfortable liberal/secular scholars, writers like Allama Shibli Numani and Syed Sabahuddin Abdur Rahman do not fight shy of talking about the reign of Aurangzeb. For instance, Abdur Rahman points out that non-Muslim writers generally refer to Aurangzeb as a biased ruler, but his policy of recruitment of his officers belies such a characterization.

According to him, the king believed that religion should not interfere in matters of governance, and nor should biases have any place in such things. In support of this position, the ruler even cited the Quranic instruction: *lakum dinakum wa liya-din* ('To you your religion, to me mine'). Abdur Rahman even speculates that if Muslim rulers had not adopted such a policy towards non-Muslims, perhaps their government would not have lasted for so long.[56]

Abdur Rahman contests Jadunath Sarkar's views on Aurangzeb's religious policy and largely extends Shibli Numani's older and more established position in Muslim intellectual circles. He questions Sarkar's motives in projecting Aurangzeb as a villain and Shivaji as a hero. He is particularly outraged by Sarkar's suggestion that the Mughal monarch behaved in the light of the Quran and the teachings of Islam, which condone violence, and thus, alienated non-Muslims from the Mughals, leading to the emergence of Shivaji as a saviour of the Hindus, and the subsequent fall of the Mughal empire.

For Abdur Rahman, Aurangzeb's orders to destroy some temples were not aimed at suppressing Hindus in general. For, if that was the case, he would not have given so many land grants to Hindu temples. The author asserts that the attacks on places of worship should be understood in their localized context and that such examples should not be used to provoke one set of people against another. According to him, scholars like Sarkar contributed to the divisive agenda of the British and were rewarded with honours in return.[57] Abdur Rahman's work is a rare example of a detailed critique of Sarkar's writings, when the liberals have now given up on both Aurangzeb and Sarkar.[58] Sarkar's contributions also do not figure in two recent collections of classic historiographical interventions on the eighteenth century.[59] On the other hand, taking a liberal Muslim position, Syed Jamaluddin rebukes Abdur Rahman and Muslims in general for 'unnecessarily' making a ruthless ruler like Aurangzeb an academic 'liability' and for according saintly status to him.[60]

However, Aurangzeb is indeed venerated in the devotional

Muslim milieu and counted amongst the pantheon of pious figures, mainly Sufis—a list that also includes a despotic Sultan like Mahmud of Ghazna. The names of all of these so-called pious men are uttered or inscribed with the suffix '*rahmatullah-alaih*' ('God's mercy be upon him'). This is not only true for oral traditions, but also for popular literature that circulates around Sufi centres. Rashid Hasan Khan has pointed out that the replacement of the respectful phrase *zill-e subhani* (Shadow of God) with *zill-e shaitani* (Shadow of Satan) for Aurangzeb in some versions of Jafar Zatalli's composition, *Akhbarat-e siyaha-e darbar-e mualla*, is a later interpolation by the copyists,[61] which also means that there were people, possibly Shi'ites, who, unlike Sunnite/Sufi circles, did not venerate the emperor.

In general, however, Zatalli used words as weapons,[62] and he could be devious in his use of phrases. Many abusive epithets were deployed by him; expletives of the kind that one still hears, with varying degrees of improvisations, in many parts of north India and possibly in the Deccan, and other regions as well. Some examples are *gaand se dosti, punchh se bayr* (friendship with the buttock, animosity with the tail);[63] *sipahi ka maal, jhaanth ka baal* (soldier's property, pubic hair).[64] Stand-alone expressions of disgust such as chut (vagina), gand (buttock), lauda (penis), *bhonsri* (vagina) and jhaanth (pubic hair) were also thrown in freely.[65] Several other proverbs used by Zatalli are still deployed in Urdu-Hindi circles with little or no embarrassment: *unt ke munh mein zira* (a cumin seed in a camel's mouth);[66] *naach na janun angan tedha* (when you do not know how to dance, [don't] blame it on the crooked courtyard/floor);[67] *kutta tedhi punchh hai, kabhi na sidhi ho* (a dog has a crooked tail that can never be straightened).[68]

Projecting himself as the object of sarcasm, Zatalli also wrote a poem, *Dar bayan-e dilawari* ('Description of Bravery'), in which he ridiculed the hollow claims of the greatness and bravery of Mughal nobles and warriors. Zatalli's critical comments on the pretensions and insincerities of the Mughal elite once again anticipate similar remarks by the next generation of Urdu poets in Delhi such as Sauda, and, thus, connect him to the tradition of sorrowful *shahr-e ashob* poetry in Urdu, which laments the decline of the Mughal empire and with this, its purportedly refined culture and unmatched aura.[69]

It is also important to note here that Zatalli's critique substantiates and corroborates the accounts of contemporary and near-contemporary chroniclers and historians. In the opinion of one modern writer, since the age was one of political decline and economic distress, there runs a thread of gloom through much of the contemporary historical writing.[70] It is suggested that the degenerated nobility reduced the king to a hapless pawn in the game of politics. The deposition and death of Farrukh-Siyar demonstrated the final triumph of ministers and nobles over the emperor. It is also noted, though erroneously, that the later Mughals had received no thorough education in the art of government and, therefore, they proved unequal to the task of dealing with the crises that continuously threatened Mughal dominion.[71] The contemporary writers, who saw the empire caught in the turmoil of civil strife and its vast structure ultimately breaking down in the wake of political threat both from within the empire and outside, condemned the unwise policies of the later Mughal rulers and their inefficient administration.[72]

The reported degeneration of the nobility, mainly through corruption and, what was perceived as immorality, further compounded the problem. However, these reports of the chroniclers and historians are to be studied with caution as their assessments of Mughal politics at this time are invariably coloured by their own ethnic and sectarian backgrounds as well as professional interests. For instance, opinion was divided on the role of the Sayyid brothers, influential nobles in Mughal court politics. While Khafi Khan condemned the Sayyid brothers, Qasim Lahori defended them.[73] Court politics, struggles amongst the nobility and the weakened personal authority of Mughal princes transformed Mughal sovereignty into a useless parade of rulers, which did not make any difference, and, by implication, contributed to the political decline of the Mughals. The awe and grandeur of the Mughal household, led by the emperor, had diminished and the imperial image was dented.

Yet, modern scholars are aghast at Zatalli's coarse expressions and uncouth remarks on the state of affairs. This could be because Zatalli basically affects their own sensibilities and disturbs the usual understanding of Mughal culture as being 'polished', an idea acquired through both academic tomes as well as popular literature. Even if we ignore that portion of Zatalli's account which is identified as vulgar for his exposure of what was perceived to be sexual misdemeanours—especially of rampant homosexuality amongst the Mughal nobility—his work provides an important commentary on Mughal society in a period of political flux. The alleged acts of transgressions were probably not unheard of under Akbar or for that matter under Shah Jahan, but it was now possible for Zatalli to talk about it in writing, and in Urdu, the language of Mughal camps and bazaars. The personalities of the rulers and chiefs could now be questioned in public as norms of decorum and propriety in the Mughal court culture underwent a considerable change.

Also, Zatalli's poems, *Dar bayan-e tawakkul* ('On the Declaration of Trust [in God]'), *Dar ahwal-e istaghna* ('On Conditions of Content') and *Qinat-nama*, reveal his attempts to withdraw from a world he was uncomfortable with, and to take refuge in religion. Therefore, this set of writings brings out another dimension of the poet's strategy—renunciation of the world and trust in God. Such self-righteousness brought about a sense of arrogance as well. As he says in *Dar bayan-e tawakkul*, 'How does it matter if you cannot afford a pyjama? Stand alone proudly flaunting your loin cloth' (*agar shalwar na bashad, kis ko ghum hai/langota khainch kar sab se akad rah*).[74] Zatalli further proclaimed in *Dar ahwal-e istaghna*:[75]

na zar na zewar-o-naqad wa na kotha ajnas
na jashn-e 'id na sair-e dashara daram mun

That is, deprived of wealth (*zar*, *zewar*: gold and jewellery), he was unable to enjoy the festivities of 'Id and Dussehra, yet he no longer cared about his poverty and lack of interest in good things in life (*gharib-o-ajiz-o-miskin zatalli am jafar/hazar shukr, na zor-o-na zahra daram mun*).[76] This emotion is typical of Muslim men aiming for *buzurgi* or saintliness in old age. Zatalli himself wrote a pietistic and parsimonious *Budhapa-nama*, as mentioned earlier. His decreasing strength and failing health in old age was contrasted with the beauty and grace of youthfulness in his *Joban-nama*, which in turn was presented as a temporary phase in life. The poet wondered how could he preserve his youth by coaxing or cajoling it not to go (*ise pher kiyun-kar mana-kar rakhun /jawani gayi, kiya rijha-kar rakhun*).[77]

Not surprisingly, the poet also composed a *na't* or eulogy for Prophet Muhammad. The na't includes the following couplet:[78]

> *muhammad paar utaran haar sab ka*
> *muhammad sarwar-o-salar sab ka*
> (Muhammad is the liberator of all
> Muhammad is the commander of all.)

As pointed out earlier, for all his indiscretion, the poet was careful enough not to attack any icons of Islamic religiosity, certainly not the Prophet, though objectionable remarks on qazis, ulama, muhtasib and other guardians of the faith, mainly of the dominant Sunnite strand, are found throughout his work. On the other hand, he paid tributes to the first four rightly-guided caliphs. It is possible that Zatalli came from a Shi'ite background or might have been a *tafzili*, one who privileged the fourth caliph, Ali, over the first three (Abu Bakr, Umar and Usman), but unlike the Shias, did not condemn the others.[79]

Jafar Zatalli knew that he was treading on a controversial ground, so he reminded himself of the danger of revealing all his secrets—a suggestion of the kind recommended for Sufi mystical experiences or in juristically sanctioned policies of concealing one's belief, *taqiyya*, which are followed by hapless

Shi'ites or other marginal groups, especially when faced with violent opposition.[80] It may also be pointed out here that the concealment of religious identity, or taqiyya, can be a flawed strategy. For the danger is that a silent and weak person, group of people or community might eventually get absorbed in the vocal and dominant community without any resistance. In other words, a vocal majority can subdue a silent minority.[81]

Despite deference for politically privileged religious icons, in a political context like that of the early decades of the eighteenth century, and possibly for the whole period of Mughal rule, mocking the rulers could be as harmful as an act of blasphemy in most parts of the Muslim world. Indeed, as mentioned earlier, Zatalli paid with his life for telling it all in salacious language. It is doubtful, however, that he would have been spared if he were polite in his criticism. We have already discussed earlier how the critics of Akbar's policies, whether ulama, Sufis or, even rationalists, could be eliminated for daring to disagree with the dominant opinion.[82]

The execution of Zatalli, or for that matter, of any other critic or opponent of the Mughals could not hide the fact that their power and legitimacy had taken a beating in many regions of the realm. The Jats, Sikhs, Satnamis and a host of Hindu zamindars and Muslim chiefs were frequently asserting their independence and the Mughal nobles were unable to establish their imperial domination and authority. A detailed analysis of the dismemberment of the Mughal empire is out of the purview of this work, but we will take up the question of the violent Mughal–Sikh conflict and, more generally, the varying, and often turbulent relationship between Islam and Sikhism in the next chapter.

It might be appropriate to end this chapter with Jafar's signature line on a bond paper as a witness (*hazir zamini*), which reads,[83] '*lallu pattu, walad indhan jangli, mutawattin andher nagri, mulazim-e sarkar-e chaupatabad*'. Jafar signed his name as a loquacious sycophant and son of a wild beast, who lived in *andher nagri* (literally, city of darkness) and worked in the service of the ruler of *chaupatabad* (a ruined or despicable habitation). Apart from the outrageous description of the Mughal capital Shahjahanabad, where he lived, as chaupatabad, Jafar's idiom is reminiscent of the popular Indic proverb for situations of anarchy, '*andher nagri, chaupat raja*' (city of darkness, inefficient ruler). At the end of the document, Jafar also identifies himself as *ahmaq walad be-waquf* (stupid son of a fool). In the language of the current popular culture, he was simply *bindas* or cool.

Surely, Jafar transgressed all limits of moral conduct in Mughal India in his writings, at least, in terms of the distinction between the elite, refined and measured literary culture of the Mughal court on the one hand, and the crude and popular outpourings of the subalterns and marginal people on the other. Historians generally tend to privilege the former—the formal and onstage performance of the rulers and courtiers. Even though political culture, essentially dominated by the elite, is important for our understanding of Islam in the Indian environment, should literature of the kind that Zatalli produced be swept under the Persian carpet? Should historians continue to blur the distinctions between Mughal self-image and the actual social and cultural practices of the time? Is it illegitimate to counterpoise Zatalli's observations with dominant Mughal ideals? Historians and literary scholars are scared of asking such questions of crucial import that can lead to a more holistic understanding of Mughal India. Much of the scholarship thus remains bound to the framework of official chronicles. Any attempt to break the shackles is dismissed as transgression and vulgarity, which should better be ignored, if not suppressed altogether. To move on, the next chapter will explore religious and literary entanglements at the level of mysticism and religiosity as well as popular literature.

7

The Sufi-Bhakti Milieu
Later Transformations

Islam and Sikhism

Sikhism is generally perceived to be a militant form of Hinduism that emerged as a response to the onslaught of Islam in medieval India. The protracted struggle between the Sikhs and the Mughals through the seventeenth and eighteenth centuries and, more recently, the horrors of Partition have contributed to this perception. This is despite the fact that Sikh leaders have struggled to protect the community both from violent Hindu attacks in the recent past, as well as from peaceful absorption into 'ceremonial Hinduism'. By contrast, those who are oblivious to identity politics involving the Sikhs—such as the general population of the West, whether America or Europe—tend to mistake a Sikh for a Muslim. Indeed, the Sikh man's turban, his beard, the long traditional robe, the community's religious scriptures, the practice of *langar* (community kitchen), the architecture of a gurudwara and the rejection of idol worship are some of the features shared with Islam. No wonder then that Sikhs are under attack from ignorant Americans and Europeans for their alleged 'resemblance' with Osama Bin Laden and other look-alike Muslims who may not necessarily subscribe to violent political Islam.

I will argue in this chapter that the similarities between Sikhism and Islam, both at the level of ritual practices and cultural characteristics or features, are not accidental. I will point to some very important Islamic influences on the career of the first Sikh religious leader, Guru Nanak, and, more generally, to Indian Islam's relationship with Sikhism during the formative years of the religion as one with a Book of its own. This association with Sikhism continues to be emphasized in Muslim religious and literary traditions, both elite and popular, despite the divergent and often conflict-prone history of the two communities over the past four centuries. Examples from an influential tradition of Muslim writings in Urdu where Guru Nanak is venerated as a holy man par excellence are included in this chapter.

The origin and development of Guru Nanak's religious ideas can be located in the Sufi-Bhakti milieu of late fifteenth- and early sixteenth-century north India, though many Sikh devotees might be averse to such a proposition. Before taking my argument any further, it is important to understand the process of what is loosely termed as 'syncretism' and 'synthesis' in religious and cultural spheres during the Lodi and Sur regimes of the late fifteenth and early sixteenth centuries—the period when Guru Nanak flourished.

As we discussed earlier, the Sufis played a prominent role in this process of syncretism in the Subcontinent.[1] The doctrine of 'wahdat-ul-wujud' (monism as a reality) had brought the Sufis close to certain streams of non-Muslim thought. The Sufis not only popularized yogic practices amongst their followers, but also drew attention to the similarities in the spiritual terminologies of Muslims and Hindus. The contribution of the Sufis to the growth and development of vernacular literature and devotional music is equally noteworthy . At times, however, the Sufis did take as fanatical a position as that of any orthodox alim or theologian in medieval India. Sources refer to a large number of tales of miraculous combats between Sufis and their non-Muslim opponents. The narratives of a Sufi's triumphs over his antagonists, often leading to the conversion of the adversary to Islam, intend to prove his superior spiritual stature. Reports of conversions by a Sufi sheikh brought him immense prestige and authority in his wilayat. The image of Sufi sheikhs as disseminators of Islam was thus built and maintained for posterity through these narratives. The Sufis' influence over their contemporary society and politics was also immense. They made significant contributions towards the consolidation of Afghan power in their own regions and spiritual jurisdictions, and imposed restrictions and limitations on the political authority, even as they enjoyed widespread popularity.

The influence of Islam, or for that matter, of any other system of ideas on Nanak's teachings has been refuted by a leading Sikh historian, J.S. Grewal, who has remarked that the Guru's ideas had 'a sure degree of originality' as they were a product of 'illumination' upon him.[2] A more objective scholarship, however, recognizes the importance of the religious heritage from which Nanak benefited, but highlights the transformation of that inheritance by the Guru as having led to the formation of Sikh religion.[3] On the other hand, while noting that in its initial inspiration the Sikh movement showed a genuine monotheistic eclecticism in which the Islamic influence was clearly discernible, another scholar, Aziz Ahmad, doubts whether the 'syncretic appeal' of the medieval religious leaders has had any lasting influence. He also points out that the transformation of Sikhism from an eclectic faith into one with anti-Muslim overtones is perhaps the most tragic instance of the failure of syncretism in India.[4]

Indeed, Sikh accounts both lament and extol the prolonged episode of the 'struggles' and 'sacrifices' of their Gurus against alleged Mughal oppression by Akbar's successors. Such a formulation neglects the fact that the religio-political community of the Sikhs, comprising prosperous Khatri traders and upwardly mobile Jat peasants, was gradually emerging as an alternative political culture in medieval India. Ironically, the evolution of the separatist, as against the syncretistic, community or *panth* of the Sikhs with its distinct cultural boundary markers, was taking place during Akbar's—of all emperors'—reign! It was only a matter of time before the Mughal administrative machinery geared up to keep the Gurus and their *masands* (revenue agents) in check. However, the masands were eventually perceived as constituting a challenge to the office of the Guru himself and their role was dissolved by the time of the founding of the Khalsa by the tenth guru, Gobind Singh. The Guru directed his followers to make donations to him directly and not to anyone else representing him or the community.[5]

A more sympathetic Sikh view claims that while Akbar's catholicity protected the Gurus and their followers from open violence, it could not obviate the nefarious designs of their enemies. It is lamented that with Akbar's death, the withdrawal of imperial protection came rather suddenly, accompanied by violence.[6] There is a case here for the Gurus' innocence, compared to the allegations of uncalled-for violence practised by the rulers who were increasingly pandering to the pressures of the Islamic orthodoxy, or for that matter, due to personal predilections of an 'orthodox' Muslim ruler such as Aurangzeb; however, not many scholars might accept such a proposition.

It is important to note here that three key events took place within the first two centuries of Sikhism's emergence, which shaped its distinctive features: (i) a series of ten Gurus, from Guru Nanak to Guru Gobind Singh (d. 1708), provided leadership to the community; (ii) the compilation of the scriptures, *Guru Granth Saheb*, by the fifth Guru, Arjan, in 1603–04; and (iii) the foundation of the Khalsa by the tenth Guru, Gobind Singh, in 1699. The Gurus' encounters with the Mughals led to a considerable distancing between Sikhism and Islam in general. This is even reflected in contemporary scholarship on Sikhism, which tends to conform to the demands of the religious orthodoxy. The emotional and sensitive nature of some of the issues means that they cannot be discussed and debated freely even in 'dispassionate' academic circles.

A recent collection of articles reveals the tensions involved in discussing this process of cultural and religious appropriations.[7] As mentioned earlier, historically, the need to carve out a distinctive identity and a political realm of their own brought the Sikhs into violent conflict with their opponents, chiefly the Mughal rulers and by extension, Muslims in general. Thus, even as adherence to the peaceful teachings of Guru Nanak, namely the worship of the True God, remained the central dogma of the Sikh panth, armed struggle (*danga*) for sovereign power (*miri* or *patshahi*) became the war cry for the Khalsa, which has led to the celebration of the sacrifices of many a Guru, hailed as martyrdom (*shahidi*). In such a context, the re-presentation of selected Sikh writings, such as Sainapat's *Sri Guru Sobha*, Koer Singh's *Gurbilas Patshahi Das*, Kesar Singh Chibber's *Bansavalinama Dasan Patshahian Ka*, Bhai Santokh Singh's *Suraj Prakash* and Ratan Singh Bhangu's *Guru Panth Prakash*, as instances of the praising, compromising, Brahminizing, re-asserting or valorizing of the Khalsa tradition appears to be too neat an arrangement of a complex history, involving Sikhs as well as Muslims, Hindus and others living in Punjab.[8]

In an attempt to iron out historical complexities, non-Sikh scholarship has largely been dismissed, either as unimportant or biased, unless the call for armed Sikh struggle in extraordinary situations is supported by the authors concerned. Thus, while modern writings by scholars like Teja Singh and Ganda Singh have been appreciated, a Muslim author like Abdul Latif has been dismissed as biased against the Sikhs and thus, unimportant. As noted above, such an approach is conditioned by, and is subservient to, the dictates of the guardians of Sikh religion who have, at various times in the past, recommended maintaining a distance from Muslim and Hindu cultural and linguistic legacies, or advocated the doctrine of the independent growth of Sikhism as the third panth, while asserting an unbroken continuity in the divinely ordained preaching of the ten Gurus. Thus, rather than question and critique a dynamic religious tradition dispassionately, the scholarly enterprise is reduced to understanding and interpreting it within a limited framework.[9]

However, such politics notwithstanding, verses attributed to the thirteenth-century Chishti Sufi sheikh of Punjab, Farid-ud-Din Ganj-i-Shakar, variously referred to as Khwaja Farid/Baba Farid/Sheikh Farid are included in the Sikh scriptures and could never be expunged altogether. The *Guru Granth Saheb* has over a hundred verses attributed to Sheikh Farid, only slightly less than those credited to saint-poet Kabir, for instance. Traditionally, in Sikh, and in Punjabi tradition more generally, Farid is venerated for his devotional poetry included in the *Granth Saheb*. It is sometimes suggested that Sheikh Farid of the Sikh scriptures could as well be a sixteenth-century poet and descendant of the original Chishti Sufi Baba Farid who lived in the thirteenth century. There are few takers for this view even among historians. There is almost a consensus that Farid of the Sikh scripture is the thirteenth-century Chishti saint. In any case, the shared heritage is reflected in the inclusion of devotional songs of a large number of monotheistic poets belonging to diverse mystical traditions in the *Guru Granth Saheb*, which was first compiled in the early seventeenth century. Later editions, including the final version prepared in the early eighteenth century, did not expunge the compositions of religious leaders outside the fold of the chain of Sikh Gurus, including Baba Farid, despite the emerging political difficulties.[10]

Sikhism's later transformation from a syncretic religion to one that was hostile towards Islam, or for that matter, the division of Kabir's followers into Hindu and Muslim Kabirpanthis, did not stop the process of syncretic borrowing from diverse religious traditions. Despite pressures from Hindu and Muslim reformist and revivalist movements, syncretism in popular belief has survived in India. A common feature in most of the existing syncretistic cults is the worship or veneration of a galaxy of saints—legendary or otherwise. Many of these saints had followers from across the boundaries of institutionalized religions, even though some followers retained their association with their 'parent' religion. No wonder, reports of violence between Hindu and Muslim followers for funerary rights over the dead bodies of these saints and Gurus recur throughout the history of medieval India. The followers of Nanak, like that of

Kabir, fought a pitched battle before a 'divine' intervention reportedly resolved the crisis (more on this later).

The making of the Khalsa with strict markers of identity was in a measure connected to Mughal–Sikh conflicts through the seventeenth and eighteenth centuries, which completely vitiated relations between Sikhism and Islam.[11] Taking stock of Muslim–Sikh relations in Punjab since the time of the early Gurus, W.H. McLeod suggests that the widespread hostility between the two groups emerged during the political flux of the eighteenth century, when the markers of difference were outlined in a fashion that ranged from the bizarre to the horrible. The eighteenth-century Sikh codes of belief and conduct, the *rahit-namas*, came up with all kinds of instructions that ensured a complete rupture between the two religions, and inter-communal relations reached its nadir in the horrendous aftermath of the Partition of India.[12]

Large-scale confrontations over political power transformed Sikhism from a syncretic religious tradition that drew heavily from the beliefs and practices of Islam to outright hostility towards the latter. As mentioned earlier, Sikh tradition both laments and celebrates the 'martyrdom' of the Gurus that occurred during recurrent clashes with the Mughals. Despite political violence and the standardization of Sikhism as a religion of the Book, independent of Islam and Hinduism, Guru Nanak's image as a holy man comparable to a Sufi sheikh survives in the Muslim tradition. This is contrary to the formulation initially advanced by colonial authors—in a stark reminder of what is traditionally characterized as 'divide and rule'—that Muslim accounts misrepresented and denigrated the Guru.[13]

Significantly, even in a political account of the early-eighteenth-century conflict between the Sikhs, led by Banda Bahadur, and the Mughals, a fine distinction is made between Guru Nanak's career and the later development of Sikhism in relation to the Mughal power. The late-eighteenth-century historian and intellectual at large, Ghulam Husain Tabatabai mentions in his celebrated *Siyar-ul-Muta'khkhirin* that Guru

Nanak was a disciple of a Sufi saint and, therefore, a Sufi in his own right. However, Ghulam Husain continues, Nanak's followers corrupted his teachings and went on to start a new cult of Sikhism, which had been at loggerheads with the Mughals for most of its existence in the Punjab region.[14] It may be pointed out here that to say that Nanak could have been a Sufi might now be considered as his denigration in the circle of his followers.

In the latter half of the eighteenth century, Ghulam Husain Tabatabai was no ordinary figure. He belonged to a large group of Persianate-Mughal gentlemen who were quick to realize the significance of the new politics that was emerging in the latter half of the eighteenth century with the British playing a major role. These were the enlightened early modern Muslim figures, some of whom had not only travelled widely within the Indian Subcontinent, but also beyond, including Europe, and certainly to England. They should neither be treated as collaborators of the colonial regime, for colonialism had not happened as yet, nor as spokesmen for any Muslim group. Ghulam Husain and his contemporaries moved comfortably from the company of the Mughal emperors of Delhi and the nawabs of Lucknow, to the zamindars of Banaras, Kayastha bureaucrats of Patna and the nazims of Murshidabad, even as they negotiated profitably with the firangi officials of the East India Company. Many of the above formulations on the intellectual milieu of the eighteenth century are derived from the recent works of Partha Chatterjee, where he makes a distinction between the 'early modern' and 'colonial modern' in the eighteenth and nineteenth centuries.[15]

The late-eighteenth and early-nineteenth-century Urdu poet, Nazir Akbarabadi, on the other hand, does not fall in the category of the portfolio intellectuals of this period. He can be located in the conventional Sufi-oriented religious and literary tradition of Hindustan, which is known for its inclusive, non-confrontational approach to the diversities of beliefs and practices.[16] Nazir Akbarabadi's eulogy to 'Baba Nanak Shah' is analogous to that of a Sufi like Baba Farid.[17] A few lines from his long *Madah Nanak Shah Guru* are worth considering:

hain kahte nanak shah jinhen wo purey hain agah guru
wo kamil rahbar jag mein hain yun raushan jaise mah guru

maqsud murad ummid sabhi bar late hain dilkhwah guru
nit lutf-o-karam se karte hain ham logon ka nirbah guru

is bakhshish ke is azmat ke hain baba nanak shah guru
sab sis nuwa ardas karo aur har dam bolo wah guru

(Literally, the one who is referred to as Nanak Shah is the all-knowing Guru
He is a perfect leader and is illuminated the world over like the moon.

One longs for the Guru who fulfils our desires, wishes and expectations
He looks after us through his perpetual grace and generosity.

Such is the exalted presence of Baba Nanak Shah Guru
That one should bow one's head in submission and chant his praise all the time.)

The terms and phrases used by Nazir will be intelligible to those who are exposed to the various popular religious traditions originating in northern India. His idiom not only cuts across the linguistic boundaries of Urdu, Hindi and Punjabi, but also blurs the distinctions between religious leaders belonging to Sikhism, Sant and Sufi traditions, and, contrary to McLeod's understanding of Muslim writings, is far from polemical. In a measure, this may reflect further in Nazir's celebration of the Sufi Sheikh Farid's social and religious roles in society.

Born into a respectable family some time in 1175 at Kahtawal near Multan, Sheikh Farid, then known as Masud, was mystically inclined even as a student, which had earned him the sobriquet *diwana bachcha*. A leading saint of the Chishti order of Sufism, Farid occupies an important position in the social, cultural, religious and literary history of medieval Punjab. His tomb at Ajodhan, now called Pak Pattan in Pakistani Punjab, is a major pilgrimage centre. Yet, it appears that his career remains marginal to the mainstream discourse on the historical scholarship of the region, even though occasional tributes are paid to him by scholars working on the evolution and growth of Punjabi language and literature: some even call him the father of Punjabi literature and the sheikh enjoys the same status in the history of Urdu literature. Elsewhere, I have analysed anecdotes in Sufi literature related to Sheikh Farid's role as a healer and protector of the people, his relations with the Muslim political and religious establishment, and his attitude towards non-Muslims. I have also suggested that our understanding of the process of the making of the saint and his widespread popularity will be richer if we take into account the legends associated with Sheikh Farid even though they appear incredulous to the rational mind.[18]

Returning to Nazir Akbarabadi's compositions, even though the 'subaltern' poet who located himself in the bazaars of Agra is often not considered in the canonical tradition of Urdu poetry with its later penchant for elitist sophistication, his celebration of Krishna Bhakti further strengthens the case for the existence of a composite popular culture. Devoid of political pressure, religiosity at the popular level seems to have been fairly inclusive of a variety of religious perspectives. This does not necessarily mean that the followers of gurus and saints were completely innocent of identity politics. Also, unlike the emphasis in certain modern writings, religious identities were not completely fuzzy before the governmentalization of politics and society in the colonial period.

This brings us to another set of works, *Qisas-i-Hind*, which was sponsored by the colonial regime in Punjab as a three-volume school-level textbook on Indian history.[19] The *Qisas-i-Hind* has emerged as a literary classic, but our interest here is in the chapter on Guru Nanak, entitled 'Baba Nanak Saheb' in the second volume of the text. This volume was written by the celebrated Urdu literary critic, Muhammad Husain Azad. Even though Muhammad Husain did not include Nazir Akbarabadi in his magnum opus, a biographical dictionary of Urdu poets, *Ab-i-Hayat*, his portrayal of Nanak's image in the *Qisas-i-Hind* hardly differs from Nazir Akbarabadi's, except in his recognition of the later transformation of Sikhism from a monotheistic and ascetic religious cult into a militarily strong political community. The users of *Qisas-i-Hind* could have been Muslims or Sikhs or Hindus.

Written on the lines of a 'nationalist' history, some details from Muhammad Husain's synthesis of the information on Guru Nanak and on Sikhism in general are worth recounting here. He notes that though the *firqa* (sect, cult or community) of the Sikhs emerged in the reign of Zahir-ud-Din Muhammad Babur, the founder of the Mughal empire, they flourished for long as ascetics devoted to the mystical idiom of sulh-i-kul (or the Sufi concept of perfect peace, later appropriated by emperor Akbar as an inclusive political ideology of his regime in the latter half of the sixteenth century[20]). Ignoring what happened under Jahangir and Shah Jahan, Muhammad Husain Azad jumps to the reign of Alamgir Aurangzeb when the Sikh outlook started changing to the extent that by the time of Farrukh-Siyar and Muhammad Shah, the Sikhs had picked up swords to carve out a kingdom for themselves. This is certainly bad history, but Muhammad Husain's emphasis was on knowing the life and teachings of Guru Nanak as the founder of the sect.

According to Muhammad Husain, Nanak was the son of a Khatri named Kalu, who lived in a village called Talwandi, where the latter maintained the revenue and other administrative records of the village under the Lodi Sultanate. Husain recounts that there was so much hullabaloo at the time of Nanak's birth that it reminded people of visits by grand dignitaries of the Sultanate such as an amir or wazir. As the child grew older, arrangements were made for his education—the subjects taught to him included Persian and mathematics required for everyday transactions, which he mastered quickly—but he was not favourably disposed towards the affairs of this world. Despite Kalu's efforts, Nanak did not take up trading as a vocation, nor did he enjoy being in the employ of Nawab Daulat Khan, a relation and official of Sultan Ibrahim Lodi at Kapurthala.

His marriage with a Khatri girl from Batala was successful only to the extent that two sons, Sri Chand and Lakshmi Das, were born to him, and he had no intention of being a run of the mill family man.

Muhammad Husain's account of Guru Nanak here is very similar to that of a peripatetic Muslim dervish:

> *Baba nanak saheb . . . hamesha sayyahi mein rahte aur safar ke parde mein tark-i-duniya karke yad-i-ilahi ka lutf uthate aur buniyad aqidè ki tauhid ke saath sulh-i-kul par thi, is liye batein aisi dil nashin aur khatir pasand thiin ke sab sun-sun kar khush hote the aur har mazhab ke log nazr-i-azmat se dekh kar suhbat ko ghanimat samajhte the.*
>
> (Baba Nanak Saheb spent a lot of time travelling and used his sojourns as a pretext to leave the trappings of this world to devote his time to the pleasure of remembering God. Since the basis of his faith was monotheism and peace with all, his utterances were fabulous and heart-warming and had a wide appeal. People from across religious affiliations enjoyed listening to his conversations, viewed him with awe and found his company to be a blessing.)

Muhammad Husain says that even as people belonging to different religions sought out the blessed company of Nanak, the basis of his own faith was monotheism with 'perfect peace' of the kind practised in India and elsewhere by the Sufis. Following the mystic path, Nanak reportedly devoted himself to long and often excruciating meditation (*faqirana reyazatein*), which once included praying immersed in the river Beas near Sultanpur for three days at a stretch. This place later became a major centre of pilgrimage for the Sikhs and is called Sant Ghat. Nanak also spent time meditating under a tree (*ek darakht ke niche baith kar bhagwan ki tapasya karte rahe*), identified by his followers as 'Baba ki bairi'. Eventually, the Guru gave up on his home and family to renounce the world altogether (*gharz isi tarah rafta rafta bilkul duniya se qata talluq ho gaya aur ghar baar sab chhut gaya*).

Despite the help from Nawab Daulat Khan of Sultanpur, Nanak's father and subsequently, his father-in-law, failed in their efforts to 'reform' the man who was growing to be a guru. His affinity towards Sufism and contacts with Muslims notwithstanding, Nanak's religious attitude tended to be ambivalent. He certainly did not fit in the formal, institutional Sunni Islam with its emphasis on namaz and other rituals, often allegedly performed without sincere devotion to Allah. Muhammad Husain Azad records relevant anecdotes in this connection:

> *Kahte hain ek din baba nanak saheb ko nawab apne saath masjid mein le gaye, nawab tow namaz mein masruf hua, baba nanak saheb alag baithe rahe, jab nawab namaz se farigh hua tow puchha ke nanak! Tum khuda ki namaz mein hamare saath sharik na huye? Baba nanak saheb ne kaha ke tumhara dil tow qandhar mein ghode ki kharidari kar raha tha, namaz kiske saath padhta. Nawab bhi munsif admi tha, usne saaf kah diya ke fil-waqe' mera khayal thikana na tha.*
>
> (It is said that once the Nawab took Baba Nanak Saheb to a mosque. Even as the former got busy in praying, namaz, Nanak sat through at a distance. Once the Nawab had finished his namaz, he turned to Nanak and asked him why did he not join in praying with him. Baba Nanak Saheb retorted that since the Nawab's attention was diverted towards the purchase of horses in Qandhar he had nobody to accompany for namaz. The Nawab sincerely admitted that he was unable to concentrate on his prayers.)

A similar episode involving the lack of sincerity of the prayers of a local qazi, who was forcing Nanak to go to mosques for prayers is reported by Muhammad Husain. Nanak's ability to know the workings of the mind of the qazi and his this-worldly concerns, even as he led the prayer, silenced the latter. Such episodes that expose the falsity of the claim of Muslim religious leaders to guide the people on the right path of Islam also recur in Sufi hagiography. In Nanak's case, it also reveals how he negotiated with the pressure on him to formally embrace Islam by joining Muslims in their prayers, etc. Nanak, as someone who recognized the notion of the unity of God, was treading a dangerous path where he could be confronted to declare his allegiance to Islam in no uncertain terms. Instead of giving such an opportunity to the ulama or qazis, he found fault with their own commitment to Islam—a clever strategy also deployed by the Sufis. Ordinarily, his refusal to perform namaz by declaring that he was not a Muslim could have led him into a serious situation where the charge of apostasy could be levelled against him. There are examples of the execution of certain non-Muslim religious figures in the Sultanate period who recognized Islam as a true religion, with the unity of God and Muhammad being His prophet as the fundamental creed, but who refused to convert to Islam as they maintained that their own faith was also perfectly valid. This was not acceptable to the ulama who insisted that only Islam was true, or haqq, all other religions were falsehood, or batil. This was not exceptional for Islam, as leaders of many other religions or cults also claimed to be representing the Truth. This question was at the heart of the debate in Akbar's ibadat-khana, as we saw in chapter four.

The *Puratan janam-sakhi* version of Nanak's encounter with the qazi includes the bold declaration of the Guru: 'There is neither Hindu nor Mussalman'. This was reported to Daulat Khan, who dismissed it as the kind of utterances one might get to hear from a faqir. The qazi, however, took a more serious view of what appeared to him to be a rejection by Nanak of Islam's claim to superiority as well as the distinctions between Hindus and Muslims as separate communities. Daulat Khan agreed to question Nanak, but found nothing offensive in the reply that he received.[21] The matter was apparently hushed up and Muhammad Husain preferred not to include this part of Nanak's inquisition of sorts in his narrative.

Another example of Nanak maintaining an ambiguous position with regard to Islam is the report of his travelling to Mecca, where he reportedly slept with his legs in the direction of the Ka'ba. Muhammad Husain has left out the account of a miracle in which the caretakers of the Ka'ba witnessed the holy place moving in whichever direction Nanak's legs were dragged. The earliest version of the report of the Guru's visit to Mecca and the miracle associated with it is found in Bhai Gurdas's early account of the life of Guru Nanak. Later, seventeenth-century *janam-sakhi*s (biographies) recount the episode with some satisfaction.

In Muhammad Husain's biographical sketch, amongst the many miracles of the Guru, one was his perceived ability to fly in the air, a common motif in mystical traditions. Nanak could then reportedly travel across long distances, and could also get a particular place transported to him wherever he stayed. In a similar vein, Ka'ba coming over so that a Sufi saint could circumambulate it is reported in Sufi hagiographies, tazkiras. But Nanak is known to have toured extensively along with his two companions, Bala (a Hindu) and Mardana (a Muslim Dom). The latter represented Nanak's intimate contact with Islam. Muhammad Husain discusses Mardana's wisdom in sacrificing everything for the Guru's company—abandoning his family, facing poverty and hunger, and helping his master in his prayers by singing devotional poetry and playing musical instruments (*jab baba nanak saheb yad-i-ilahi mein baithte thhe tow mardana rabab baja kar aur tasawwuf aur marifat ke bhajan ga kar dil raushan kiya karta*).

According to Muhammad Husain's account, Nanak stayed at Aimanabad once during his travels. It was there that he was captured, along with his followers, by the invading Mughals led by Babur. He was, however, able to win the confidence of Mughal soldiers by reciting Sufi poetry, clearly in Persian:

> *Is alam mein bhi unke muwahhidana kalamon ne apne nur ka jalwa dikhaya, yani sipahiyon ko jab malum hua tow badshah mazkur ke paas le gaye. Babur un se achhi tareh pesh aya aur un ki batein sun kar bahut mahzuz hua . . . kahte hain ke use baba nanak saheb ne dua bhi di thi aur kaha tha ke saat pusht tak teri aulad ki badshahat is mulk mein qayam rahegi.*

> (Even in such a condition [of captivity], his monotheistic compositions created a flutter and the soldiers brought him to the presence of the emperor. Babur behaved with him properly and was delighted to hear his discourses . . . It is said that Baba Nanak Saheb, in turn, had blessed the emperor and prophesied that his descendants would rule the country for seven generations.)

This report is contrary to Nanak's criticism in *Babur-vani* of the depredations caused by Babur's invasions in Punjab.

As indicated above, many of the anecdotes presented by Muhammad Husain Azad could as well be found in the janam-sakhis dealing with Guru Nanak. It is also important to note here that two of the earliest editions of the most popular janam-sakhi of Bhai Bala were published by Muslim contemporaries of Muhammad Husain: Hafiz Qutub Din (1871) and Maulvi Mahbub Ahmad (1890). These connections are considered unimportant by scholars like McLeod and others, who emphasize confrontations between Muslims and Sikhs historically. Also, by deploying a rigorous positivist methodology for historical research and by looking for 'absolute truth' based on 'facts', McLeod considers the janam-sakhis to be of little value for a historical study of Nanak. For him, later traditions, full of legends and miracles, are utterly misleading and, therefore, useless. In taking such a position, the historian has done away with a whole tradition of religious beliefs with all its inclusions and exclusions determined by social and political contexts.

Returning to Muhammad Husain Azad's narrative, the author says that Nanak came back from his travels to settle down in his last years at Gurudaspura, where he built a *dharamshala* (note the author does not call it a khanqah, a Sufi's dwelling place) and called the place Kartarpur. He called his family and also collected his disciples there. Soon he passed away at the age of seventy (*chand roz un-logon ko apne pand-o-nasaih se faiz bakhshi ki thi ke paigham ajal ka aya aur sattar baras ki umar mein duniya se inteqal kiya*). According to Muhammad Husain, since his followers comprised people from diverse religious backgrounds, they eventually fought over his dead body. Whereas the Muslims amongst them claimed that they would bury him (*tajhiz-o-takfin*) after performing the funeral prayers (*namaz janaza*), the Hindus wished to cremate him following their own rituals (*hindu kahte the ke ham kirya karam karke jalayenge*).

Eventually the corpse disappeared:

> *Is takrar ne aisa tul khaincha ke ladai tak naubat pahunchi, lekin jab nash par se chadar uthai tow wahan kuchh bhi na tha, akhir faisla yeh hua ke adhi chadar hinduon ne lekar jalai aur adhi musalmanon ne lekar qabar mein dafan kar di.*
>
> (The argument took an ugly turn, leading to the possibility of violence, but when the sheet covering Nanak's body was removed there was nothing there. Ultimately, it was decided that half the sheet be taken by Hindus for burning and the remaining half, buried by Muslims.)

Like the struggle over the dead body of Kabir, the above conflict between the Hindu and Muslim followers of Guru Nanak speaks volumes about their alleged ignorance of their identities as Muslims and Hindus. Reflecting on the quarrel, Muhammad Husain pays tribute to the levelling field of Punjab and the time and notes:

> *Magar zamane ki gardish un sab par ghalib hai, chunke maqam mazkur darya-e rawi ke kinare par tha, is liye pani ki taghiyani qabr aur samadh donon ko baha kar le gayi.*
>
> (Since the vicissitudes of time dominated over temporary emotions, the site of the contestation being on the bank of the river Ravi, a heavy tide washed away both the grave and the tomb.)

Muhammad Husain quickly sums up his account by mentioning the chain of Gurus—following Nanak's nomination of his disciple, Lahna Khatri, known as Guru Angad, over the claims of his disobedient sons—who eventually transformed the community of Nanak's followers into an armed band fighting for political power. The Sikh leader Banda Bahadur strengthened Guru Tegh Bahadur and Guru Gobind Singh's struggle to further encroach upon Mughal territories, even as violence and death recurred. Muhammad Husain concludes:

> *Yeh tino saheb apne mutaqidon ke dilon mein aisa josh-o-kharosh paida kar gaye ke woh firqa jiski buniyad faqat faqr aur sulh-i-kul par rakhi gayi thi, ek bahadur mulk-gir giroh ho gaya, aur ek din woh hua ke kul mulk punjab salha sal ke liya is firqe ke tasallut mein agaya.*
>
> (These three personalities created such fervour in the heart of their followers that the sect that was founded on the basis of piety and peace with all was converted into a group of courageous people striving for territorial aggrandizement, and a day came when the whole country of Punjab came under their control for years to come.)

Even in the compositions of a politically conscious and active poet like Sir Mohammad Iqbal, popularly known in Urdu circles as Allama Iqbal, Guru Nanak emerges as a major religious leader, social reformer and even a harbinger of divine unity and truth.[22] Iqbal begins his extremely popular poem, *Hindustani Bachchon ka Qaumi Geet* (in *Bang-i-Dara*, *c.* 1905) with these lines:

> *chishti ne jis zamin mein paigham-i-haq sunaya*
> *nanak ne jis chaman mein wahdat ka geet gaya*
> *mera watan wahi hai, mera watan wahi hai*
>
> (Literally, the land where the Chishti heralded the message of truth
> The garden in which Nanak sang the song of unity
> That is my homeland, that is my homeland.)

It is important to note here that in Iqbal's understanding of the history of India, Nanak and Chishti Sufis (here identifiable with Khwaja Muin-ud-Din Ajmeri) not only stand side by side, but also are high on the significance of their contributions in shaping its religious character. The proclamations of haqq or truth and wahdat or unity of existence, at least of God, show a remarkable commonality in India's religious or mystical traditions; this is as true of wujudi Sufis as of Bhakti saints. Wahdat can as well mean the political unity between Hindus, Muslims and Sikhs in the Indian nationalist context, though as we know, Iqbal eventually drifted away to take a separatist position, supporting the two-nation theory which led to the Partition of 1947.

It is often asserted that the origins of many Sufi mystical practices can be traced to Buddhist influences in Central Asia and Afghanistan, as also in India through yogis and other mystics. Iqbal's reference to Nanak in the above poem is not an isolated case of showing deference to the Guru by a poet who also happens to be from Punjab. Iqbal, in fact, wrote an entire poem devoted to Nanak, wherein he laments how the Indians ignored the blessings of God brought by generations of saintly figures, where he mentions Gautam Buddha in particular, to live in darkness, inequity and other evils. However, he says, there emerged another figure, Nanak of Punjab, a *mard-i-kamil*, the Sufi ideal of a perfect man, who raised the slogan of divine unity, *tauhid*, again, and shook the country of Hind, out of its slumber (*Bang-i-Dara*, *c.* 1908):

phir uthi akhir sada tauhid ki panjab se
hind ko ek mard-i-kamil ne jagaya khwab se

Thus, both literary and popular religious traditions have shown a remarkable flexibility in the wake of later hostility between Sikhism and Islam, insofar as the celebration of social and religious roles of Guru Nanak is concerned. In other words, implicit in the detailed treatment of Nanak in Nazir Akbarabadi's poetical works, as also in the hugely popular collection of essays,

Qisas-i-Hind, and the politically-charged compositions of Allama Iqbal, is a shared cultural and religious heritage, which tended to get ruptured for political and dogmatic reasons. This is particularly important, as in this case, examples have been given from a literary tradition, Urdu, which is often condemned as the communal or ghettoized language of Islam in the Indian Subcontinent. In a measure, this identification of Urdu with Muslim separatism has led to the neglect of material that provides a different perspective on Nanak's career. This may be due to the erroneous assumption since colonial times that Muslim writings have always been hostile towards Sikhism, and, indeed, towards all non-Muslims. Such a position persists in current research on Sikhism. The Urdu-Muslim sources remain out of the range of material used by leading scholars, even as the value of some medieval Persian writings (such as the *Dabistan-i-Mazahib*) on the Sikh Panth has been recognized.

This can be understood further in terms of the identity question as generations of Sikhs in Punjab and elsewhere have used the Urdu language for their own intellectual transactions and have certainly known Muslim writings on Nanak. However, politics demands that they should not recognize the presence of this literary tradition, even as respect for a Muslim figure like Baba Farid can be flaunted at times. Indeed, there is a huge body of literature in Urdu from the nineteenth century onwards on Sikhism generally, which also remains largely neglected. As in several other cases, modern historical scholarship on the theme is hostage to contemporary politics. Nineteenth- and twentieth-century Urdu literature, though itself a victim of the politics of the time, provides a welcome relief from what is accepted as standard knowledge on the relationship between Islam and Sikhism. This set of writings can help us reconsider three major themes in Sikh studies: (a) the life and teachings of Guru Nanak; (b) the making of the Sikh scriptures; and (c) the Mughal–Sikh conflict. Existing literature on these themes remains poorer for want of willingness on the part of scholars of Sikhism to integrate 'Muslim' material.

To conclude, the Guru was as much a guide for Hindus and Muslims as he has been for the Sikhs of later generations. Modern Sikhs might find it scandalous, but Nanak could as well have been appropriated by the Sufis, Ismailis or the Vaishnavites. He moved away to be regarded as the founder of a separate religion.[23]

Refashioning Devotional Islam

In this section, we will study the transformations that medieval Sufi traditions have undergone in modern times. Rather than presenting a grand or linear narrative of the changes that might have possibly taken place, the complexities involved in the process are highlighted. Even though examples will be given to illustrate how a pre-modern religious tradition attempted to 'bypass' modernity—Western modernity to be more accurate—or to come to terms with it, in order to safeguard itself, my main concern is to draw attention to the kinds of difficulties faced by 'traditional' Muslim communities since the nineteenth century. Is Sufic Islam really an answer to their problems? Here, I have limited myself to asking some pertinent questions, instead of attempting to proffer any solution to this predicament.

As mentioned earlier, Sufism emerged as a Sunnite response to sectarian schisms in the early centuries of the Abbasid Caliphate. It identified in Abbasid Muslim society a lack of moral integrity amongst people professing to be the true believers of Islam and attributed this to the materialism and worldliness of the time. Turning away from the anxieties of attachment to this world, whether private or public, Sufis called for self-reflection or soul searching, the remembrance of God beyond ritual prayers at mosques, meditation in solitude and wandering around as dervishes to Muslim cities and non-Muslim or semi-Islamized hinterlands. From their journeys, physical or metaphorical, they returned with claims of having personally experienced the truth of Islam, of the loving God and of the righteousness of the path of the Prophet (thus strengthening the position taken by Sunnite ulama or the theologians). As religious exemplars, then, Sufis were supposed to guide the Muslims, ignoring or tolerating human weaknesses, and also bringing non-Muslims into the fold of Islam. Their claims for religious and, at times, political authority could run them into trouble with the ulama, who interrogated their religious practices and resorted to violence to keep them in check.

As discussed in chapter two, Sufi institutions flourished in medieval India under the direct/indirect support and patronage of Muslim rulers, even as many Sufis struggled to protect themselves from being reduced to the position of courtiers. Reports of collaboration and conflict between Sufis and rulers bring out the complexities in the relationship between the two. The older suggestions concerning Sufis' attitude towards politics, such as the argument about Chishtis staying away from the state and Suhrawardi involvement in politics in the Delhi Sultanate, appear a bit too simplistic. The medieval Muslim rulers required legitimacy for their rule and did so, among other things, by invoking the support of leading Sufis of the realm; the latter needed the protective umbrella of Muslim rulers to carry on with their practice of Islam in areas where they flourished. Contestations for controlling a spiritual territory (wilayat) involved not only non-Muslim opponents, but also those from within the various strands of Muslim mystic movements, as also from the Islamic orthodoxy, that is, the Sunni-Hanafite ulama.[24]

The Sufi traditions in the Indian environment through the medieval period (*c*. thirteenth to eighteenth centuries) are known for accommodating, appropriating and absorbing mystical ideas and practices from a wide variety of sources. The Sufi orders contributed immensely to the evolution of a range of art forms. This is particularly true of literature (in several Indic vernaculars), music, dance, etc., all of which involved complex negotiations for adaptations, inclusions and exclusions of forms which ranged from the elegant to the grotesque.[25] Interactions and appropriations involved complex negotiations at various levels of social and political strata as well as competing religious domains. They also involved a lot of conflict and contestation over what were the most legitimate forms of spirituality. The Sufis' attempts to prove the superiority of their discipline and the 'truth' of Islam, compared to the 'falsehood' of other religious traditions, such as the ones represented by Brahmins and yogis, led to debates, disputations, and, if Sufi hagiographies and discourses are to be believed, the competitive performance of miracles. In Sufi memory, their victories in these combats helped them establish their authoritative position in the localities in which they settled.

These contestations often involved the conversion of the adversary and his followers to Islam. While such episodes of miraculous encounters and conversion might have been exaggerated in Sufi tazkiras, they reveal the attempt to propagate the image of Sufis as disseminators of Islam.[26] This image gets further support from the claims of Muslim communities in various regions of having converted to Islam at the hands of Sufis who are acknowledged as the patron saints of their respective areas. Indeed, in many cases, conversion to Islam involved a long process of cultural accretion around a major shrine or pilgrimage centre.[27]

Thus, conversion involved (i) in exceptional cases, a sudden transformation of the heart of an individual to accept the righteousness of Islam; (ii) having faith in the saintliness of a Sufi, expressed by visits to the dargah (shrine), following the rituals and eventually, the acceptance of the creed of the patron saint and his 'representatives' (keepers of the shrine/descendants of the Sufi); and (iii) recognition of the superiority of Islam after 'testing' the knowledge and miraculous powers of a Sufi, followed by reciting the kalima, or the profession of faith in Islam, a decisive moment both in the life of the convert and the Sufi concerned. This is what many Sufi hagiographies emphasize, though all three types of cases are found in Indo-Persian sources.

The slow process of Islamicization is being recognized in current research as the most plausible way in which large sets of Muslim communities emerged in the Indian Subcontinent through a long period of Islamic acculturation around popular Sufi shrines, though there may not have been any specific recorded moment of conversion involving a large population. Also, by contrast, centres of Muslim power, such as the Delhi–Agra region have a lower concentration of Muslims, belying the general perception that Islam spread through the sword of Muslim rulers under the guidance of the ulama. However, this might well be a Delhi–Agra-centric view, for regional Muslim polities such the ones in the Deccan and Bengal did enjoy considerable power during the Sultanate period (though the Sultanate in Bengal dominated the western part, whereas the large community of Bengali Muslims emerged in the eastern region[28]).

Islamization and conversion to Islam thus involved complex negotiations, which further contradicts the older view that only large sections of low-caste Hindus were attracted to the egalitarianism and notions of brotherhood in Islam, as embodied by Sufi institutions such as khanqahs, jamatkhanas and dargahs.[29] Normative Islam does have certain ideals emphasizing egalitarianism in society, but as Islam spread to various regions, it got embedded in local social structures; and hierarchies—based on birth, wealth and power—became an integral part of Muslim communities,[30] as is the case with caste amongst Muslims in India. The Sufi ideals proved to be inadequate to fight inequalities in society, even though one comes across instances of Sufis expressing their helplessness in the matter or recommending invocations for divine interventions through prayers, charms, amulets, etc., and occasionally even resorting to miracles for delivering justice.

Like many other forms of religiosity, devotional Islam around Sufi centres has been under tremendous pressure from the nineteenth century onwards. The passing away of older Muslim polities and the establishment of colonial rule meant that the crucial political support that Sufic Islam enjoyed was lost. The response to colonial transformations in politics and society was manifold:

(i) One response attempted refashioning devotional Islam, a view represented by Sufi figures like Ahmad Raza Khan Barelwi, who took a rigid view of the sources of Muslim traditions—his fatwa could put to shame many a 'fundamentalist' opponents of the time;[31]

(ii) The second was fierce opposition to colonial rule and support to the demand for a separate homeland for Muslims (see Gilmartin's study on Sufi establishments in Punjab)[32]—this was contrary to a more puritanical, reformist Muslim group that owed allegiance to Deoband (see the discussion on the Dar-ul-Ulum Deoband later in this chapter) and supported the Indian nationalist struggle led by the Congress (though some sections of the Deobandi ulama supported the Muslim League as well);[33]

(iii) In postcolonial contexts, Sufi fraternities have gone global with new branches of 'Indian' Sufism being opened up in the West and African countries;[34]

(iv) In more recent times, Sufi traditions have moved to the unlimited space of the World Wide Web. This attempt to reach out is reflected in the large numbers of internet sites on Sufis and Sufi-related forms of Islam. Sooner, rather than later, Sufi-healers, or as I like to call them, e-babas, might do good business. The traditional forms of expression such as *kitabat* (calligraphy) are being replaced by computer-mediated images in new cyber-Islamic environments.[35] As we will see in the concluding chapter, Muslim religious and political networks are using the internet extensively.

The ability to reach out and connect with an audience in the acceptable language of the time has been one of the remarkable features of Sufism through the ages. Despite sustained onslaughts by secular-rationalists and reform-minded Islamists (Wahhabi/Deobandi), devotional Islam has been able to survive because of its capacity to adapt to changing social and political contexts.

Historically, this is characterized by a kind of 'double-movement' in which Sufic Islam got entrenched in the dominant culture of the time and place, while being mindful of the terms of reference of Islam, derived from the Quran and the Traditions of the Prophet.[36] Even as Sufi traditions claim to be following the path shown by the Prophet, they are distinguished from other Islamist groups by their sensitivity towards historical Islam as represented by veneration for saintly figures of earlier generations and attempts to safeguard customs and traditions of earlier times, thus allowing for concessions demanded by situations and socio-cultural difference.

The qawwals or Sufi musicians still sing verses in Arabic, Persian, Urdu, Hindi and Punjabi in a variety of genres. Purists might heap scorn at this and the patron-saint of Sufi qawwali, Amir Khusrau, and his preceptor, Nizam-ud-Din Auliya, may be turning in their graves, but the saint and his disciple would have been the first to recognize the need to reach out to people with the most accommodative face of Islam, irrespective of the religious affiliations of the audience. Non-Muslims continue to constitute a large segment of the devotees of Sufi shrines in modern times, even as Muslim disciples might be drifting away from Sufism due to contemporary political demands.

The medieval centuries witnessed the emergence of a number of reformist Sufis who ensured that the shifts were within the range of what was considered to be acceptable within Islam. The Naqshbandi Sufis, Sheikh Ahmad Sirhindi in the late sixteenth and early seventeenth centuries and Shah Waliullah in the eighteenth century, are two figures respected across Sufi silsilas.[37] In modern times, however, reformers from Sufi tradition have deviated too far from core Sufi practices to be counted as Sufis any more. The early-nineteenth-century jihad movement led by Sayyid Ahmad Shahid, trained in the Waliullahi tradition, is a case in point. According to Marc Gaborieau, Sayyid Ahmad was a millenarian charismatic figure whose political thought was rooted in medieval Islam.[38] The Barelwis, as much as the British, condemned him as a Wahhabi. The Barelwis, in fact, question the celebrations of his *shahadat* (martyrdom) at the hands of the Sikhs in the early 1830s and dubbed him as a *maqtul*, somebody who was simply murdered. Similarly, Tablighi Jama'at can hardly be called a Sufi movement, though it is often erroneously confused as one.

One figure, who challenged colonialism and Islamic fundamentalism in modern times, while still remaining within the fold of Sufism, was the leader of Ahl-i-Sunnat wal Jama'at, Ahmad Raza Khan Barelwi. Following Ahmad Raza Khan's tirade against reformist Islam in the nineteenth and early twentieth centuries, devotional Islam that flourished around Sufi ideals of medieval times is now disparaged as 'Barelwi Islam' or *barelwiyat*. Contrary to the erroneous notion that the Barelwis were a retrogressive and moribund people whose 'worship' at Sufi shrines smacked of polytheism (*shirk*), Usha Sanyal's study of Barelwi literature, chiefly the juristical rulings (fatwa) of Ahmad Raza Khan, brings out a more fanatic and obdurate character of the movement insofar as their insistence on strict adherence to the Quran and hadis was concerned. The fundamentalist or revivalist character of Barelwi Islam comes to the fore in the fatwa war which Ahmad Raza Khan fought with other forms of Islam such as the Ahmadiya/Qadiyani, and with the Wahhabis, a generic term applied to describe Muslim groups whose beliefs were perceived to be false, batil, and inspired by the fundamentalist dispensation of Saudi Arabia. Ahmad Raza Khan charged the Deobandi and Wahhabi ulama with having gone beyond the pale of Islam and called them kafirs because, according to him, they took a position that was antithetical to Allah and the Prophet.[39] The reformist Wahhabi leaders, in turn, levelled the same set of charges against the Barelwis.

However, the Barelwi obsession with the path of the Prophet (*sunna*) and their concern—though in a reactionary way—to follow or 'revive' the pristine purity of Islam, not only made them distance themselves from the supposedly corrupt, everyday Islam of other Muslims (who were actually condemned as kafirs), but also from the Hindus who were termed as killers, oppressors and actively belligerent infidels/kafirs. The Barelwi leader's scathing remarks against Hindus were not based merely on a textual analysis of early sources of Islam. They can be located in the context of the increasing tension in Hindu–Muslim relations in British India. Much of this tension stemmed from Hindu reassertion in the form of the *shuddhi* movement and a violent, vigorous campaign against cow slaughter (other contentious issues have included music being played in front of mosques, the Urdu/Hindi divide, etc.). Ahmad Raza, in fact, reminded Muslims of Hindu atrocities committed against them during riots over the refusal of sections of Hindus to settle for anything less than a total ban on cow slaughter. As a consequence, the Barelwis maintained a distance from the Congress, which was condemned by Ahmad Raza as a 'party of kafirs and polytheists'. Indeed, in a bizarre reversal of the prevailing order, Ahmad Raza treated all kafirs, including Brahmins, as untouchables.

This aversion towards the Congress is reflected in the fierce Barelwi opposition to the Muslim–Congress alliance during the Khilafat and Non-cooperation movements. Though Khilafat leaders were aware of the unmistakably Hindu stance of the Congress with its deployment of non-Islamic tools and idioms of protest against the Raj, they believed that this marriage of convenience was useful for fending off Western hegemony. Ahmad Raza, on the other hand, opposed such collaboration as it meant sacrifice of principle for tactical gain. He not only opposed Mahatma Gandhi addressing Muslims from the pulpit of a mosque (which symbolized Prophetic authority), but also questioned Maulana Azad's credentials as an alim, religious scholar, preferring to address him instead as 'Mister'. His followers continued to reject the possibility of any alliance with Hindus regardless of any perceived benefits. As David Gilmartin has shown about Punjab, many of them went on to support the Muslim League's demand for Pakistan. But then, by 1946, many shades of Muslims in Punjab were part of the Muslim League bandwagon.

This can be contrasted with the attitude of the Dar-ul-Ulum Deoband, founded in the late nineteenth century with some

Sufic antecedents, but which drifted quite far from it to be characterized as a Wahhabi institution leaning towards the Indian nationalism of the Congress.[40] The political stance of an influential faction of the Deoband school is formulated in the *Muttahida Qaumiyat aur Islam* (*Composite Nationalism and Islam*), first published in Urdu in 1938 by a politically active theologian, Husain Ahmad Madani (1879–1957).[41] This little tract has long enjoyed the status of a classic articulation of the idea of inclusive nationalism, which is defined by the Maulana as a united front of Muslims and Hindus struggling to undo the yoke of British colonial rule in the first half of the twentieth century. This support of a section of Sunni religious leaders to the movement for Independence led by the Indian National Congress is often compared with the campaign for a separate Muslim state advocated and led by utterly irreligious intellectuals and politicians like Mohammad Iqbal and Mohammad Ali Jinnah, besides the more orthodox Barewli ulama. For some, Deobandi opposition to the demand for Pakistan revealed that there was no contradiction in strictly following the tenets of Islam and working side by side with Hindus to attain the political objective of driving away the British from the Indian Subcontinent.

Challenged by separatist leaders like Iqbal, Madani deployed his training as a theologian to justify his standpoint in the light of the Quran and used examples from the career of Prophet Muhammad. He argued that the word *qaum* (nation) was used in the Quran for any group of people having the same kinship as well as linguistic, territorial or professional ties, and not for Muslim followers of the Prophet alone. Thus, according to him, nation was not based merely on religious affiliation. In a rather anachronistic and conflationary formulation, he noted that the 'foundation' of nationalism was laid by the Prophet when he entered into an agreement with various Muslim and non-Muslim inhabitants, including certain Jewish tribes, of Medina; indeed, for Madani, Muslims and Jews comprised a 'nation' under the Prophet.[42] Using such examples of tactical cooperation with non-Muslims on the basis of race, colour, language and territory, the cleric insisted that a joint struggle of Muslims and Hindus was a legitimate plan that could defeat the enemies of Islam and advance Muslim interests in political and economic fields without compromising religious practice and personal law. He called for the destruction of European powers by administering a dose of their own medicine to them—nationalism, which, he lamented, was used to dismember the Ottoman Empire.

Celebrating Madani's formulation of composite nationalism as a political ideal, given the diversity of religious beliefs in the Subcontinent, Indian 'nationalist' historians and political propagandists have ignored the limitations of the project. The theologian was clear that the duration of the use of such an idea—rising above the considerations of exclusive religious and community interests—was 'temporal and special'.[43] For Madani, composite nationalism was required in India so long as Muslims were in a minority; they could not be expected to fight with the British and Hindus simultaneously. In such a situation, it was advisable to fight against an enemy of Islam with the help of another. In contexts where Muslims were numerically stronger and controlled political power, there was no need to enter into such a political alliance and make compromises. Even though Madani considered India to be a *dar-ul-aman* (land of peace), and Islam to be a flexible and accommodative religion, he castigated the 'falsehood', 'intolerance', 'insensitivity', 'illegitimacy' and 'immorality' of other religious traditions, including Christianity, Judaism and Hinduism,[44] not sparing even Buddhism with which Islam had hardly any political confrontation, but which could be competing for low-caste Hindu converts in modern times. (It might be possible that many reformist Hindu figures such as Dayananda were speaking in an identical language.) Madani also suggested that composite nationalism and pan-Islam were not incompatible, and to his credit, he maintained, in principle, that in case of a direct clash of interests between the two, Muslims were to ideally go with political alliance rather than religious solidarity. This last point was the hallmark of a political expression by a Muslim leader who was rabidly antagonistic towards anything that could be identified with either Western modernity (such as university education and sartorial styles) or Hindu influence at the social and cultural level (reflected in rituals or practices at Sufi shrines, for instance).

Thus, contrary to later celebrations, the scope of the idea of composite nationalism was limited to fighting the British rather than defining political and cultural loyalties for a lasting project to build a secular public culture in the Subcontinent. To be fair to Madani, secular ideals have risen in a particular intellectual lineage and Madani was hostile to that lineage. Moreover, opposition to separatism and the Partition of 1947 stemmed from his understanding that the interests of Islam could be safeguarded better in a united India than in fragmented nation states. The idea of pan-Islam, fighting against Western/Christian powers and establishing the diktats of Islam as a way of life have been extended in recent times by the Taliban, often trained in Deobandi madrasas in Pakistan. It is also true that the Dar-ul-Ulum Deoband has no control on the madrasas opened by its graduates or by those broadly adhering to the kind of Islam advocated by it,[45] either in India or Pakistan, or for that matter in Bangladesh. Yet, Deoband has not distanced itself fully from extremist forms of political Islam, nor has it shed its image as the most puritanical Sunni Islamic seminary in South Asia today, though some recent fatwas issued from this institution have condemned the invocation of Islamic idioms by terrorist groups. Yet, the dichotomy between the theoretical position of Islam on issues of modern concerns, expressed through occasional fatwas, and the requirements of the time is difficult to grapple with. Given the pressures arising from the political situation, within India and globally, traditional Muslim institutions are undergoing a process of churning and, at least, a tactical distancing from violence and terror cannot be ruled out.

We have seen how Sufic Islam could be no less intolerant in certain contexts. Coming from the leader of a movement that associated itself with the Sufi tradition of Islam, Ahmad Raza Khan's blatantly anti-Hindu approach is disappointing from the point of view that Sufi institutions always worked for syncretism and synthesis, a position that is unfortunately not bolstered by concrete evidence. Instead, as mentioned above, a kind of elective affinity was at work. Leading Sufis of early Islam in India, though advocating peaceful coexistence, were also very concerned about establishing the supremacy of Islam over other religious traditions. Ahmad Raza believed he did not deviate from the path of the Sufi masters of the past.

This brings us back to questions concerning Sufi attitudes towards non-Muslims, conversion, Islamization and the long-term cultural accretion around Sufi shrines. Sufi literature clearly reveals how the Chishtis, for instance, were not averse to the idea of conversion of non-Muslims to Islam, either directly at the hands of a leading pir or through a long process of Islamic acculturation in localities sacralized by the shrines of medieval saints.[46] In a recent study, Carl Ernst and Bruce Lawrence have set aside all these issues to suggest that 'colonial' and 'modern' Chishtis were compelled by the challenges of the time to seek converts to Chishti Sufism and, thereby, to Islam. They also note that modern Chishtis were drawn into complicated political relations with non-Muslims as a result of the dissolution of old imperial structures when British colonialism began to take hold in India. Sulayman Taunsawi, for instance, urged his followers to participate in resistance against Sikh aggression in Punjab, and so, 'apparently for the first time in the annals of Chishti history, we have spiritual biographies drawn into partisanship on behalf of one political group (Muslim) over another (non-Muslim)'.[47] In saying so, the authors ignore the evidence of Nizam-ud-Din Auliya sending his khalifas, or spiritual successors, to participate in political or military campaigns. The Chishti claims of the role played by Muin-ud-Din Ajmeri in the Turkish conquest also remain ignored. The letters written to rulers by leading Chishtis of subsequent generations, like Nur Qutb-i-Alam in Bengal and Abdul Quddus Gangohi in northern India also reveal their involvement in politics and their attitude towards non-Muslims who were condemned as kafirs.[48]

However, the suggestion by Ernst and Lawrence on how the 'modern' Chishtis have responded to the challenges of colonialism and modernity by appropriating new forms of communication, beginning with print, followed by sound recordings, films, television programmes, and more recently, the internet, is significant. The latest communication technology has been used to contest ideological challenges from 'Orientalists', Muslim fundamentalists and secular modernists.[49] Increased travel and better communication infrastructure have also facilitated a new degree of geographical extension and networking.[50] From this perspective, the notion of the 'decline' of Sufism as well as the accusation that the Barelwi Muslims are indifferent towards the challenges of modern times are indeed misleading. The protagonists of Sufism have shifted the arena of combat from the towns (qasbas), localities (*muhallas*), mosques and graveyards (*qabaristans*) to the World Wide Web. Online Sufi healers are now catering to 'spiritually hungry' people across the globe.

In conclusion, one can ask a few questions based on the foregoing discussion. What is the nature of transformation that medieval Sufi tradition has undergone in modern times? Despite assertions to the contrary, both from its followers and the detractors, Sufism has changed and adapted to the requirements of modern times for being meaningful and relevant. It will be interesting to investigate the kind of compromises the movement has had to make to meet the demands of the time. The distinctions between Sufism and other forms of Islam in terms of responding to the social and political challenges in a given context also need attention. The question is, how does a Sufi respond to a situation compared to an alim? The continued popularity of Sufic Islam—despite attacks from chauvinistic Western modernism, fundamentalist Islamic reformism or revivalism, and an aggressive Hinduism/Hindutva of the RSS and its affiliates—baffles its antagonists. Sufi shrines continue to command respect from non-Muslims in a situation where mosques can be destroyed, state machinery permitting.

Further, does giving space to an alternative form of worship and devotion for God, as is the case in several strands of Sufism, essentially mean deviating outside the fold of Islam altogether, or is there a possibility of remaining within the bounds of Islam and yet being tolerant of other kinds of religiosity? Certain Sufi groups have shown that tolerance is not always incompatible with the foundational categories of their faith, which also reminds us of the question of whether there is a theoretical premise in Islam for Muslims to live in peace with non-Muslims—zimmis, ahl-i-kitab or kafirs—or can Muslims only fight with others? More topical is the question of whether various forms of Islam and terrorism are really synonymous, as we are made to believe by Western powers.

Also, should shariat-driven Islam necessarily and exclusively provide the social and political ideal for Muslims for all time to come, or are there other ways of negotiating with the cotemporary world that are considered equally legitimate, even if they are not specifically sanctioned by the Quran and Traditions of the Prophet, two major sources of the shariat? In other words, why should a distant and theoretical Islam be privileged over the lived Islam of various regions? Sufi traditions are known to have historically dealt with the contradictory pulls of moving with time and place on the one hand, and the righteous path of the Prophet located in early-seventh-century Arabia on the other.

Further, it is important to delineate the ways in which Sufis combined their experiences with the demands of normative Islam in certain specific contexts. How did they handle seemingly contradictory prescriptions—of (a) commanding right and forbidding wrong and (b) to you your religion, and to me, mine—to be considered 'good Muslims' both in the society in which they lived and in the estimation of Allah whom they worshipped? Why cannot a Muslim live in peace with himself or herself without bothering about the righteousness or falsehood of other religious beliefs and practices? Is it a must for all Muslims, including Sufis, to serve as missionaries for Islam and do Muslims have it in them to attract others to one of the various interpretations of their faith, without using force or resorting to persuasion? Is every Muslim a possible missionary and what does Islam offer to a potential convert in modern times? Finally, is asking such questions heretical in Islam as well as in academia today?

The above questions are difficult, but legitimate problems for further investigation. Faced with schisms and violence in public life, many Sufi traditions recommend withdrawal and meditation, though the possibility of active retaliation cannot be ruled out in certain contexts. Yet other occasions have marked the graceful refashioning of Sufi traditions. This is as true of modern times, as of the pre-modern, though distinctions of time often seem to get blurred in the lived experiences of Islamic communities, including traditional Sufi fraternities as well as the followers of revivalist movements.[51]

8

Reason and Faith in Islam

The black heritage of 9/11 has generated widespread interest in Islam. This concluding chapter addresses some contemporary questions about Islam and Muslims, though like most 'good' Muslims, I have a tendency to go backward in time. I will examine the various forms of Islam, both in terms of divergent doctrinal positions and varied lived experiences of Muslims. This inquiry is informed by the contemporary concern of how sectarian, ethnic and social differentiations amongst Muslims are being set aside to create a false notion of a monolithic Islam in certain political contexts. Muslims across the globe who have little or no interaction and hardly any shared everyday practices, stand united over some issues of symbolic significance such as the alleged desecration of the Quran, mud-slinging on the life and career of Prophet Muhammad or the imposition of a political system that does away with the shariat, or Muslim law, which purportedly gives Muslims a distinct identity. The 'fundamentalist' or Islamist groups advocating the 'cause' of Islam have tended to take up such pan-Islamic issues.

I use the word 'fundamentalist' in the sense of an individual or institution that dwells on the perceived need to return to the so-called golden period of Islam under the Prophet and his successors (the *khulafa-i-rashidin*) in the first century of Islam. This is possible, it is asserted, by strictly following the shariat, based on the Quran and the Traditions of the Prophet. It rejects what it considers later accretions to Islam and seeks to sanitize Islamic history across time and space. Many modern Muslim intellectuals have warned against the use of the term 'fundamentalism' in Islam and term it misleading. I would like to follow Youssef M. Choueiri's classification of religious and political movements in modern Islam—such as revivalism, reformism and radicalism—as diverse manifestations of what can be called fundamentalism, Islamism, Wahhabism, or, more academically, political Islam. Such an appreciation of the religious and political mobilization in Muslim societies should not necessarily be confused with Christian fundamentalism, which emerged in the context of the organized religious hierarchy of the Church and secularization of the state and society in the West.[1] In the social sciences, we have learned to use clearly defined categories to group a range of phenomena that meet the definition, even while recognizing that several instances in a category can differ from each other. In this manner, it is possible to use the same term 'fundamentalism' for Hindu, Sikh and Muslim religio-political movements.[2]

I wish to draw attention to how Islamists exploit notions of perceived violence against Islam by trying to show to the Muslim public how the Christian West and also Jews (generally referred to in tandem as, *yahud-o-nasara*) continue with their historic tirade against Islam. They argue that the religion and, therefore, Muslim identity can only be protected by fighting a jihad (holy war) and reviving the golden age of Islam; that is by going some fourteen centuries backward in time. From this perspective, even though Muslim revivalist and reformist groups might be using modern technologies and speaking in the language of democracy, etc., Afghanistan's experience with the Taliban has shown that the Islamist claim for a space in contemporary politics, both within the 'Muslim world' and outside of it, could lead to disastrous consequences. The American belligerence in Afghanistan and Iraq can certainly provide legitimacy to certain forces speaking in the languages of political Islam, but this cannot hide the darker sides of the latter's own record.

By taking such a position, one can ask whether Islamic groups that invoke the norms and ways of life recommended in the Quran do so merely for mobilizing Muslims as a group rather than for implementing those norms in real life. Secondly, do all invocations of Quranic law by Islamic groups imply a Talibanist position? Even as these questions need to be investigated, liberal Muslim intellectuals who attempt to explain Muslim behaviour, particularly of Al Qaida-type attacks, need to guard themselves against falling into the trap of fundamentalist Islamic movements. The intolerance shown by these Islamic social and political networks is not only unacceptable to the world, but also to Muslims in general. Left to themselves and when not provoked by emotionally charged issues such as the ones mentioned earlier, Muslims have little respect for such solidarity groups and would prefer to move with the times and lead completely irreligious lifestyles with space for tolerating social differences. They are certainly not itching for bloodshed all the time; yet, the widespread violence within Islamic societies, including cases where America or the West are not involved, requires investigation. In order to understand whether and to what extent violence and terrorism are inherent to Islam, we need to distinguish Muslim societies from Islamist movements, which may be society- or state-centred on the one hand, and localized/transnational on the other. Despite terror tactics and moral claims, the limited appeal of such movements amongst Muslims in general reveals that there is a tension over resuscitating past traditions and living in the present. We need to know in what contexts certain Muslim groups, or all of them, react the way they do.

As a response to the American crisis following 9/11, Mahmood Mamdani's recent work shows the CIA's dubious presence everywhere—what is known as working for the 'Great Satan'. Mamdani goes with the general view that holds the United States responsible for creating the monster called 'Islamic terrorism', which has not only displaced moderate forms of political Islam, but is also treating its erstwhile mentor in Afghanistan and elsewhere—the United States itself—as enemy number one. Mamdani has actually illustrated in great detail how American foreign policy over the last thirty years or so is responsible for all kinds of problems in most parts of the world.[3] However, blaming 'Islamic terrorism' on America and contemporary global politics is not enough for understanding the complexities of the Muslim situation. What we need to recognize is that there is a long historical struggle within Muslim societies between the moderates/liberals/progressives and Islamist hardliners over the form of Islam that must prevail and how it can be implemented.

As Robert Hefner suggests, America-centric reflections on why Muslims hate 'us' are understandable and necessary, but it would be erroneous to overlook the fact that violence was directed not merely against America, but against moderate and democratic-minded Muslims around the world as well. The 9/11 attack was but the latest chapter in a long struggle between moderate Muslims and radical Islamists for the hearts and minds of Muslims. Further, for Hefner, there is no clash of civilizations between Islam and the West. The really decisive battle is the one taking place *within* Muslim societies, where ultra conservatives compete against moderates and liberals to win over the Muslim public.[4]

To an extent, it is true, as argued by scholars like Olivier Roy, that 'Islamism' is a brand of modern political Islamic fundamentalism that claims to recreate a true Islamic society not simply by imposing the shariat, but by establishing first an Islamic state through political action. Islamists see Islam not as a mere religion, but as a political ideology, which should be integrated into all aspects of society (politics, law, economy, social justice, foreign policy, etc.). To Islamists, an Islamic State should unite the umma, or the community of Islam as much as possible, without being restricted to a specific nation within a geographical boundary. Only such a utopian state can attempt to recreate what is perceived as the golden age of the first decades of Islam, as mentioned earlier, and supersede tribal, ethnic and national divides, whose resilience is attributed to the believers' abandonment of the true tenets of Islam or to colonial policy in later times.[5] One is reminded here of Partha Chatterjee's formulation that contrasts the 'utopia' or homogeneous time of (Western) modernity (as proposed by Benedict Anderson and others) with that of the heterogeneity of the vast postcolonial world (using Foucault's heterotopia as a model).[6] Following Chatterjee, one can say that it is morally illegitimate to uphold universalist ideals of nationalism and expect Muslim leaders to blindly kowtow, while ignoring the situation of Muslims under the colonial regime or succumbing to the pressures of a Hindu-Indian nationalism of recent times.

Further, it is often argued that the new brand of supranational neo-fundamentalism is more a product of contemporary globalization than of an Islamic past. Yet, its appeal to Muslims is rooted in a certain tradition: Muslim regimes such as the Sultanate and the Mughals were generally seen as potential homes for Muslims elsewhere; someone like Mohammad Iqbal used this idiom later; and Islamist movements have popularized it in recent generations. Using international languages, travelling easily by air, studying, training and working in many different countries, communicating through the internet and mobile phones, some people are able to think of themselves as 'Muslims' and not always as citizens of a specific country. It is a paradox of globalization that modern supranational networks and traditional, even archaic, infra-state forms of relationships have been brought together.[7]

The role of electronic communications and the media is, indeed, significant in this context. A search run on the internet returns millions of sites on Islam. These include a large number of comprehensive resources that cover an entire gamut of themes and issues on Islamic history, doctrines, societies and culture. Many of these websites are maintained by fundamentalist Islamic groups and individuals presenting their version of the faith, countering those uploaded by the 'enemies' of Islam, particularly in the Christian West. One will notice that a lot of effort is made to appeal to Western users. Such use of cyberspace by 'orthodox'

Muslim organizations with diverse sectarian affiliations within Islam, reveals their willingness to adopt electronic technology for propaganda and preaching. Islamists, thus, continue to adapt to advanced technology even as they seek to travel backwards in search of a political ideal. There are also apprehensions in the West about the recruitment of vulnerable young Muslims by alleged jihadi groups through email and other web-based networks; often, of course, these apprehensions are caused by the aggressive anti-Islamic propaganda of the dominant Western powers, which are unable to get away with many of their own flawed strategies.

It will be useful to explore the representations of Islam on the internet, mainly those constructed and maintained by those adhering to fundamentalist Islam, using the term as defined earlier. The content of the sites maintained by such groups includes material pertaining to the basic tenets of Islam, the life of the Prophet, the history of the early caliphate, the formulation of a monolithic Islamic culture and debates and discussions on current issues. It will be important to locate the sources of this content and identify the social and intellectual backgrounds of the writers or creators of the web pages. A rapid perusal of some of these pages indicates that they were composed by individuals with some training in natural sciences and mathematics. This may be due to their early exposure to computers and cybernetics, even as ordinary Muslims and those trained in social sciences and humanities struggle to use email and other web-based services.

In this context, the Islamic orthodoxy's approach towards the internet may also be taken into account. The conservative Islamic seminaries in India (Dar-ul-Ulum Deoband, Nadwat-ul-Ulama Lucknow) have multilingual websites. The widespread use of the internet reminds one of the enthusiastic acceptance of printing technology in the nineteenth century by this same group. However, two other powerful media—radio and television—were resisted for long, before Muslim religious leaders allowed their use for news and current affairs programmes, and also for the dissemination of knowledge about

Islam. Gradually, there was a softening of this orthodox attitude, and entertainment was also incorporated into the accepted list. It was suggested that like using radio for listening to news and running commentaries of cricket matches, watching the 'live telecast' of matches on television could be permitted. But the viewers were to close their eyes or look somewhere else during the advertisements, especially when women (no matter whether properly covered or not) appeared on the screen. Surely, only very few blindly indoctrinated persons would follow the ulama's suggestions about watching television. While most people enjoy what they get to see, dedicated Islamic television channels have also emerged that guide Muslims through the straight path of Islam.

The internet also allows access to books, cassettes, CDs and related products of culture and entertainment industries as online merchandise. E-commerce sites, however low their volume of transactions may be, indicate the demand for and availability of 'Islamic' products that provide distinctive cultural boundary-markers for Muslims across the globe. The geographical expanse of such a project thus stretches to the unrestricted space of the World Wide Web. The focal point, however, remains seventh-century Arabia and through it, the representation of Islam and Muslims as being against the largely Western 'other'.

It may be mentioned that the historical context of the making of Islam is important for our understanding of Muslim culture. In a recent work, Jonathan Benthal attempts to show that the inherent intolerance of Islam towards pagans and infidels exists in all contexts. He argues that even 'though an overall process of self-criticism has been pioneered by many outstanding individuals and is gradually gathering institutional support, this rarely extends to a sympathy with the Qur'anically abhorred forces of "shirk" and polytheism'.[8] Here, it may be important to remember that all civilizations are complex entities and Islam has been a complex civilization too; simple generalizations will not hold.

We have to recognize the complexity of Muslim societies in order to understand how, say, someone like Osama bin

Laden can get rather extensive material and social support among Muslims across regions.[9] Yet large sections of Muslims, particularly the liberals, are aghast over what is happening in the name of Islam. Though much of the present situation can be explained in terms of contemporary politics—especially the emergence of the West and lately, American foreign policy, as has been mentioned earlier—it also has something to do with the historical legacy of Islam and struggles within Muslim societies as well. In this context, it is important to remind oneself of the various forms of religious and intellectual traditions and contestations for power in the Abbasid Caliphate that formed the core of what is identified as Classical Islam, which emerged in the period between the eighth and twelfth centuries. The caliphate shaped the contours of Islamic societies in different regions in times to come. Even though regional groups of Muslims may have their own peculiarities and historical trajectories, the dominant features, particularly in matters of religion and politics, are shared. Many of the categories and terms and concepts—whether shariat, kafirs or jihad—which keep recurring in discussions on Islam, first emerged during the process of the consolidation of Islamic institutions. Within a century of the rise of Islam in Arabia, large parts of the Middle East, Iran, Central Asia, the Maghreb and Africa were brought under one political umbrella of a resurgent new faith. Even as the Abbasid caliphs based in Baghdad controlled a large territory and were legitimated by the Sunni majority, Fatimid Egypt and Umayyad Spain also contributed to the formation of Classical Islam.[10]

The contestations for power led to schisms, often violent, and there emerged the legitimist Shias, extremist Khwarijis, quietist Murjias, rationalist Mutazilas and the sharia-minded literalist Sunnis—all of whom claimed to be the most righteous Muslims, the most truthful members of the community of Prophet Muhammad, proverbially divided into as many as seventy-two sects (as reportedly prophesied by the Prophet himself).[11] The adjectives used above for identifying the characteristic features of different sects will make sense to those who are aware of Islamic traditions and the history of Islamic civilization in the Middle East between the eighth and twelfth centuries. Very briefly, in the contestations for capturing the political power of the caliphate, the Shias raised the question of the legitimacy of those in power and claimed that only a descendant of the Prophet through his daughter, Fatima, and her husband, Ali, could be the legitimate leader or imam of the Muslims (hence the use of 'legitimist' above). A section of the supporters of Ali protested against his passive approach in dealing with political opponents and moved away from him and resorted to violence (referred to as 'extremists'). The other group was opposed to violence and struggles for political power and avoided getting involved in the debate regarding righteousness and legitimacy (identified as 'quietists'). The sharia-minded literalist Sunni ulama wanted a very particular, literal reading of the Quran and the Traditions of the Prophet as the guiding texts. The matrix of difference between these firqas or sects was political to start with, but later took the form of rigid doctrinal positions and sectarianism. Further forms of differentiations—social, intellectual and juristical—will be explored below.

Of these sects, the Sunni orthodoxy came out as the most powerful group after a bitter struggle with the 'heretics', especially the Mutazilas. Hanbalis, one of the four schools of Sunni jurisprudence (the others being the Hanafi, Shafi'i and Maliki), gained politically and had the mob of Baghdad with them. Still, material prosperity (through war booty coming from the frontiers, regular agrarian revenue and flourishing trade and commerce) and political stability in the cities provided resources for peaceful intellectual pursuit. Provided the ulama were not provoked through questioning of established fundamental beliefs, tremendous progress could be made in the fields of natural sciences, literature and philosophy.

The region was already under heavy Greek influence, with major intellectual centres being located in Egypt and Syria. Iranian contributions to eastern Islam were also noteworthy. Al-Farabi, Ibn Sina, Juwaini, Nizam-ul-Mulk, Ghazali—all of them came from Iran, Khurasan and parts of Central Asia, mainly Samarqand and Bukhara. To state it briefly, at least three phases can be clearly distinguished for Iran: what came from the pre-Islamic traditions; the Abbasid period when Sunnis prevailed; and later, when the Shia Central Asian group captured Iran and imposed the Shia faith ruthlessly.[12] The actual administration and bureaucracy of the Abbasid Caliphate, also came under Persian control through the famous Barmakid family and others. The major centres of madrasa learning, besides Baghdad, were in Khurasan. Sufi systematization, the emergence of orders or *tariqas* and attempts to go beyond simple explanations into philosophy—all of these trends mainly originated in Iran to start with, and were related to the Iranian 'national' revival in learning and culture (with due apology to the theorists of modern nationalism), which helped the Persians conquer their Arab conquerors as also the Mongols later. With the disintegration of the Abbasid Caliphate, Turkish militia carved out their own Sultanates, but the bureaucracy and intelligentsia mainly remained under Persian control. Though Abbasid prosperity had facilitated the advancement of a sophisticated elitist culture, much of the actual initiatives were taken by non-Arabs after the first century of Islam. Arab warlords and caliphs patronized or supported one or the other forms of Islam so long as their own authority was not questioned or challenged. Thus, the political conditions allowed a lot of space for diverse schools of Islamic religious and political thought to flourish.

All the key figures of the Greek philosophical tradition—Socrates, Plato, Aristotle—were well known to medieval Islam. Muslim philosophers in the Middle East, Iran, Egypt and Spain collected, translated, critiqued and selectively appropriated aspects of the Greek philosophical system, including portions dealing with religious matters, either to challenge Islam or to attempt a synthesis. They included Al-Farabi, Ibn Sina and Ibn Rushd. As a group, they had completely dismantled, at least academically, all the foundational categories of Islam: God's omnipotence, prophet-hood, revelation, miracles, resurrection, Day of Judgment, and heaven and hell. Even as sections of intellectuals and philosophers sought to use political power to establish their views and findings as the ruling ideology, the most potent political challenge came from the Shias. Their two-fold strategy included the one by the quieter, mainstream Twelver Shias, who, at times, adopted the doctrinally sanctioned precaution of concealing religious beliefs (called taqiyyah in the vocabulary of the jurists), but still emphasized *talim* or the need for the exclusive religious authority of the infallible imam, a descendant of the Prophet through his daughter, Fatima, and her husband, Ali, traced down twelve generations when the last imam, Mahdi, supposedly went into hiding. The aggressive Ismailis, who broke away from mainstream Shia tradition over the issue of the legitimate contender for the seventh imam and supported the candidature of Ismail, resorted to violence and assassination to capture political power and establish their creed. The Ismailis may no longer be considered aggressive now, as the context has changed. Indeed, certain branches of Ismaili tradition present the most liberal face of Islam in modern times. They could just as well be resorting to taqiyyah, or a tactical concealment of their faith in order to protect themselves.

The Sunni response to the challenge, both intellectual and political included: (a) the official ulama's use of power to suppress 'heresies' or the questioning of established beliefs, referred to as fitna; (b) *Kalam* or Islamic scholasticism, which represented a rather naïve attempt on the part of a section of sharia-minded religious leaders to defend religion rationally, but which could not withstand the sophisticated standards of inquiry proposed by the philosophers, scientists and mathematicians. Eventually getting discredited, the Kalamists (or Mutakallimun in Arabic) were accused of exposing their beliefs and faith to ridicule by the rationalists; (c) Sufism, which identified the problem in Abbasid Muslim society as the lack of moral integrity amongst people who professed to be true believers of Islam, and attributed it to the materialism and worldliness of the time. As mentioned earlier, shunning all anxieties of attachment to this world, whether private and public, Sufis called for soul-searching, the remembrance of God beyond ritual prayers of mosques, meditation in solitude and wandering around as dervishes. Eventually, they would return, claiming to have personally experienced the truth of Islam, of the loving God and the righteousness of the path of the Prophet. Thus, Muslim mystics were supposed to guide the Muslims, ignoring or tolerating human weaknesses, and also to bring non-Muslims to the fold of Islam. As we saw earlier in this book, their claims for religious and, at times, political authority could run them into trouble with the ulama, who interrogated their religious practices and sought to suppress them.[13]

In this context, it will be useful to study the writings of two influential scholars in some detail: (a) on defending theology, as represented by the mystically inclined, eclectic, Sunni revivalist, Baghdad-based scholar of Iranian origin, Imam Ghazali (d. 1111); and (b) in defence of philosophy, led by the Cordova-based jurist turned philosopher, Ibn Rushd (d. 1198). The raging debate between the conservative theologians and the rationalist philosophers in Classical Islam and its results might help us understand the legacy of Islam and its impact in later times to some extent.

Ghazali engaged with various forms of intellectual and religious traditions in the late-eleventh- and early-twelfth-century Abbasid Caliphate. In his *Deliverance from Error*, Ghazali condemned the liberal philosophers; criticized the aggressive Imamist Ismailis (Batinis, interiorists); scolded the naïve Kalamists; chided the official ulama for not only rejecting attempts at understanding the truth of Islam without giving them a proper, detailed hearing, but also for expecting servile conformism from all Muslims (whether learned scholars or ordinary masses); and praised the self-sacrificing Sufis for following the righteous path of the Prophet after a rigorous, excruciating process of knowing the existence of God through spiritual experience, *marifat*. Using his own early exposure to Hellenistic epistemology, Ghazali not only argued that the philosophers, particularly those concerned with metaphysical questions, had not studied the texts properly, but also accused them of spreading evil and unbelief. Typical of the general tendency amongst the ulama, Ghazali called for the suppression of philosophers and other 'heretics' in order to protect the 'ignorant' masses from being misled by them.

The foundational categories of Islam, as interpreted from the Quran and portions of the authoritative hadis reports, emphasize egalitarianism and brotherhood at the social level. At the intellectual level, however, distinctions were recommended between the Muslim masses, who were supposed to practise what they were told was true Islam, and those who had the 'expertise' (knowledge and intellect) to arrive at an understanding of the truth of Islam through their own study and reflection, particularly when the message of the scriptures was not entirely clear; that is, those who could apply their imagination, *qiyas*, and interpret, ijtihad, in legal terms. But as Islam spread quickly over a wide geographical expanse, the Islamic recommendation for equality and egalitarianism was abandoned in favour of local social and political hierarchies. Historically, then, hierarchy has prevailed in Islamic societies in almost all spheres—political, intellectual and social.[14] Intellectually, the 'community' of Islam (umma) has included three distinct groups: the philosophers, the theologians and the masses. The philosophers questioned everything (including Greek philosophy which they drew on); the ulama/theologians called for blind conformism (taqlid) to the rulings of the jurists (imams) and the masses were supposed to blindly follow the Islamic juridical decrees or fatwas.

Seeking to free themselves from the rather literal reading of the sources of Islamic law, philosophers tried to harmonize science, religion and philosophy by placing each of these in its proper place, both in the sphere of knowledge and action. The first philosophers in Islam (Al-Kindi, Al-Farabi, Ibn Sina, Ibn Rushd) were sincere Muslims and interpreted religion in the light of their scientific and philosophical knowledge,[15] even as they acknowledged the existence of God, prophet-hood and the

Day of Judgment. So what was at stake then? The dispute for political power (for influence over rulers or for rulership in their own right) between the theologians and philosophers never ceased from the ninth century onwards. The ulama and fuqaha (jurists), being in closer touch with the illiterate masses, were able to influence them more deeply. The Muslim rulers (caliphs and Sultans), in turn, needed the ulama's support for legitimating their rule and wanted to be seen as the protectors of the shariat. Consequently, the philosophers were left to the rage of the masses. Many reports of the persecution of philosophers and burning of their books are found in the intellectual history of Islam.[16]

Ghazali wrote in his introductory note to his *Incoherence* volume that the philosophers (referred to as idiots, heretics, hide-bound atheists) either blindly and uncritically followed the Greek masters or completely misunderstood them. He also alleged that the translations of their works were full of interpolations, which could lead to disputes and contestations. He, however, focused on Al-Farabi and Ibn Sina, the two most 'faithful' translators and 'original' commentators on Aristotle's philosophy.[17] His purpose was 'to disillusion those who think too highly of the philosophers, and consider them to be infallible'. He wrote, 'I will refute what they believe, by showing that it is a mixture of diverse elements which come from such schools as Mu'tazilah, the Karamiyah, the Waqifiyah, etc. My attitude towards these sects themselves is that, while it is not necessary for me to defend any of them, we are all equally opposed to the philosophers. *For we differ among ourselves only in regard to the details; whereas the philosophers attack the very foundation of our religion.* Let us, therefore, unite against the common enemy; for at a critical juncture, we must forget our private quarrels' (*emphasis added*).[18]

Ghazali listed twenty charges against the philosophers in his *Incoherence*. He argued that because the philosophers could not carry out the 'apodictic demonstration' according to conditions they had postulated in logic, they differed a great deal about metaphysical questions and thus it is in the metaphysical sciences that most of the philosophers' errors are to be found.

Of the twenty errors pointed out by him, three are characterized as 'unbelief' and the remaining seventeen as 'innovations'. The three issues, which according to Ghazali, were opposed to the fundamental beliefs of all Muslims, include (a) God knows only universals and not particulars; (b) their belief in the eternity of the world, both past and future; and (c) that men's bodies will not be re-assembled on the Last Day, but only disembodied spirits will be rewarded and punished, and the rewards and punishments will be spiritual, not corporal. Ghazali identified all these as blasphemous and insisted, 'No Muslim has ever professed any of their [philosophers'] views on these questions'.[19] On other matters, such as the philosophers' denial of the attributes of God, their doctrine is seen as being close to that of the Mutazila and, therefore, according to Ghazali, they are innovations rather than unbelief.[20]

Responding to the theologians' accusations, Ibn Rushd defended philosophers and called for the need to deploy 'intellectual reasoning' on complex metaphysical subjects, just as Muslim jurists were expected to resort to 'juridical reasoning' in matters of law for which there was no clear guidance in the sources. According to him, it was possible for the practitioners of law and philosophy to commit errors: if they came up with something good which was in accord with the 'truth' of Islam, it would be appreciated (even if it came from people who did not belong to the religious community of Islam); and if their interpretations were found to be wrong, they might be excused and better forgotten.[21] This approach was different from that of the ulama who cursed the philosophers and intellectuals and called for burning their books.

It is important to note here that Ibn Rushd himself conformed to the basic tenets of Islam on (a) God and His creation; and (b) the truthfulness of Divine Law. He backed his arguments with several verses from the Quran and quotations from the Prophetic Traditions. Himself a Malikite jurist, Ibn Rushd classified Muslim intellectuals into three categories, depending on their standing and expertise: (a) the rhetorical class of the overwhelming multitude (ulama and jurists?); (b) the dialecticians (Muslim scholars who expounded the principles of religion using Greek logic and Aristotelian categories); and (c) the demonstrative class (philosophers, by nature and training). He recommended that the demonstrative arguments of the philosophers—in such complex and sensitive matters as the nature and limits of God's knowledge, or on the eternity of the world, or on resurrection and life after death—were not to be shared with the dialectical class and never with the general masses.[22]

Ibn Rushd suggested that Ghazali's condemnation of the philosophers, mainly of Al-Farabi and Ibn Sina, was not definite, for the theologian had also clarified that calling people unbelievers for violating the unanimity of a juridical position could only be tentative. In his bid to reconcile philosophy with law, Ibn Rushd also called for an elitist distinction between ordinary people and learned jurists in matters of interpretations of the sunna or prophetic reports. According to him, differences of opinion over metaphorical interpretations of complex legal issues were intellectual prerogatives and their crude popularization by religious leaders like Ghazali meant committing an offence against the basic principles of law and against philosophy, no matter how good his intention was.[23]

However, in line with the intolerance of the liberals (like the Mutazila earlier and the secularists in modern times), Ibn Rushd, who pleaded that philosophers were to be excused even if they committed errors, called upon the official ulama to forbid access to Ghazali's books, which contained learned matter, to the general public, just as he felt that they needed to forbid 'demonstrative' books to those who were not considered capable of understanding them.[24] In a sense, this was aimed at minimizing schisms and sectarian divisions in Islam. He wrote: 'It was due to interpretations—especially the false ones—and the supposition that such interpretations of the Law ought to be expressed to everyone, that the sects of Islam arose, with the result that each one accused the other of unbelief and heresy. Thus the Mutazilites interpreted many [Quranic] verses and Traditions, and expressed their interpretations to the multitude, and the Ash'arites did the same, although they used such interpretations less frequently. In consequence, they threw people into hatred, mutual detestation, and wars, tore the Law to shreds, and completely divided people'.[25] Thus, Ibn Rushd sought political patronage and use of political power even for his elitist 'discourse'. He paid homage to his patron, the Almohad ruler, Abu Yaqub Yusuf (ruled, 1163–84), by appreciating that he was crucial for 'the removal of many of the evils, ignorant ideas, and misleading practices, and for opening a way to many benefits, especially to the class of persons who have trodden the path of study and sought to know the truth'.[26] Eventually, however, the theologians succeeded in cornering political power over the medieval period and managed to suppress reason or anything that went beyond blind conformity to the rulings of the jurists. Science and philosophy got marginalized in Islam. One can legitimately wonder, however, why the philosophers did not gain power long enough to make a lasting difference (more on this below).

It might be useful at this point to briefly compare the developments in Christianity, Islam and Hinduism. Christianity did two things: one, build a religious hierarchy called the Church, with the obligation of obedience; and, two, institute the mechanism of the great religious conference to consider divisive issues and come to a consensus which, then, became the doctrine for all Christians. The system worked more or less efficiently till the Reformation. Hinduism, on the other hand, largely acknowledged the multiplicity of doctrines and left the question of their validity to individual believers. Islam's difficulty has been that it has neither developed the means to enforce doctrinal uniformity among believers nor abandoned the belief that a single faith can really be made to prevail by wiping every other faith out. There is no central authority whose fatwas can be binding on all Muslims all over the world despite the general portrayal of Islam as a homogeneous religion.

Besides the question of violence over wresting control of political power to establish a particular interpretation of shariat as the universally applicable state law, Muslim societies in general are characterized by an open, outgoing style. They had several strands: one was intellectual openness, as indicated earlier, justified by the Quran and the Prophet's command to acquire knowledge, even from China if need be. In the early generations, they also turned to the Byzantine empire, which was closer at hand. Insofar as the Quran is concerned, early Islam identified itself with Christian Byzantium, than the pagan Sassanid Persia (more on this below). As mentioned earlier, the rich diversity of Greek thought also helped open countless windows. However, under various historical conditions, those options were closed one after the other. The victory of the conservative ulama sodality was an important reason for this. The second distinctive feature of medieval Muslim societies was commercial enterprise. The old Muslim lands mediated between Europe, India and China through commerce, both over land and through sea. The increasing European control over the maritime trade from the sixteenth century onwards meant that the Arab, Persian and other Muslim merchants were slowly marginalized. Thirdly, through the middle ages, Muslims forged huge empires. In most contexts, Muslim rulers drew local skills and resources into their regimes and accommodated differences judiciously, for instance, as in the case of Muslim rulers in medieval India.

The emergence of the West and other processes of modern history, chiefly colonialism, put Muslims everywhere on the defensive politically. These things happened at a great pace, compressed into three or four centuries, and took Muslims by surprise. Occasionally, they came to terms with the change or 'decline' from their perspective, but their initiatives lacked institutional backing. Minus political power and commerce, Islam was left not with institutions, but only with its law, the shariat, as interpreted by the ulama. The shariat came to be defined as final and immutable, not readily open to reinterpretation to suit changing circumstances. In modern times, vast numbers of

Muslims have been caught in a dilemma: while the old world which they once dominated has disappeared, an enormous pride in political and creative achievements of the past has remained along with the idea that if it happened once, it can be done again, a proposition periodically expressed by revivalist and reformist movements. However, instead of back-up institutions within which to take stock of the evolving situation, there are numerous clergy, trained in madrasas at a very low cost and equipped with few intellectual tools other than a particular interpretation of the shariat. An extraordinary lack of institutional infrastructure means that there are hardly anything beyond madrasas and khanqahs to provide guidance to Muslims, both in any case emerging as bastions of religious orthodoxy of different types. The philosophers and liberal intellectuals could only establish elite clubs or reading groups and as eccentric scholars, they were accused of being unconcerned about the ways of the world in which they lived. This is, however, understandable given the ulama's generally hostile reaction to anything that sounds like deviation from established norms.

By contrast, early modern Europe adapted quickly to the rapid changes in politics and economy. It also appropriated from Islam Arabic renderings of medieval science and philosophy (something which the ulama now celebrate, claiming as their own). Islam and Christianity have indeed had a shared history. Jesus is primarily a Middle Eastern figure and one of the most respected prophets in Islam.[27] It might be too far-fetched to think of Christianity and Islam as sister religions—just as it is heretical to claim that Islam is a sect within medieval eastern Christianity. Even though the Quran acknowledged the Biblical prophets, Islam considers itself a distinct 'religion' and Muhammad's life marked a clear departure from Christianity; yet Muslims remained open to other influences.

Political transformations and the governmentalization of society meant that Europe was going to have, through the sixteenth to eighteenth centuries, a different trajectory altogether. As noted previously, Michel Foucault's formulations are not entirely irrelevant here. It will be interesting to explore to what extent this departure was propelled by Aristotle's *Politics*, while the coterminous Muslim world remained caught in the older Platonian *Republic*[28] (this is not to underestimate Europe's intellectual history from the tenth century onwards). This view might help us go beyond the usual formulation that the middle ages witnessed a struggle between science and religion, and that science emerged victorious in the Christian West and religion won the war in the Islamic East. It may also be noted that though science emerged in the West, Christianity itself was never really eclipsed. It has continued to expand and a great many Christians practise their religion privately, rather than going to Church and making public assertions of faith. And traditionally, Christian questions and ideas continue to be recycled in literature and in writings on ethics and suchlike.

It is not that Muslims have reached the end of the road. Islam does have the historic resources of ideas and precedents to work its way out of the present quagmire.[29] In a very interesting and sensitive handling of the complex ways in which Muslims of Chitral district of northern Pakistan, on the border with Afghanistan, are negotiating with their times, anthropologist Magnus Marsden has shown how Muslims here, both in rural areas and in urban settings, had evolved creative and distinctive ways (through music, satire, mimicry) of living together despite the occasional violence and tension over sectarian differences and new forms of Islam (represented by young male students returning from lower Pakistani madrasas where they are exposed to radical Islam, such as that practised by the Taliban). There is no dearth of 'open-minded local intellectuals' here, who not only critique established Islamic doctrinal traditions, but also resist the diktats of the young graduates from Islamic seminaries,[30] just as Muslims in general have coped with the challenges of modernity, globalization, etc. However, one may guard against reading too much into Marsden's account, even though his text can also be read as one documenting a case of an incipient transformation. In a multi-generational perspective, cumulative ideological pressure may result in clear, directional changes. An ideologically informed new generation can discard traditional values and bring about rapid changes in society, even as old-timers complain or helplessly watch the process of social transformation. The Talibanization of Pakistan is a case in point.

On the Indian side of the Subcontinent, a huge Muslim population has been facing difficulties at the hands of aggressive Hindu majoritarianism. Muslims are being asked to pay in the present for what their 'ancestors' as rulers in medieval centuries allegedly did to the Hindus. However, saner voices are advocating for a more generous politics and society: one that is sensitive to those rendered defenceless for reasons of history, gender, age, caste and creed. The Indian secular constitution and law does guarantee the rights of marginalized people, despite occasional lapses on the part of ruling parties.[31]

Contemporary pressures, as in the Indian case from Hindu communalists, tend to unite Muslims into a monolithic community; otherwise, the two broad sects of the Shias and Sunnis are further sub-divided into many sects. Shias have their Bohras, Khojas, Ismailis and the more numerous Asna-Asharis, with each of them forming a close-knit community with distinct boundary-markers. Indian Sunni Islam is equally fragmented. Besides the four schools of Sunni jurisprudence, or mazahib, such as the Hanafi, Hanbali, Maliki and Shafi'i (and Ja'fri in the Shia case), there are traditional Muslims with their adherence to various forms of Sufic Islam (who also claim to be the true followers of the path of the Prophet, Ahl-i-Sunnat wal Jama'at, and are reviled by their opponents as Barelwi or even the juridically scandalous *Mushrik*), reformist Muslims influenced by the Tablighi Jama'at (identified also as Deobandis and sometimes as Wahhabis), the fundamentalist followers of the Jama'at-i-Islami (another form of Wahhabism), and the more dogmatic Ahl-i-Hadis. Indeed, there has been a lot of tension, conflict, even violence over which one is the most righteous and must dominate over and shape Muslim life.

To summarize, the resurgence of violent political Islam and Islamist groups, parties and terror networks should not necessarily imply that the problems facing Muslim societies today are a purely modern concern. Even as modern politics is important, we will do well to understand the historical trajectories of the making of Islam. As we saw earlier, despite the space for tolerating difference and the variegated nature of Muslim societies across time and place with all their achievements, in situations of political crisis, adherence to a monolithic, political Islam emerges as a dominant ideology. The proponents of shariat-bound Islam would like to capture power once again, in order to establish what is, in their opinion, the correct form of Islam that invokes a particular reading of the Quran and the prophetic Tradition. Liberal interpretations of Islam and Muslims who have resisted the totalizing nature of Islamic orthodoxy (of whatever school) would be the immediate victims. Historically, when it comes to questioning established beliefs, sharia-minded Islam have had the last word. When they had power, they crushed all their opponents, when they had none, they still had a lot of followers to blast their way to 'heaven'. Faith prevails over reason.

One option for dealing with the contemporary crisis in Islam could be to revive the Ibn-Rushds by studying ancient Islamic thought and illustrating its relevance for projects necessary in the present and future. The emphasis on the philosophers countering the Islamist celebration of the role played by Ghazali in saving Islam and Muslims from deviations induced by Greek and other traditions of learning could bring out other complex features of Muslim societies, which tend to get ignored in many superficial discussions of contemporary political Islam. But unlike the secularists/modernists, I am not blindly supporting the 'rationalists'. I only wish to show how they were marginalized or lost the struggle for power in terms of influencing the rulers. More importantly, I also wish to reconsider how rationalists like the Mutazila could be so very intolerant towards those who refused to subscribe to their doctrines, and they too used political power to suppress their opponents. It may be possible that in deploying an Islamic rationalist tradition as an answer to political Islam, one might be giving way to intolerance of another kind; for, as they say, power corrupts and corrupts absolutely. However, a more informed understanding of the question of why certain Muslim groups behave the way they do demands calm reflection on the historical trajectories of Islam.

In conclusion, what I have said earlier is not a matter of kufr (infidelity) or *iman* (faith), and, therefore, there can be no fatwa against those who wish to differ. The lesson from the history of Islam is that debates and discussions are often confused with disputations or even fitna (sedition), which has led to all kinds of consequences, including the use of political power to crush any dissenting voice or reaction. Intolerance has been the cause of disgrace, infamy and anarchy. Impatience, as reflected in extremist violence, is far from the solution either. On the other hand, as the wise men of medieval Islam put it: *as-sabru miftah-ul-fakhr* (Patience is the key to glory)!

Notes

Chapter 1: Islam and Indian History

1. See Richard M. Eaton's important study, *The Rise of Islam and the Bengal Frontier, 1204–1760* (New Delhi: Oxford University Press, 1994).

2. For an exhaustive survey of extant material heritage, see Mehrdad Shokoohy, *Muslim Architecture of South India: The Sultanate of Ma'bar and the Traditions of Maritime Settlers on the Malabar and Coromandel Coasts; Tamil Nadu, Kerala and Goa* (London and New York: Routledge Curzon, 2003).

3. For an insightful 'internal' critique by a self-professed secularist historian of the 'inner tension that often characterizes secular histories' and the limitations of 'secular teleology' even in the finest works on ancient and medieval India, see Neeladri Bhattacharya, 'Predicament of Secular Histories', *Public Culture*, 20: 1 (2008), pp. 57–73.

4. Some scholars view the latter half of this period as 'early modern' in a global, comparative framework. For an argument in favour of the use of the term 'early modern' for even the fifteenth century, see Sanjay Subrahmanyam, *Penumbral Visions: Making Polities in Early Modern South India* (New Delhi: Oxford University Press, 2001), pp. 253–65. For a re-conceptualization of the differentiation between the 'early modern' and the 'colonial modern', see Partha Chatterjee, 'The Early Modern and Colonial Modern in South Asia: A Proposal for a Distinction', Paper presented at the Centre for Studies in Social Sciences, Calcutta, July 2004.

5. For a study of how painting and architecture have been neglected as sources for the political history of medieval India, see

Monica Juneja, 'Introduction', in *Architecture in Medieval India: Forms, Contexts, Histories* (New Delhi: Permanent Black, 2001). For a recent work, addressed to general readers and students, that liberally deploys exquisite pictures of paintings, monuments and other artefacts, see Annemarie Schimmel, *The Empire of the Great Mughals: History, Art and Culture* (New Delhi: Oxford University Press, 2005).

6. Muzaffar Alam, *The Languages of Political Islam in India*, c. *1200–1800* (New Delhi: Permanent Black, 2004), p. 27. This work also includes Alam's important distinction on competing forms of Islamic law and political theory and his ideas about a theoretical premise for a broad-based medieval Muslim polity.

7. Ibid., p. 42.

8. See chapter three.

9. Alam, *Languages of Political Islam,* p. 47.

10. Ibid., pp. 48–49.

11. Ibid., pp. 114, 134–35.

12. Ibid., pp. 124–25, 127, 147.

13. See chapters two and three.

14. See also, Bhattacharya, 'Predicament of Secular Histories'.

15. For a criticism of the Mughal-centric approach to the study of medieval Indian history, see Sanjay Subrahmanyam, 'The Mughal State: Structure or Process? Reflections on Recent Western Historiography', *Indian Economic and Social History Review*, 24: 3 (1992), pp. 291–321.

16. For a fresh look at the Afghan period, see Raziuddin Aquil, *Sufism, Culture, and Politics: Afghans and Islam in Medieval North India* (New Delhi: Oxford University Press, 2007).

17. For a traditional, political history of Bengal, see Jadunath Sarkar (ed.), *The History of Bengal, Muslim Period, 1200–1757* (Patna: Academica Asiatica, 1973); Syed Ejaz Hussain, *The Bengal Sultanate: Politics, Economy and Coins (AD 1205–1576)* (New Delhi: Manohar, 2003). Also see Richard Eaton's impressive study, *The Rise of Islam and the Bengal Frontier*. For a study of devotional Islam in the Deccan, see Richard M. Eaton, *Sufis of Bijapur, 1300–1700, Social Roles of Sufis in Medieval India* (Princeton: Princeton University Press, 1978); also see Carl W. Ernst, *Eternal Garden: Mysticism, History and Politics at a South Asian Sufi Centre* (Albany: State University of New York Press, 1992); Simon Digby, *Sufis and Soldiers in Awrangzeb's Deccan: Malfuzat-i-Naqshbandiyya* (New Delhi:

Oxford University Press, 2001); Nile Green, *Indian Sufism since the Seventeenth Century: Saints, Books and Empires in the Muslim Deccan* (London: Routledge, 2006).

18. Alam, *Languages of Political Islam*, p. 144.

19. Ibid., preface, p. ix.

20. For a similar approach, see Carl W. Ernst and Bruce B. Lawrence, *Sufi Martyrs of Love: The Chishti Order in South Asia and Beyond* (New York: Palgrave Macmillan, 2002). For a different view, see Raziuddin Aquil, 'Conversion in Chishti Sufi Literature (13th–14th Centuries)', *Indian Historical Review*, 24: 1–2 (1997–98), pp. 70–94.

21. Mohammad Habib, *Life and Thought of Ziyauddin Barani*. The work has been printed several times and here, we will be using the last version in this book, included in Mohammad Habib, *Politics and Society During the Early Medieval Period, Collected Works of Mohammad Habib*, Vol. II, edited by K.A. Nizami (New Delhi: Peoples Publishing House, 1981), pp. 286–366. Also see the reprint (in *Politics and Society*, Vol. II, pp. 418–32) of Mohammad Habib's 'Introduction' to *The Political Theory of the Delhi Sultanate (Including translation of Ziauddin Barani's Fatawa-i-Jahandari, circa, 1358–9 AD)* by Mohammad Habib and Afsar Umar Salim Khan (Allahabad: Kitab Mahal, n.d.).

22. Barani anticipated modern political theorists in his discussion on the exceptional situation when laws, in this case, the shariat, could be suspended and the rulers acquired extraordinary powers. Also see, in this context, Giorgio Agamben, *Homo Sacer: Sovereign Power and Bare Life,* English translation by Daniel Heller-Roazen (Stanford: Stanford University Press, 1998); Agamben's *State of Exception*, English translation by Kevin Attell (Chicago: University of Chicago Press, 2005).

23. For more on this, see chapter three. Much of what Barani wrote in this text was 'theoretical' and does not necessarily reflect on 'reality'. For a useful, general survey of writings on the theme of the 'Circle of Justice', see Linda T. Darling, '"Do Justice, Do Justice, For That is Paradise": Middle Eastern Advice for Indian Muslim Rulers', *Comparative Studies of South Asia, Africa and the Middle East*, 22: 1–2 (2002), pp. 3–19. For an important exposition of the tensions between religious egalitarianism and social stratification in classical Islam, see Louise Marlow, *Hierarchy and Egalitarianism in Islamic Thought*, Cambridge Series in Islamic Civilization (Cambridge: Cambridge University Press, 1997).

24. For an earlier, dismissive approach towards Sirhindi's career written from a secularist perspective, see S.A.A. Rizvi, *Muslim Revivalist Movements in Northern India in the Sixteenth and Seventeenth Centuries* (New Delhi: Munshiram Manoharlal, 1993). For information on Shah Waliullah, see S.A.A. Rizvi, *Shah Wali-Allah and His Times* (Canberra: Ma'rifat Publishing House, 1980). For a more sensitive treatment of reformist and revivalist movements in medieval India, though from a separatist standpoint, see Aziz Ahmad, *Studies in Islamic Culture in Indian Environment* (Oxford: Clarendon Press, 1964).

25. Michel Foucault, 'Governmentality', in *The Foucault Effect: Studies in Governmentality*, edited by Graham Burchell et al. (London: Harvester, 1991), pp. 87–104; see especially Foucault's eleventh lecture (17 March 1976) in *'Society Must Be Defended'. Lectures at the College De France, 1975–76*, edited by Mauro Bertani and Alessandra Fontana, translated by David Macey (New York: Picador, 2003).

26. We will be referring in this book to examples from a series of caliphates; the 'rightly-guided' first four caliphs who succeeded the Prophet in the first century of Islam, the caliphate of the Umayyads, which resembled a dynasty with its base in Damascus, and the Abbasid Caliphate, which ruled from its capital, Baghdad.

27. For a synthetic discussion of these crucial connections, see Saïd Amir Arjomand, 'Perso-Indian Statecraft, Greek Political Science and the Muslim Idea of Government', *International Sociology*, 16: 3 (2001), pp. 455–73.

28. Foucault, 'Governmentality', p. 89.

29. Arjomand, 'Perso-Indian Statecraft', p. 471.

30. See chapters two and seven.

31. See Abel on 'Zimmis' in *Encyclopaedia of Islam*, New Edition, Vol. II (Leiden: Brill, 1991).

32. Originally used in the sense of 'to obliterate', 'to cover' and 'to conceal' in old Arab poetry and in the Quran, the word 'kafir' is applied to the unbelieving Meccan 'infidels' or idolators, who endeavour to refute and revile Prophet Muhammad. During the early Meccan period, a waiting attitude towards idolators was recommended, but later on, Muslims are ordered to keep apart from them, to defend themselves from their attacks and even to make offensives against them. In most passages of the Quran, the reference is to unbelievers in general who are threatened with God's punishment. Later sources also refer to them as unclean and jihad (holy war) against the unbelievers

of a *dar-ul-harb* (enemy land) is obligatory. For more information, see W. Bjorkman, 'Kafir', *Encyclopaedia of Islam*, New Edition, Vol. 4, pp. 407–09.

33. Jadunath Sarkar, *Studies in Aurangzib's Reign* (London: Sangam, 1933).

34. I.H. Qureshi, *The Muslim Community of the Indo-Pak Subcontinent, 610–1947* (Delhi: Renaissance Publication House, 1985).

35. Irfan Habib, 'Introduction: Commemorating Akbar', in Iqtidar Alam Khan (ed.), *Akbar and His Age* (New Delhi: ICHR and Northern Book Centre, 1999).

36. Iqtidar Alam Khan, 'The Nobility under Akbar and the Development of his Religious Policy, 1560–80', in Richard M. Eaton (ed.), *India's Islamic Traditions, 711–1750* (New Delhi: Oxford University Press, 2003).

37. Satish Chandra, *Essays on Medieval Indian History* (New Delhi: Oxford University Press, 2003).

38. See Iqtidar Alam Khan, 'Nobility under Akbar and the Development of his Religious Policy'; and M. Athar Ali, *The Mughal Nobility under Aurangzeb* (New Delhi: Oxford University Press, 1997).

39. Richard Eaton, 'Temple Desecration and Indo-Muslim States', in Eaton's *Essays on Islam and Indian History* (New Delhi: Oxford University Press, 2002).

40. See Katherine Butler Brown's excellent essay, 'Did Aurangzeb Ban Music? Questions for the Historiography of his Reign', *Modern Asian Studies*, 41: 1 (2007), pp. 77–120.

41. See chapter seven.

42. Raziuddin Aquil, 'The Study of Islam and Indian History at the Darul Musannefin, Azamgarh', in Raziuddin Aquil and Partha Chatterjee (eds.), *History in the Vernacular* (Ranikhet: Permanent Black, 2008).

43. Richard Eaton, 'Introduction', in Eaton (ed.), *India's Islamic Traditions*.

Chapter 2: Sufi Traditions and the Emergence of Islam in the Subcontinent

1. For an up-to-date and analytically oriented thesis on the growth and development of the Islamic mystical tradition in the Abbasid

Caliphate and its spread to many parts of the Muslim world during the period between the ninth and the twelfth centuries, see Ahmet T. Karamustafa, *Sufism: The Formative Period*, The New Edinburgh Islamic Surveys (Edinburgh: Edinburgh University Press, 2007).

2. The term 'orthodoxy' is being used here and elsewhere in this book for the official ulama, often referred to as the *ulama-i-su*, or 'worldly ulama', who insisted on implementing the Sunni Hanafite interpretation of Islam and sought to use political power for this purpose.

3. For a fourteenth-century reference to the Sufi practice of *chilla-i-makus*, see Amir Khwurd, *Siyar-ul-Auliya* (Islamabad: Markaz Tahqiqat-i-Farsi Iran wa Pakistan, 1978).

4. Important studies by scholars like Aziz Ahmad, Muzaffar Alam, Richard Eaton, Carl Ernst, Bruce Lawrence, M. Mujeeb, K.A. Nizami and S.A.A. Rizvi, among others, provide good introductions to Indian Sufism. For detailed references, see Bibliography.

5. For a thought-provoking counter-narrative, see Eleanor Zelliot, 'A Medieval Encounter Between Hindu and Muslim: Eknath's Drama-Poem *Hindu-Turk Samvad*', in Richard M. Eaton (ed.), *India's Islamic Traditions*, pp. 64–82.

6. For existing literature on the Delhi Sultanate, see A.B.M. Habibullah, *The Foundation of the Muslim Rule in India,* revised edition (Allahabad: Central Book Depot, 1961); K.A. Nizami, *Religion and Politics in India During the Thirteenth Century* (New Delhi: Oxford University Press, 2002); I.H. Siddiqui, *Afghan Despotism in India* (Aligarh: Three Men, 1961); K.S. Lal, *History of the Khaljis*, revised edition (Delhi: Munshiram Manoharlal, 1980); Agha Mahdi Husain, *Tughluq Dynasty* (Delhi: S. Chand, 1976); Mohammad Habib and K.A. Nizami (eds), *A Comprehensive History of India, V, Part One, The Delhi Sultanate* (Delhi: Peoples Publishing House, 1992); Peter Jackson, *The Delhi Sultanate: A Political and Military History* (Cambridge: Cambridge University Press, 1999). Catherine B. Asher and Cynthia Talbot's *India Before Europe* (Cambridge: Cambridge University Press, 2006) offers a fine synthesis of the political and cultural history of medieval India before European intervention.

7. Important analyses of 'historical' texts from medieval India can be found in Mohibbul Hasan (ed.), *Historians of Medieval India* (Meerut: Meenakshi Prakashan, 1968) and in Harbans Mukhia, *Historians and Historiography During the Reign of Akbar* (Delhi: Vikas Publications, 1976).

For the older tradition of varied and interesting forms of history writing in medieval Islam, see Chase F. Robinson, *Islamic Historiography* (Cambridge: Cambridge University Press, 2003).

8. Mohammad Habib, *Politics and Society*, pp. 385–433. Subsequent scholars like M. Mujeeb, K.A. Nizami and S.A.A. Rizvi, among others, have generally reiterated Habib's position.

9. Raziuddin Aquil, 'Miracles, Authority and Benevolence: Stories of *Karamat* in Chishti Sufi Literature of the Delhi Sultanate', in Anup Taneja (ed.), *Sufi Cults and the Evolution of Medieval Indian Culture* (New Delhi: ICHR and Northern Book Centre, 2003), pp. 109–38.

10. For a review of secondary literature, see Raziuddin Aquil, 'Sufi Cults, Politics and Conversion: The Chishtis of the Sultanate Period', *Indian Historical Review,* 22: 1–2 (1995–96), pp. 190–97.

11. Also see Aquil, *Sufism, Culture, and Politics.*

12. *Tabaqat-i-Nasiri* of Minhaj-us-Siraj, edited by Abdul Hayy Habibi, Vol. 1 (Kabul: Historical Society of Afghanistan, 1963–64), pp. 397, 399–400; and Amir Khwurd's *Siyar-ul-Auliya*, p. 57.

13. *Tabaqat-i-Nasiri*, p. 400.

14. Ibid., pp. 400–01.

15. Eaton, *Essays on Islam and Indian History*.

16. *Zawabit* (regulations, rules, precepts) + *mulki* (of or relating to empire or government). The expression appears in the mid-fourteenth century text, *Fatawa-i-Jahandari* by Ziya-ud-Din Barani. The author insisted that *sharia* law was inadequate for running the Sultanate and wrote that a new extra-religious law needed to be evolved. 'Zawabit' were indeed of a secular nature and were certainly not theocratic. For more on Barani and his political ideas, see chapter three.

17. For information on Qutb-ud-Din's enthronement, see Minhaj-us-Siraj's *Tabaqat-i-Nasiri,* p. 417.

18. For information on the life of the saint, see Ihsanul Haq Faruqi, *Sultan-ut-Tarikin* (Karachi: Dairah Mu'inul Ma'arif, 1963).

19. For biographical material on Muin-ud-Din Chishti, see Amir Khwurd's *Siyar-ul-Auliya*, pp. 55–58. Also see P.M. Currie, *The Shrine and Cult of Muin al-Din Chishti of Ajmer* (New Delhi: Oxford University Press, 1989).

20. *Siyar-ul-Auliya*, pp. 56–57.

21. Ibid., p. 57.

22. For Islamic theoretical positions on dar-ul-harb and dar-ul-

islam, see A. Abel, *Encyclopaedia of Islam*, New Edition, Vol. II, pp. 126, 127–28.

23. For this and other references to the visit to Muin-ud-Din's tomb at Ajmer in the fourteenth century, see Simon Digby, 'Early Pilgrimages to the Graves of Muinuddin Sijzi and other Indian Chishti Shaikhs', in M. Israel and N.K. Wagle (eds.), *Islamic Society and Culture: Essays in Honour of Aziz Ahmad* (Delhi: Manohar, 1983), pp. 95–100.

24. For biographical material, see *Siyar-ul-Auliya*, pp. 58–67; and *Siyar-ul-Arifin* of Shaikh Jamali. Ms., IO Islamic 1313, OIOC, British Library, London, fols. 31b–43a. Also see, S.A.A. Rizvi, *A History of Sufism in India*, Vol. I, *Early Sufism and its History in India to 1600* AD (New Delhi: Munshiram Manoharlal, 1978), pp. 133–38.

25. *Siyar-ul-Auliya*, p. 64.

26. Ibid., p. 65.

27. For the caliph's comparable approach, see Saïd Amir Arjomand, 'Transformation of the Islamicate Civilization: A Turning-Point in the Thirteenth Century?', *Medieval Encounters*, 10: 1–3 (2004), pp. 213–45.

28. Ziya-ud-Din Barani notes that Sultan Nasir-ud-Din was a mere *namuna*, as the reins of power were in the hands of Balban, then known as Ulugh Khan; see *Tarikh-i-Firuz-Shahi* of Ziya-ud-Din Barani, British Museum Ms. 6376, OIOC, British Library, London, fols. 12b–13a.

29. *Tarikh-i-Firuz-Shahi*, fols. 23b–24a.

30. Ibid., fols. 26a–28a, 38a–45a.

31. Ibid., fols. 13b–17b.

32. *Siyar-ul-Auliya*, pp. 89–90; *Siyar-ul-Arifin*, fols. 56b–57a; *Jawahir-i-Faridi* of Ali Asghar Chishti (Lahore: Victoria Press, 1884), pp. 204, 214–15. For more on Balban's religiosity and his veneration of the Sufi saints, see *Tarikh-i-Firuz-Shahi*, fols. 21b–22a. For biographical material on the sheikh's life, see *Siyar-ul-Auliya*, pp. 67–101; *Siyar-ul-Arifin*, fols. 43a–65b. Also see K.A. Nizami, *The Life and Times of Shaikh Fariduddin Ganj-i-Shakar* (Aligarh: Muslim University, 1955); Richard Eaton, *India's Islamic Traditions;* Raziuddin Aquil, 'Episodes from the Life of Shaikh Farid-ud-Din Ganj-i-Shakar', *International Journal of Punjab Studies,* 10: 1–2 (2003), pp. 25–46.

33. *Jawahir-i-Faridi*, pp. 215–18. Also see *Khazinat-ul-Asfiya* of Maulwi Ghulam Sarwar, Vol. I. Kanpur, n.d, p. 301.

34. *Siyar-ul-Auliya,* pp. 76, 195.

35. Ibid., pp. 100, 200.

36. For an early biography of the saint, see Muhammad Jamal Qiwam, *Qiwam-ul-Aqa'id*, translated by Nisar Ahmad Faruqui from the original Persian into Urdu (Rampur: Idarah Nashar-o-Isha'at, 1994). Also see the collection of his conversations in *Fawa'id-ul-Fu'ad*, compiled by Amir Hasan Sijzi, Persian text with an Urdu translation by Khwaja Hasan Sani Nizami (New Delhi: Urdu Academy, 1990); *Siyar-ul-Auliya*, pp. 101–65; *Siyar-ul-Arifin*, fols. 75b–100b; K.A. Nizami, *The Life and Times of Shaikh Nizamuddin Auliya* (Delhi: Idarah-i-Adabiyat-i Delli, 1991).

37. For an authoritative collection of Nasir-ud-Din's malfuzat, see *Khayr-ul-Majalis*, compiled by Hamid Qalandar, edited by K.A. Nizami (Aligarh: Muslim University, 1959). For early tazkiras, see *Siyar-ul-Auliya*, pp. 246–57; *Siyar-ul-Arifin*, fols. 126a–130b. Also see K.A. Nizami, *The Life and Times of Shaikh Nasiruddin Chiragh* (Delhi: Idarah-i-Adabiyat-i Delli, 1991).

38. Aquil, 'Miracles, Authority and Benevolence'.

39. For the practice and defence of sama in Chishti circles, see Carl W. Ernst and Bruce B. Lawrence, *Sufi Martyrs of Love*, pp. 34–46.

40. For an early-fifteenth-century recorded version of the saint's remark (*'dehli as tu dur ast'*), see *Tarikh-i-Mubarak-Shahi* of Yahya bin Ahmad bin 'Abdullah Sarhindi, edited by M. Hidayat Hosain (Calcutta: Asiatic Society, 1931), pp. 96–97.

41. The episode of the bestowal of kingship on Muhammad Tughluq is recorded in a Chishti hagiography, *Qiwam-ul-Aqa'id* (compiled *c.* 1350), p. 96.

42. Richard M. Eaton, *Sufis of Bijapur*; Simon Digby, 'The Sufi Shaykh as a Source of Authority in Medieval India', *Purushartha,* 9 (1986), pp. 55–77, and his 'The Sufi Shaikh and the Sultan: A Conflict of Claims to Authority in Medieval India', *Iran,* 28 (1990), pp. 71–81; Muzaffar Alam, 'Assimilation from a Distance: Confrontation and Sufi Accommodation in Awadh Society', in R. Champakalakshmi and S. Gopal (eds), *Tradition, Dissent and Ideology, Essays in Honour of Romila Thapar* (New Delhi: Oxford University Press, 1996), pp. 164–91; and Aquil, 'Miracles, Authority and Benevolence'.

43. Digby, 'The Sufi Shaykh as a Source of Authority', and 'The Sufi Shaikh and the Sultan'; Aquil, 'Miracles, Authority and Benevolence'.

44. *Siyar-ul-Auliya*, pp. 89–90.

45. *Siyar-ul-Arifin,* fols. 97b–99b.

46. *Siyar-ul-Auliya*, p. 89.

47. *Tarikh-i-Firuz-Shahi*, fols. 153a–b.

48. Nizami, *Life and Times of Shaikh Nizamuddin Auliya*, p. 110.

49. Nizam-ud-Din Auliya sent Wajih-ud-Din Yusuf with Ala-ud-Din Khalji's army for the conquest of Chanderi, a strategic place on the route to the Deccan. Yusuf stayed on at Chanderi after its conquest, *Siyar-ul-Auliya*, pp. 296–97.

50. Nizam-ud-Din Auliya's leading disciples Amir Khusrau and Amir Hasan Sijzi participated in the campaigns. Khusrau's reports reflected the mood in the army.

51. For a biography of the sheikh, see K.A. Nizami, *Life and Times of Shaikh Nasiruddin Chiragh*.

52. *Fawa'id-ul-Fu'ad*.

53. Ernst and Lawrence, *Sufi Martyrs of Love*.

54. Writings on Khusrau abound, but most of them read like propaganda literature; for a scholarly handling of the literature by and on Khusrau, see Sunil Sharma, *Amir Khusraw: The Poet of Sultans and Sufis* (Oxford: Oneworld, 2005). Sunil Sharma's more important biography of a neglected poet of an earlier period of political flux and displacements may be mentioned here, *Persian Poetry at the Indian Frontier: Mas'ud Sa'd Salman of Lahore* (New Delhi: Permanent Black, 2000).

55. Yohanan Friedmann, 'Islamic Thought in Relation to the Indian Context', first published in 1986, reprinted in Richard Eaton (ed.), *India's Islamic Traditions,* pp. 50–63.

56. Ahmad, 'Epic and Counter-Epic in Medieval India', first published in 1963, reprinted in Richard Eaton (ed.), *India's Islamic Traditions,* pp. 37–49.

57. Friedmann, 'Islamic Thought in Relation to the Indian Context'.

Chapter 3: Muslims and Kafirs in the Delhi Sultanate

1. I first presented certain ideas explored in this chapter at 'Rethinking a Millennium: International Seminar in Honour of Professor Harbans Mukhia', New Delhi, 2–4 February 2004; a version

of that paper was later published as 'On Islam and *Kufr* in the Delhi Sultanate: Towards a Re-interpretation of Ziya' al-Din Barani's *Fatawa-i Jahandari*', in Rajat Datta (ed.), *Rethinking a Millennium: Perspectives on Indian History from the Eighth to the Eighteenth Century, Essays for Harbans Mukhia* (Delhi: Aakar Books, 2008), pp. 168–97.

2. Stuart Hall, 'Cultural Studies and its Theoretical Legacies', in Lawrence Grossberg, Cary Nelson and Paula Treichler (eds), *Cultural Studies* (New York and London: Routledge, 1992), pp. 277–94.

3. Ziya-ud-Din Barani, *Tarikh-i-Firuz Shahi*.

4. Barani may have been born not later than 1285 and probably earlier as he mentioned having read the whole of the Quran during the reign of Sultan Jalal-ud-Din Khalji (1290–96); see Peter Hardy, 'Barani', *Encyclopaedia of Islam*, New Edition, Vol. 1, pp. 1036–37. For a detailed account of Barani's career with a lot of adverse remarks, see Mohammad Habib, 'Life and Thought of Ziyauddin Barani' in his *Politics and Society*, Vol. II, pp. 286–366. We will also refer to Habib's 'Introduction' to *The Political Theory of the Delhi Sultanate* by Habib and Khan, reprinted in Habib's *Politics and Society*, Vol. II, pp. 418–32.

5. Baran is the old name of Bulandshahar, an ancient town situated on the main route from Agra and Aligarh to Meerut in Uttar Pradesh. The name 'Baran' was derived from the name of its legendary founder, Ahirban. The discovery of copper plate inscriptions from the fifth century and much older coins establishes this town's antiquity. Its earliest recorded association with Muslims dates back to its conquest by Sultan Mahmud of Ghazna in 1018; see A.S. Bazmee Ansari, 'Bulandshahr (Baran)', *Encyclopaedia of Islam*, New Edition, Vol. 1, pp. 1299–1300.

6. Mohammad Habib writes that Muhammad Tughluq appointed Barani as his *nadim* (courtier) in late 1334. Curiously, Habib notes that it was an office of much profit and no responsibility and not one suited to a man with self-respect. He then goes on to quote the account of the courtier's position and duties as recorded in Nizam-ul-Mulk Tusi's *Siyasat-nama*. He notes that Nizam-ul-Mulk's description matched with 'Barani's own confessions'. Nizam-ul-Mulk writes that there were certain advantages the Sultan enjoys with a courtier. First, as a friend of the king, he is with him day and night, and is in the position of a bodyguard of the king; if danger arises, the courtier sacrifices his life and uses his body a shield to protect the king. Secondly, it is possible

for the king to say a thousand things, in jest and seriously, to the courtier, which he cannot say to the wazir and to the officers of his government for they are holders of high posts and managers of his affairs. Thirdly, like spies, they inform the king of the actions of his *maliks*. Fourthly, they can speak boldly about the good and the bad aspects of state policy.

The nadim also needs to be high-born, accomplished, good in manners, pleasant in appearance, orthodox in faith, worthy of confidence and pure in his ways. He should also be able to tell plenty of jocular as well as serious stories. Finally, he must be the king's constant companion in drinking, enjoyment, *majlis*es, hunting and playing; see Habib's *Politics and Society*, Vol. II, pp. 339–40, where he cites Nizam-ul-Mulk Tusi's *Siyasat-nama*, edited by Agha Abbas Iqbal (Tehran, 1320).

7. *Qiwam-ul-Aqa'id*, pp. 96–97. Also see chapter two of this book.

8. Barani admits that when he was imprisoned in Bhatnir fort after the death of Muhammad Tughluq, his enemies complained to Firuz Shah Tughluq and accused him of using a thousand poisonous words. According to Habib, the complaint could have been true: 'Barani as a writer is too fond of abusive phrases, many of which are only intelligible when translated literally from Persian into Plain Hindi. But while in the *Firuz Shahi* there is some literary flavour about his abuses, in the *Jahandari* they are merely coarse.' See Habib's *Politics and Society*, Vol. II, p. 420.

9. Shahid Amin, 'Alternative Histories: A View from India', SEPHIS—CSSSC lecture, Amsterdam/Kolkata, 2002, p. 7. Amin comments here on Mohammad Habib's Presidential Address, Indian History Congress, December 1947.

10. Habib, *Politics and Society*, Vol. II, pp. 422–23.

11. Ibid., Vol. II, p. 419.

12. *Tarikh-i-Firuz Shahi,* pp. 20–21.

13. Habib, *Politics and Society*, Vol. II, p. 421.

14. Ibid., Vol. II, p. 422, emphasis in the original.

15. Ibid., Vol. II, p. 429.

16. Defending the rule of the Sultan, Imam Ghazali wrote that the decline of the caliphate did not mean that the people should stop obeying the law, dismiss the qazis (jurists), declare all authority to be valueless and pronounce the acts of those in high places to be invalid.

He clarified that the office of government in different regions in this case, would be legally executed by Sultans who professed allegiance to the caliph by mentioning the latter's name in the khutba (sermons) and the sikka (coins), and in whose name they would maintain stability and order. Ghazali also recommended support for and submission to unjust and ignorant rulers, as attempts to depose them could prove counter-productive. Further, Ghazali also effected a fusion of the Islamic ethic and Sassanian norms of governance. For a detailed exposition of Ghazali's views on good governance, see F.R.C. Bagley, *Ghazali's Book of Counsel for Kings* (Oxford: Oxford University Press, 1964). The noted historian, Ibn Khaldun, has also defended the transformation of the caliphate into kingship for he felt the qualities of the caliphate survived in the preference for Islam and its ways, and adherence to the path of truth. See A.K.S. Lambton, *State and Government in Medieval Islam: An Introduction to the Study of Islamic Political Theory* (Oxford: Oxford University Press, 1981), p. 173. For Ibn Khaldun's life and works, see also M. Talbi, 'Ibn Khaldun', *Encyclopaedia of Islam*, New Edition, Vol. 3, pp. 825–31.

17. Like Ghazali, Nizam-ul-Mulk Tusi also attempted to combine something of the Islamic ideal with the Persian notion of the ideal ruler; see Nizam-ul-Mulk Tusi's, *The Book of Government or Rules for Kings, The Siyasat-nama* or *Siyar al-Muluk* of *Nizam-ul-Mulk*, translated from the Persian by Hubert Darke (London: Routledge & Kegan Paul, 1960).

18. Habib and Khan, *Political Theory*, p. 28.

19. M. Habib, 'The Campaigns of 'Alauddin Khalji Being the English translation of "*The Khaza'in-ul-Futuh*" of Amir Khusrau', reprinted in *Politics and Society*, Vol. II, pp. 149–270, esp. pp. 149, 152, 163 (n. 3).

20. Barani wrote that the noble, free-born, virtuous, religious, of high genealogy and pure birth are worthy of offices and posts in the government of the king. They alone are capable of virtues like kindness, generosity, valour, good deeds, truthfulness, keeping of promises, protection of other classes, loyalty, clarity of vision, justice, equity, recognition of rights, gratitude for favours received and fear of God, Habib and Khan, *Political Theory*, pp. 97–98.

21. For the author, the low-born who practise baser arts and meaner professions are capable only of vices such as immodesty, falsehood, miserliness, misappropriation, wrongfulness, lies, evil-speaking,

ingratitude, dirtiness, injustice, cruelty, non-recognition of rights, shamelessness, impudence, blood-shedding, rascality, jugglery and Godlessness, Habib and Khan, *Political Theory*, p. 98.

22. Ibid., p. 97.

23. Habib, *Politics and Society*, Vol. II, pp. 419–20.

24. Ibid., Vol. II, p. 420.

25. Ibid.

26. Ibid.

27. Ibid., Vol. II, p. 430.

28. *Siyar-ul-Auliya* of Amir Khwurd, p. 322.

29. Ibid., p. 323.

30. Ibid.

31. Ibid.

32. Habib, *Politics and Society*, Vol. II, p. 288.

33. Habib and Khan, *Political Theory*, p. 18, n.13.

34. For the Chishti Sufis' relations with the Sultans of Delhi, see chapter two of this book; also see two of my essays, 'Sufi Cults, Politics and Conversion' and 'Miracles, Authority and Benevolence'.

35. *Siyar-ul-Auliya*, p. 323.

36. Ibid.

37. For more on this, see chapter two of this book.

38. *Siyar-ul-Auliya*, p. 541.

39. Ibid.

40. Abdul Haqq Muhaddis Dehlawi, *Akhbar-ul-Akhyar*, translated into Urdu by Subhan Mahmud and Muhammad Fazil (Delhi: Adabi Duniya, 1990), p. 222.

41. Ibid., pp. 222–24.

42. Ibid., p. 225.

43. Habib, *Politics and Society*, Vol. II, p. 431.

44. Ibid.

45. Habib and Khan, *Political Theory*, pp. 5–6. Treating Sultan Mahmud as his 'hero', Barani addresses the later Sultans as Mahmud's sons and attributes many statements on good governance and the cause of Islam to the former. According to Habib, Barani knew little or nothing about the Sultan Mahmud of history. In fact, 'his ignorance is appalling. But Mahmud has to bear the whole burden of Barani's philosophy, though he would have repudiated it from A to Z'; from Habib, *Politics and Society*, Vol. II, pp. 420–21. It may be mentioned

here that Habib himself prepared a completely sanitized account of Mahmud's career and his Indian campaigns, first published in 1927 as a book and reprinted in *Politics and Society*, Vol. II, pp. 36–104. For a more insightful study, see Romila Thapar, *Somanatha: The Many Voices of a History* (Delhi: Viking, 2004).

46. Mukhia, *Historians and Historiography,* chapter one.

47. See chapter one of this book.

48. Habib and Khan, *Political Theory,* p. 43.

49. Ibid., pp. 43–44.

50. Ibid., p. 44.

51. Partha Chatterjee, 'Peasants, Politics and Historiography: A Response', *Social Scientist*, 11: 5 (May 1983), pp. 58–65.

52. Scanning a complex or unfamiliar scene, the individual tries to sort out simple and general categories rapidly in terms of images which fall into social stereotypes. On encountering a black or an Arab man on the street, a white person registers threat, and does not search for more visual codes. The judgment is instant and the results surprising; thanks to the classifying powers of what Roland Barthes termed 'image repertoire', people shut out further stimulation. Confronted with difference, they quickly become passive. By using an image repertoire to withdraw from others, the individual feels more at ease. For a discussion on these issues in a very different context of the city of New York, comprising all kinds of individuals and social groups, see Richard Sennett, *Flesh and Stone* (London: Faber and Faber, 1994), pp. 355–59, 365–66.

53. For the Chishti Sufis' attitude towards non-Muslims, see Aquil, 'Conversion in Chishti Sufi Literature'; also see, chapter two of this book.

54. Habib and Khan, *Political Theory,* p. 44.

55. Ibid., pp. 44–45.

56. Ibid., pp. 45–46.

57. Ibid., p. 46.

58. Friedmann, 'Islamic Thought', p. 52.

59. Habib and Khan, *Political Theory,* p. 46.

60. Ibid., pp. 46–47.

61. Cl. Cahen, 'Dhimma', *Encyclopaedia of Islam*, New Edition, Vol. 2, pp. 227–31.

62. Friedmann, 'Islamic Thought', pp. 52–53.

63. Ibid., p. 53.

64. Habib and Khan, *Political Theory,* p. 47.

65. Ibid.

66. Ibid.

67. Friedmann, 'Islamic Thought', p. 61.

68. Habib and Khan, *Political Theory,* p. 48.

69. Ibid.

70. The uncut forelocks restriction refers to a hair-style considered fashionable among well-groomed Arab men, which derived from the practice among the descendants of the Prophet to maintain their hair long. Therefore, the restriction ensured that a non-Muslim would not pass off as a respectable Muslim gentleman.

71. See chapter four of this book.

72. *Muntakhabu't-Tawarikh, by 'Abdu'l-Qadir ibn i Muluk Shah known as Al-Badaoni*, Vol. II: 'The Reign of Akbar, from 963 to 104 AH', translated into English by W.H. Lowe, first published 1899 (Delhi: Idarah-i Adabiyat-i Delli, 1973), p. 227.

73. F. Steingass, *A Comprehensive Persian–English Dictionary* (New Delhi: Munshiram Manoharlal, 1996), pp. 899–900.

74. *Muntakhab-ut-Tawarikh* of Badauni, Vol. II, p. 227, n. 5.

75. Ibid., Vol. II, p. 228.

76. Cahen, 'Dhimma'.

77. For more on the duties of the muhtasibs, see chapter five of this book.

78. Habib and Khan, *Political Theory,* p. 48.

79. Ibid., pp. 39–40. For a criticism of Barani's view that the shariat cannot be implemented as the rule of law, see Syed Sabahuddin Abdur Rahman, *Hindustan ke Salatin, Ulama aur Mashaikh ke Talluqat par ek Nazr* (Azamgarh: Darul Musannefin, 1964), p. 37.

80. See chapter one of this book.

81. *Fawa'id-ul-Fu'ad*, Vol. IV, Fortieth Meeting.

82. Habib and Khan, *Political Theory,* pp. 48–49.

83. *Fawa'id-ul-Fu'ad*, Vol. II, Twenty-third Meeting.

84. Eaton, 'Temple Desecration and Indo-Muslim States'.

85. See Aquil, *Sufism, Culture, and Politics*, chapter four.

86. Eleanor Zelliot, 'A Medieval Encounter Between Hindu and Muslim', pp. 64–82.

87. *Fawa'id-ul-Fu'ad*, Vol. IV, Fortieth Meeting.

Chapter 4: Islam and Heresies in Mughal India

1. *Muntakhab-ut-Tawarikh* of Mulla Abdul Qadir Badauni, Persian text edited by Maulavi Ahmad Ali, Kabir al-Din Ahmad and W. Nassau Lees, Vols. I–III (Calcutta: Bibliotheca Indica, 1865); *Muntakhabu't-Tawarikh*, by 'Abdu'l-Qadir ibn i Muluk Shah known as Al-Badaoni, Vol. II, 'The Reign of Akbar, from 963 to 1004 A.H.', translated into English by W.H. Lowe, first published 1899 (Delhi: Idarah-i Adabiyat-i Delli, 1973). [Hereafter, Badauni, *Muntakhab-ut-Tawarikh*, II, Persian text; Eng. Trans.]. For an early assessment of *Muntakhab-ut-Tawarikh* as a historical text, see Mukhia, *Historians and Historiography*.

2. See Abul Fazl's *Akbarnama*, English translation by H. Beveridge, Vols. I–III (Delhi: Rare Books, 1972–73, reprint) and his *Ain-i-Akbari*, English translation by H. Blochmann (Vol. I) and H.S. Jarrett (Vols. II and III) (Delhi: Oriental Reprint, 1977–78, reprint).

3. Like that of Ziya-ud-Din Barani, as noted in chapter three earlier, Badauni's political commitments and intellectual contributions await a proper examination. For an earlier attempt, see Fauzia Zareen Abbas, *Abdul Qadir Badauni as a Man and Historiographer* (Delhi: Idarah-i Adabiyat-i Delli, 1987). Also see Mukhia, *Historians and Historiography.*

4. Badauni records that the construction of the ibadat-khana, consisting of four halls, had begun near the new palace at Fatehpur in the month of *Zil Qad*, A.H. 982 (1574–75), after the emperor returned from his journey to Ajmer. See Badauni, *Muntakhab-ut-Tawarikh*, II, Persian text, p. 198; Eng. Trans., p. 200.

5. Badauni, *Muntakhab-ut-Tawarikh*, II, Persian text, p. 198; Eng. Trans., pp. 200–01.

6. Quran, II, verse 256. Though the numerical value of the letters in the words included in the *ayat-ul-kursi*, '*Tafsir-i-Akbari*', that is, 'Commentary of Akbar's Time', gives the date of composition as AH 983, Badauni mentions this in his account of the previous year, that is, AH 982.

7. Badauni, *Muntakhab-ut-Tawarikh*, II, Persian text, p. 198; Eng. Trans., p. 201.

8. Ibid., II, Persian text, pp. 198–99; Eng. Trans., p. 201. Badauni himself was sympathetic towards the Mahdawis and respected Sheikh Mubarak Nagauri enough to commemorate his death with the phrase, 'The Perfect Sheikh', despite the fact that the sheikh was

the originator of the idea of the superiority of the *imam-i-adil* (the just leader), that is, Akbar, over the ulama and had also drafted the controversial document of 1579, as we shall further see below. Also see Muhammad Mujeeb, 'Badauni', in Hasan (ed.), *Historians of Medieval India*, pp. 107–08. For the millenarian movement of the Mahdawis, also see Qamaruddin, *The Mahdawi Movement in India* (Delhi: Idarah-i-Adabiyat-i Delli, 1985).

9. Badauni, *Muntakhab-ut-Tawarikh*, II, Persian text, p. 199; Eng. Trans., p. 202.

10. Ibid.

11. Ibid., II, Persian text, p. 200; Eng. Trans., pp. 202–03. Muhammad Mujeeb observes that 'Badauni is vexed enough to lose his balance, and he touches the depths of meanness in the aspersions he casts on Faizi and Abul Fazl, his benefactors throughout his career at the court. But he was not really mean.' See Mujeeb, 'Badauni', p. 109.

12. Badauni, *Muntakhab-ut-Tawarikh*, II, Persian text, p. 206; Eng. Trans., p. 209. Badauni was appointed *imam* within a year of his introduction to the court, that is 1574–75, and was expected to lead the prayers on Wednesdays. Thus, he had to be present, like the imams of the other six days, at the five daily prayers. Badauni, apparently, did not like the job. The *imamat* was eventually abolished in 1579, though Badauni retained his revenue-free grants with some deductions as we shall see later. Also see Abbas, *Abdul Qadir Badauni,* pp. 48, 64.

13. Badauni, *Muntakhab-ut-Tawarikh*, II, Persian text, p. 209.

14. Ibid., II, Persian text, pp. 206–07; Eng. Trans., p. 210.

15. Ibid., II, Persian text, p. 200; Eng. Trans., p. 203.

16. Badauni himself was a student of Abdullah Niyazi and had taken lessons from him in Imam Ghazali's *Ihya Ulum al-Din*. For an account of the early life and education of Badauni, see Abbas, *Abdul Qadir Badauni*, pp. 24–42. For Ghazali's influence on traditional Muslim scholarship in Mughal India, see chapter five of this book. Also see the concluding chapter of this book, for a discussion on Ghazali's role in combating Greek-inspired rationalist scholarship in the Abbasid Caliphate.

17. Badauni, *Muntakhab-ut-Tawarikh*, II, Persian text, pp. 200–01; Eng. Trans., p. 204.

18. Ibid., II, Persian text, p. 201; Eng. Trans., p. 204.

19. Ibid., II, Persian text, p. 202; Eng. Trans., pp. 204–05.

20. Ibid., II, Persian text, p. 202; Eng. Trans., p. 205.

21. Ibid.

22. Ibid., II, Persian text, pp. 202–03; Eng. Trans., pp. 205–06.

23. Quran, LXXXVI, verse 9.

24. Badauni, *Muntakhab-ut-Tawarikh*, II, Persian text, pp. 203–04; Eng. Trans., p. 206.

25. Ibid., II, Persian text, p. 204; Eng. Trans., pp. 206–07.

26. Ibid., II, Persian text, p. 204; Eng. Trans., p. 207.

27. Ibid., II, Persian text, pp. 204–05; Eng. Trans., pp. 207–08.

28. Ibid., II, Persian text, p. 205; Eng. Trans., p. 208.

29. Ibid., II, Persian text, pp. 205–06; Eng. Trans., p. 208.

30. Ibid.

31. Quran, IV, verse 3.

32. Badauni, *Muntakhab-ut-Tawarikh*, II, Persian text, pp. 207–08; Eng. Trans., p. 211.

33. Ibid., II, Persian text, p. 208; Eng. Trans., p. 211.

34. Ibid., II, Persian text, p. 208; Eng. Trans., pp. 211–12.

35. Ibid., II, Persian text, p. 208; Eng. Trans., p. 212.

36. Ibid., II, Persian text, pp. 208–09; Eng. Trans., p. 212.

37. Ibid., II, Persian text, p. 209; Eng. Trans., p. 213.

38. Ibid., II, Persian text, pp. 209–10; Eng. Trans., p. 213.

39. Ibid., II, Persian text, p. 210; Eng. Trans., p. 213.

40. Ibid.

41. Ibid., II, Persian text, pp. 210–11; Eng. Trans., p. 214.

42. Ibid., II, Persian text, p. 211; Eng. Trans., p. 214.

43. For an interesting account of the jokester Birbal fooling around Akbar's court and the riposte of his competitors, and for an important analysis of the 'communal' or political contents in the witty stories, see C.M. Naim's 'Popular Jokes and Political History: The Case of Akbar, Birbal, and Mulla Do-Piyaza', in Naim's *Urdu Texts and Contexts* (Delhi: Permanent Black, 2004), pp. 225–49. Naim suggests not to view the 'jokes too closely in the perspective of our contemporary concerns or lose sight of their diverse generic identities' (Ibid., p. 249).

44. Badauni, *Muntakhab-ut-Tawarikh*, II, Persian text, p. 211; Eng. Trans., p. 214. Noting that Badauni was 'orthodox, but not insensitive or narrow-minded', Mujeeb writes that the author's criticism of Akbar's

favourites and his reform should not be dismissed as 'deriving from fanaticism, ingratitude or sheer perversity'. Badauni 'utilized his command over language to vent his spleen on those who were impudent and supercilious in their attitude towards the *shariat* and who ultimately succeeded in eradicating all reverence for it from the heart of the emperor.' See Mujeeb, 'Badauni', pp. 107–09.

45. Badauni, *Muntakhab-ut-Tawarikh*, II, Persian text, p. 211; Eng. Trans., p. 215. *Surah Baqra* or the Cow: this is actually the second surah, but the first one is only a *fatiha* (introduction), so the raja's remark was not entirely out of place.

46. Ibid., II, Persian text, pp. 211–12; Eng. Trans., p. 215.

47. Ibid., II, Persian text, p. 212; Eng. Trans., pp. 215–16.

48. Ibid., II, Persian text, pp. 212–13; Eng. Trans., p. 216.

49. For an appreciative account of the project of translations of Hindu scriptures and other classical texts, see M. Athar Ali, 'Translations of Sanskrit Works at Akbar's Court', in his *Mughal India: Studies in Polity, Ideas, Society, and Culture* (New Delhi: Oxford University Press, 2006), pp. 173–82.

50. Badauni, *Muntakhab-ut-Tawarikh*, II, Persian text, p. 227; Eng. Trans., p. 232.

51. Ibid., II, Persian text, p. 227; Eng. Trans., pp. 232–33.

52. Ibid., II, Persian text, p. 251; Eng. Trans., p. 258.

53. Ibid., II, Persian text, p. 254; Eng. Trans., p. 262.

54. Ibid., II, Persian text, p. 253; Eng. Trans., p. 260.

55. Compare this view with K.A. Nizami, *Akbar and Religion* (Delhi: Idarah-i-Adabiyat-i Delli, 1989).

56. Badauni, *Muntakhab-ut-Tawarikh*, II, Persian text, p. 288; Eng. Trans., p. 297.

57. Ibid., II, Persian text, p. 255; Eng. Trans., p. 262.

58. Ibid.

59. Ibid., II, Persian text, p. 255; Eng. Trans., pp. 262–63.

60. Ibid., II, Persian text, p. 255; Eng. Trans., p. 263. As Mujeeb has noted, Badauni seems to have felt that 'while the *ulama* could not be defended' and a liberalization of Muslim way of life was essential; 'respect for the *shariat* must be maintained at all costs'. Also, if advocacy for the shariat is viewed only as an attitude of reverence for God, the Prophet and revelation, then Badauni actually 'allowed himself and would allow to others latitude for difference of opinion and for living

as one liked' (Mujeeb, 'Badauni', pp. 109, 112).

61. Badauni, *Muntakhab-ut-Tawarikh*, II, Persian text, p. 256; Eng. Trans., p. 263. Also see in this context, Kumkum Sangari's exhaustive article, 'Tracing Akbar: Hagiographies, popular narrative traditions, and the subject of conversion', in Neera Chandoke (ed.), *Mapping Histories: Essays Presented to Ravinder Kumar* (New Delhi: Tulika, 1999).

62. Badauni, *Muntakhab-ut-Tawarikh*, II, Persian text, p. 256; Eng. Trans., pp. 263–64.

63. Ibid., II, Persian text, p. 257; Eng. Trans., p. 264.

64. Ibid.

65. Mulla Muhammad of Yazd, too, was drawn up the wall of the fort in the same way. See Ibid., p. 259; Eng. Trans., p. 267.

66. Ibid., II, Persian text, p. 257; Eng. Trans., p. 265.

67. Ibid., II, Persian text, p. 258; Eng. Trans., p. 265.

68. Ibid.

69. Ibid., II, Persian text, p. 258; Eng. Trans., pp. 265–66.

70. For more on traditional Sufism in Indian history, see chapters two and seven of this book.

71. Badauni, *Muntakhab-ut-Tawarikh*, II, Persian text, p. 258; Eng. Trans., p. 266.

72. Ibid., II, Persian text, pp. 258–59; Eng. Trans., p. 266.

73. Ibid., II, Persian text, pp. 259; Eng. Trans., p. 267.

74. Ibid., II, Persian text, p. 260; Eng. Trans., p. 267.

75. Ibid., II, Persian text, p. 260; Eng. Trans., p. 268.

76. For more on this, see Sangari, 'Tracing Akbar'.

77. Badauni, *Muntakhab-ut-Tawarikh*, II, Persian text, p. 260; Eng. Trans., p. 268.

78. Ibid., II, Persian text, pp. 260–61; Eng. Trans., p. 268.

79. Ibid., II, Persian text, p. 261; Eng. Trans., pp. 268–69.

80. Ibid., II, Persian text, p. 261; Eng. Trans., p. 269.

81. Ibid., II, Persian text, p. 262; Eng. Trans., p. 269.

82. Ibid., II, Persian text, p. 262; Eng. Trans., pp. 269–70.

83. Ibid., II, Persian text, p. 263; Eng. Trans., pp. 270–71.

84. Ibid., II, Persian text, p. 263; Eng. Trans., p. 271.

85. Ibid., II, Persian text, p. 272; Eng. Trans., p. 280.

86. Ibid., II, Persian text, pp. 263–64; Eng. Trans., p. 271.

87. Badauni, *Muntakhab-ut-Tawarikh*, II, Eng. Trans., p. 275.

88. Badauni, *Muntakhab-ut-Tawarikh*, II, Persian text, p. 251.

89. Badauni, *Muntakhab-ut-Tawarikh*, II, Persian text, p. 268; Eng. Trans., p. 276.

90. Ibid., II, Persian text, p. 268; Eng. Trans., pp. 276–77.

91. Ibid., II, Persian text, p. 268; Eng. Trans., p. 277.

92. Ibid., II, Persian text, p. 269; Eng. Trans., p. 277.

93. Ibid., II, Persian text, p. 270; Eng. Trans., p. 278.

94. According to Badauni, the draft of the mahzar, when presented to the emperor, was in Abul Fazl's father, Sheikh Mubarak's handwriting. Though the others had reportedly signed against their will, the sheikh had added at the bottom of the page that he had signed his name willingly; for this was a matter which he had been anxiously looking forward to for several years. See Ibid., pp. 270, 272; Eng. Trans., pp. 278–80.

95. Ibid., II, Persian text, pp. 271–72; Eng. Trans., pp. 279–80. For a study of this document, see S. Nurul Hasan, 'The *Mahzar* of Akbar's Reign', in his *Religion, State, and Society in Medieval India*, edited and introduced by Satish Chandra (New Delhi: Oxford University Press, 2005), pp. 79–89.

96. Nurul Hasan, 'The *Mahzar* of Akbar's Reign', pp. 80–81.

97. In Nurul Hasan's opinion, 'This document is an enunciation of the religious policy of the Mughals vis-à-vis those of the Safavids, Uzbegs or the Ottomans. It released the Mughal empire from the shackles of sectarianism. The Mughal empire, being more liberal and cultured in its outlook, began to have an attractiveness for the intellectuals and freedom-loving people throughout the world of Islam' (Hasan, 'The *Mahzar* of Akbar's Reign', pp. 85–86).

98. Badauni, *Muntakhab-ut-Tawarikh*, II, Persian text, p. 272; Eng. Trans., p. 280. Characterizing the mahzar of 1579 as Akbar's attempt at the 'appeasement of Muslim orthodoxy', M. Athar Ali writes that the 'authority assigned to him was of marginal import, and yet a novelty considered dangerous in its implication by traditionalist Muslims'. Also 'Akbar's immediate attempt to take it seriously, and to abide by his newly gained religious status among Muslims by giving a Friday sermon, failed to enthuse either himself, or, apparently his audience.' See M. Athar Ali, 'Sulh-i Kul and the Religious Ideas of Akbar', in his *Mughal India*, pp. 158–72, especially p. 160.

99. Badauni, *Muntakhab-ut-Tawarikh*, II, Persian text, p. 272; Eng. Trans., pp. 280–81.

100. Ibid., II, Persian text, pp. 273–74; Eng. Trans., pp. 281–82.
101. Ibid., II, Persian text, p. 274; Eng. Trans., p. 282.
102. Ibid., II, Persian text, p. 275–76; Eng. Trans., pp. 283–84.
103. Ibid., II, Persian text, p. 276; Eng. Trans., p. 284.
104. Ibid., II, Persian text, p. 275; Eng. Trans., p. 283.
105. Ibid., II, Persian text, p. 276; Eng. Trans., p. 284.
106. Ibid., II, Persian text, pp. 276–78; Eng. Trans., pp. 284–86.
107. Ibid., II, Persian text, pp. 278–79; Eng. Trans., pp. 286–87.
108. Ibid., II, Persian text, p. 279; Eng. Trans., p. 287.
109. Ibid., II, Persian text, p. 285; Eng. Trans., p. 293.
110. Ibid., II, Persian text, p. 286; Eng. Trans., p. 294.
111. Ibid., II, Persian text, pp. 286–87; Eng. Trans., p. 295.
112. Ibid., II, Persian text, p. 287; Eng. Trans., p. 295.

113. For instance, Athar Ali writes, 'Given India's variegated culture and multiplicity of religious beliefs, what Akbar was attempting to secure was an integrated ruling class. That he also thereby took a step which could later on be invoked by India's modern nation-builders is not only a tribute to the breadth of his vision, but also an illustration of the way in which historical processes occur achieving ends which in earlier times would have been only dimly grasped, or would perhaps have remained totally undiscerned' (Athar Ali, 'Sulh-i Kul and the Religious Ideas of Akbar', pp. 169–70). The above remark is typical of a set of celebratory literature that highlights Akbar's greatness.

114. See Iqtidar Alam Khan, 'Akbar's Personality Traits and World Outlook—A Critical Appraisal', in Irfan Habib (ed.), *Akbar and His India* (New Delhi: Oxford University Press, 1997), pp. 79–96.

115. The ghastly murder has been discussed by Kesavdas, the leading Brajbhasa poet at the Bundela court, in his *Virsinghdevcharit* (Life of Bir Singh Deo). Kesavdas also wrote a celebratory account of Jahangir's career, *Jahangiryashchandrika* (Moonlight of the fame of Jahangir). For an important study of Kesavdas's work, including the embarrassing account of Abul Fazl's horrific execution, see Allison Busch, 'Literary Responses to the Mughal Imperium: The Historical Poems of Kesavdas', *South Asia Research*, 25: 1 (2005), pp. 31–54.

116. For a re-evaluation of Jahangir's reign—including the role of Islam and Timurid legacies regarding questions of sovereignty and his conscious cultivation of the image of a naturalist and aesthetic-cum-collector of *memorabilia*—see Corinne Lefevre, 'Recovering a Missing

Voice from Mughal India: The Imperial Discourse of Jahangir (r. 1605–1627) in his Memoirs', *Journal of the Economic and Social History of the Orient*, 50: 4 (2007), pp. 452–89.

Chapter 5: Recommending Right and Forbidding Wrong

1. Abdul Haqq Muhaddis Dehlawi, *Adab-us-Salihin* (titled *Uswat-us-Salihin*), translated from the original Persian into Urdu by Abdur Rahman Jami (Delhi: Adabi Duniya, 2006). [Hereafter Dehlawi, *Adab-us-Salihin*].

2. For a biography in Urdu, see Khaliq Ahmad Nizami, *Hayat-e Sheikh Abdul Haqq Muhaddis Dehlawi* (Delhi: Nadwatul Musannefin, 1953).

3. For a list of his works and related details, see C.A. Storey, *Persian Literature: A Bio-Bibliographical Survey*, Vol. I, Part I (London: Luzac, 1970), pp. 181, 194–95, 214, 427–28, 440–41, 978–79.

4. Mohammad Shafi writes that on his return from Hijaz, Abdul Haqq taught for half a century in Delhi. He won Jahangir's (who praises him in his *Tuzuk-i-Jahangiri*) and Shah Jahan's favour. See 'Abd al-Hakk B. Sayf al-Din', *Encyclopaedia of Islam*, New Edition, Vol. I (Leiden: Brill, 1986), pp. 60–61.

5. Nizami, *Hayat-e Sheikh Abdul Haqq*, pp. 241–44.

6. Ibid., pp. 246–47.

7. For Badauni's profile of Abdul Haqq, see Badauni's *Muntakhab-ut-Tawarikh*, edited by Maulavi Ahmad Ali, Vol. III (Calcutta: Bibliotheca Indica, 1869), pp. 113–17.

8. Nizami, *Hayat-e Sheikh Abdul Haqq*, pp. 223–25.

9. See chapter four of this book for a discussion on the debates under Akbar. For a brief discussion on Aurangzeb, see chapter six. Also see, chapter one for some of the important issues concerning the rule of the two emperors. For Jahangir, see Lefevre's upcoming work, including 'Recovering a Missing Voice from Mughal India'. For a richly illustrated general work on Shah Jahan and his grand architectural legacies, see Kobita Sarker, *Shah Jahan and his Paradise on Earth: The Story of Shah Jahan's Creations in Agra and Shahjahanabad in the Golden Days of the Mughals* (Kolkata: K.P. Bagchi, 2007).

10. Dehlawi, *Adab-us-Salihin*, pp. 9–10. For the adab/akhlaq

distinction in the realm of politics, see chapter one of this book; also see Muzaffar Alam's important work, *Languages of Political Islam*.

11. See Imam Ghazali, *Ihya Ulum-id-din*, translated into English by Maulana Fazlul Karim, Vols. I–IV (Delhi: Kitab Bhavan, 1982); see especially the chapter on 'Enjoining Good and Forbidding Evil', Vol. II, pp. 225–58.

12. For details of extant manuscripts and printed editions, see Nizami, *Hayat-e Sheikh Abdul Haqq*, pp. 187–88.

13. Dehlawi, *Adab-us-Salihin*, pp. 209–10; Ghazali, *Ihya Ulum-id-din*, Vol. II, p. 225.

14. For an over-emphasized formulation of the militaristic nature of jihad aimed at the expansion of Islam and, if need be, of its defence, see E. Tyan, 'Djihad', *Encyclopaedia of Islam*, New Edition, Vol. II, pp. 538–40.

15. Dehlwai, *Adab-us-Salihin*, p. 210.

16. Ibid., pp. 210–11.

17. Ghazali, *Ihya Ulum-id-din*, Vol. II, p. 229.

18. Dehlawi, *Adab-us-Salihin*, p. 211.

19. Ibid., p. 211; Ghazali, *Ihya Ulum-id-din*, Vol. II, p. 230.

20. Dehlawi, *Adab-us-Salihin*, p. 211; Ghazali, *Ihya Ulum-id-din*, Vol. II, p. 230.

21. Dehlawi, *Adab-us-Salihin*, p. 211.

22. Ibid., pp. 211–12. Ghazali quotes the fourth caliph, Ali, as saying: 'The jihad which begins before you are jihads of your hands and then the jihads of your tongue and then the jihad of your heart' (Ghazali, *Ihya Ulum-id-din*, Vol. II, p. 232).

23. Dehlawi, *Adab-us-Salihin*, p. 212.

24. Ibid., p. 212.

25. Ibid.

26. Ibid.

27. Ghazali, *Ihya Ulum-id-din*, Vol. II, p. 232.

28. For a discussion on the legitimacy of forms of music in Sufi circles of the Delhi Sultanate, see chapter two of this book.

29. Dehlawi, *Adab-us-Salihin*, p. 213.

30. For relevant discussion and references, see Aquil, *Sufism, Culture, and Politics*, chapter three.

31. For justice, see Linda Darling, '"Do Justice, Do Justice, For That is Paradise"'.

32. Dehlawi, *Adab-us-Salihin*, p. 213.

33. Ghazali, *Ihya Ulum-id-din*, Vol. II, pp. 232–33.
34. Dehlawi, *Adab-us-Salihin*, pp. 213–14.
35. Ibid., p. 214.
36. Ibid.
37. See chapter one of this book.
38. Dehlawi, *Adab-us-Salihin*, pp. 215–18.
39. Ibid., pp. 218–19.
40. Ibid., p. 220.
41. Ibid., pp. 220–25.
42. Ibid., pp. 225–26.
43. Ghazali, *Ihya Ulum-id-din*, Vol. II, p. 233.
44. Dehlawi, *Adab-us-Salihin*, p. 226.
45. For more on this, see the concluding chapter of this book.
46. Ghazali, *Ihya Ulum-id-din*, Vol. II, p. 243.
47. Ibid., Vol. II, p. 258.
48. M. Cook, 'Al-Nahy an al-Munkar', *Encyclopaedia of Islam*, New Edition, Vol. XII, Supplement (Leiden: Brill, 2004), pp. 644–46.
49. Ghazali, *Ihya Ulum-id-din*, Vol. II, p. 236.
50. Dehlawi, *Adab-us-Salihin*, p. 228. Abdul Haqq's exposition here is much more elaborate, compared to Ghazali's listing of the four conditions for the prevention of evil; Ghazali, *Ihya Ulum-id-din*, Vol. II, pp. 236–37.
51. Dehlawi, *Adab-us-Salihin*, pp. 231–32.
52. Ibid., p. 231.
53. Ibid., pp. 229–30. For more on the matrix of difference within Islam, see the concluding chapter of this book.
54. Dehlawi, *Adab-us-Salihin*, p. 231.
55. Ibid., p. 232.
56. *Fawa'id-ul-Fu'ad*.
57. Dehlawi, *Adab-us-Salihin*, pp. 235–37.
58. Ibid., p. 237.
59. Ibid., p. 238. For Ghazali, the three qualifications for someone who is allowed to prevent wrong are: (i) knowledge that the act is wrong; (ii) fear of God; and (iii) good conduct; see Ghazali, *Ihya Ulum-id-din*, Vol. II, p. 240.
60. For a discussion on the dubious nature of such an ihtisab, see Dehlawi's *Adab-us-Salihin*, pp. 216–17.
61. For more on Ghazali, see the concluding chapter of this book.
62. Ghazali, *Ihya Ulum-id-din*, Vol. II, p. 240.

Chapter 6: Violating Norms of Conduct

1. Jafar Zatalli, *Zatal-nama (Kulliyat-i-Jafar Zatalli)*, edited by Rashid Hasan Khan (New Delhi: Anjuman Taraqqi Urdu (Hind), 2003) [hereafter *Zatal-nama*].

2. Rashid Hasan Khan, introduction to *Zatal-nama*.

3. Jamil Jalibi, *Tarikh Adab Urdu, Atharvin Sadi*, Vol. II, Part I (Delhi: Educational Publishing House, 1989), pp. 90–118.

4. For more on the *ghazal* see, Harbans Mukhia, 'The Celebration of Failure as Dissent in Urdu Ghazal', *Modern Asian Studies*, 33 (1999), pp. 861–81.

5. Khan-i-Arzu, in fact, trained two generations of Urdu poets—the first set comprised Anand Ram Mukhlis, Tek Chand Bahar, Abru, Mazmun and Yakrang; and the second set consisted of such stalwarts as Sauda, Mir and Dard. For a short profile of Arzu, see Mohammad Husain Azad, *Aab-e-Hayat* (Lucknow: Uttar Pradesh Urdu Academy, 1986), pp. 115–17. For a detailed account of Arzu's career as poet, scholar, critic, linguist and lexicographer, see Jalibi, *Tarikh Adab Urdu, Atharvin Sadi*, Vol. II, Part I, pp. 148–63.

6. For a study of the life and career of Wali Mohammad Dakani (died *c.* 1720–25), who enjoys the same status in Urdu poetry as Aristotle does for Logic and is hailed as the 'Baba Adam' of Urdu poetry, as well as the impact of his celebrated *diwan* in Deccani Urdu on the north Indian Urdu literary culture in the first half of the eighteenth century, see Azad, *Aab-e-Hayat*, pp. 83–91; see also Jalibi, *Tarikh Adab Urdu, Aghaz se 1750 tak*, Vol. I, pp. 529–57.

7. It may be kept in mind that Wali's diwan came to Delhi in 1720, seven years after Zatalli's death and quickly gained wide popularity; see Jalibi, *Tarikh Adab Urdu, Atharvin Sadi*, Vol. II, Part I, p. 187.

8. As Jamil Jalibi has pointed out, even though Jafar wrote in Persian, the dominance of Hindawi is clearly discernible in his compositions, both prose and poetry; see Jalibi, *Tarikh Adab Urdu,* Vol. II, Part I, pp. 100–01.

9. Ibid., p. 108.

10. For a brief discussion of an example of a late fifteenth- and early-sixteenth-century Sufi composition, see Aquil, *Sufism, Culture, and Politics*, chapter seven.

11. See for a discussion, Rashid Hasan Khan, 'Introduction', *Zatal-nama*, pp. 29–30.

12. See Rashid Hasan Khan, 'Introduction', *Zatal-nama*, pp. 31–44.

13. *Zatal-nama*, pp. 268–312.

14. Commenting on the extant records for seventeenth- and eighteenth-century Damascus, James Grehan notes the value of little educated authors, such as soldiers, who wrote in crude Arabic that closely approximates the idioms and vocabulary of street Arabic of the time. They had no scruples about mixing colloquial expressions, Turkish loan-words and other stylistic impurities into their straightforward prose, which sometimes has an almost conversational tone. By contrast, the official files of the Islamic courts maintained a decorous silence, even as linguistic skill, both oratorical and written, was very much a part of the refined and superior image that the ulama had cultivated for themselves. They produced most of the local literature and served as the leading arbiters in all matters of taste, etiquette, and religion. See James Grehan, 'The Mysterious Power of Words: Language, Law, and Culture in Ottoman Damascus (17th–18th Centuries)', *Journal of Social History*, 37: 4 (2004), pp. 991–1015.

15. Jalibi, *Tarikh Adab Urdu,* Vol. II, Part I, p. 91.

16. See '*hijw-e shahzada Muhammad Kam Bakhsh*' in *Zatal-nama*, p. 144.

17. Ibid., p. 146.

18. See '*hasb-e haal-e khwud gufta*', *Zatal-nama*, pp. 147.

19. Ibid., p. 148.

20. Ibid., pp. 147–48.

21. '*Gand marawwa nama (hijw-e bahadur shah awwal)*', *Zatal-nama*, pp. 149–51.

22. Ibid., p. 149.

23. For more on the celebration of *amrad-prasti* or pederastic love in late Mughal India, see C.M. Naim, 'Homosexual (Pederastic) Love in Pre-Modern Urdu Poetry', in his *Urdu Texts and Contexts*, pp. 19–41.

24. As in medieval India, medieval and early modern European societies also considered words to be a form of abuse that had just as serious consequences as physical violence—the tongue being worse than the sword. However, it was mainly women who were identified for their 'dangerous' talking, for using insulting words that wounded or hurt. See for a discussion, Dianne Hall, 'Words as Weapons: Speech, Violence, and Gender in Late Medieval Ireland', *Éire-Ireland*, 41: 1 (2006), pp. 122–141.

25. For more on the Mughal male's transition from the boy-hunting emperor Babur to a son-desiring macho man Akbar, as well as the privileging of the latter as the recommended ideal, see Ali Anooshahar, 'The King who would be Man: The Gender Roles of the Warrior King in Early Mughal History', *Journal of the Royal Asiatic Society*, 18 (2008), pp. 327–40. Also see Ruby Lal, *Domesticity and Power in the Early Mughal World* (Cambridge: Cambridge University Press, 2005). For a different take on questions of gender and masculinity in medieval India, built around many later narratives of the Padmini legend, see Ramya Sreenivasan's interesting new book, *The Many Lives of a Rajput Queen, Heroic Pasts in India, c. 1500–1900* (Delhi: Permanent Black, 2007).

26. Rashid Hasan Khan, 'Introduction' to *Zatal-nama*, pp. 14–16.

27. Jalibi citing *Tazkirah-i-Shorish* in *Tarikh Adab Urdu,* Vol. II, Part I, p. 118.

28. Rashid Hasan Khan, 'Introduction', *Zatal-nama*, p. 16.

29. *Zatal-nama*, pp. 220–23.

30. Grehan, 'The Mysterious Power of Words'.

31. *Zatal-nama*, pp. 149–51.

32. Ibid.

33. See chapter four of this book.

34. *Najat-ur-Rashid*, pp. 19–20, cited in Abbas, *Abdul Qadir Badauni*, p. 39.

35. For a huge collection of essays on contemporary sexualities, coming from a variety of counter-heteronormative strands, see Brinda Bose and Subhabrata Bhattacharyya (eds), *The Phobic and the Erotic: The Politics of Sexualities in Contemporary India* (London/New York/Calcutta: Seagull Books, 2007).

36. 'Introduction', in Bose and Bhattacharyya (eds), *The Phobic and the Erotic*, pp. ix–xxxii.

37. *Zatal-nama*, pp. 213–15.

38. Ibid., p. 215.

39. Ibid., pp. 164–65.

40. Ibid., p. 165.

41. Ibid., pp. 90–91.

42. As Grehan notes for the Ottoman Damascus, the ulama stood firmly behind the social hierarchy, counselling that followers should listen to leaders, worshippers to preachers, wives to husbands, slaves to

masters, and of course, children to parents. See Grehan, 'The Mysterious Power of Words'.

43. Hall, 'Words as Weapons'.

44. *Zatal-nama*, p. 180.

45. Grehan, 'The Mysterious Power of Words'.

46. *Zatal-nama*, p. 125.

47. Ibid., p. 126.

48. Ibid., pp. 125–36.

49. Ibid., p. 136.

50. Ibid., p. 133.

51. Ibid., p. 135.

52. Ibid., p. 61.

53. Ibid., pp. 137–39.

54. Ibid., p. 139.

55. Raziuddin Aquil, 'The Study of Islam and Indian History at the Darul Musannefin, Azamgarh' in Aquil and Chatterjee (eds), *History in the Vernacular*.

56. Abdur Rahman, *Hindustan ke Salatin, Ulama aur Mashaikh*, pp. 42–43.

57. Syed Sabahuddin Abdur Rahman, *Musalman Hukmaranon ki Mazhabi Rawadari*, Vol. III (Azamgarh: Darul Musannefin, 1984).

58. Little work has been done on Aurangzeb since the publication of M. Athar Ali's *The Mughal Nobility under Aurangzeb*, first published in 1966; but see Brown, 'Did Aurangzeb Ban Music?'.

59. Seema Alavi (ed.), *The Eighteenth Century in India* (New Delhi: Oxford University Press, 2002); P.J. Marshall (ed.), *The Eighteenth Century in Indian History, Evolution or Revolution?* (New Delhi: Oxford University Press, 2003).

60. Syed Jamaluddin, 'Bazm ke Mua'rrikh', in *Tarikh Nigari: Qadim wa Jadid Rujhanat* (Delhi: Maktaba Jamia, 1994).

61. Rashid Hasan Khan, '*tamhid*' or introductory note on '*akhbarat-e siyaha-e darbar-e mualla*', *Zatal-nama*, pp. 55–56.

62. See for other contexts, Hall, 'Words as Weapons'; and Grehan, 'The Mysterious Power of Words'.

63. *Zatal-nama*, p. 59.

64. Ibid., p. 75.

65. Ibid., pp. 131, 135, 165, 180–81.

66. Ibid., p. 70.

67. Ibid.

68. Ibid., p. 85.

69. As Jamil Jalibi has noted, the impact of Jafar's style and subjects can be clearly seen in the compositions of the major Urdu satirist, Sauda. Jafar's oeuvre is also comparable to the *shahr-e ashob*, the poetry of decline; see Jalibi, *Tarikh Adab Urdu,* Vol. II, Part I, pp. 108, 115.

70. Zahiruddin Malik, 'Persian Historiography in India During the 18th Century', in Hasan (ed.), *Historians of Medieval India*, pp. 142–55, especially p. 146. Also see, Muhammad Umar, 'A Comparative Study of the Historical Approach of Muhammad Qasim and Khafi Khan', in Hasan, ed., *Historians of Medieval India*, pp. 156–64, in which both Muhammad Qasim and Khafi Khan are shown to have examined the factors leading to the eighteenth-century decay in Mughal power and authority—court factionalism is identified as the main cause.

71. Malik, 'Persian Historiography in India During the 18th Century', p. 147.

72. Ibid.

73. On reports and positions taken by historians concerning the conflict between Farrukh-Siyar and the Sayyid brothers, see Malik, 'Persian Historiography in India During the 18th Century', pp. 149–51. Also see Ghulam Husain Tabatabai's commentary on this, in Partha Chatterjee, 'The Early Modern and Colonial Modern in South Asia'; Raziuddin Aquil, 'Man of the Moment: The Intellectual Trajectory of a Persianate Mughal Gentleman in an Era of Transition, Ghulam Husain Tabatabai and his *Sair-ul-Muta'akhkhirin*', Seminar on *Arabic and Persian Studies in Bengal: Peace as Value in Literature*, organized by the Department of Arabic and Persian, University of Calcutta, in collaboration with the Asiatic Society, Kolkata, 20–22 March 2006.

74. *Zatal-nama*, p. 207.

75. Ibid., p. 210.

76. Ibid., p. 211.

77. Ibid., pp. 216–19.

78. Ibid., p. 121.

79. Ibid.

80. Ibid.

81. For a miniscule community under pressure resorting to concealment of its faith to protect itself, see Dominique-Sila Khan and Zawahir Moir, 'Coexistence and Communalism: The Shrine of Pirana

in Gujarat', in Asim Roy (ed.), *Islam in History and Politics: Perspectives from South Asia* (New Delhi: Oxford University Press, 2006), pp. 147–69.

82. See chapter four of this book.

83. *Zatal-nama*, p. 113.

Chapter 7: The Sufi-Bhakti Milieu: Later Transformations

1. Aquil, *Sufism, Culture and Politics,* chapter six. Also see chapter two of this book.

2. J.S. Grewal, *Sikh Ideology, Polity and Social Order* (New Delhi: Manohar, 1996), pp. 1–6.

3. W.H. McLeod, *Guru Nanak and the Sikh Religion*, first published in 1968 (New Delhi: Oxford University Press, 1998).

4. Aziz Ahmad, *Studies in Islamic Culture in the Indian Environment*, pp. 152–55.

5. For this reference, see Anne Murphey's important study of the early-eighteenth-century text, *Sri Guru Shobha* or the 'Splendor of the Guru' by Sainapati, 'History in the Sikh Past', *History and Theory*, 46 (October 2007), pp. 345–65.

6. J.S. Grewal, *The Sikhs of the Punjab* (Cambridge: Cambridge University Press, 1990), pp. 60–61.

7. J.S. Grewal (ed.), *The Khalsa: Sikh and Non-Sikh Perspectives* (Delhi: Manohar, 2004).

8. Ibid. For a more synthetic reading of one text in the context of the larger debates on history and literature in pre-modern or early modern India, see Murphey, 'History in the Sikh Past'.

9. Grewal (ed.), *The Khalsa*. One is also reminded here of Tony Ballantyne's critique of existing Sikh studies and his appeal to shift the focus from the dictates of the Panth to be able to engage with the broader debates in the humanities and social sciences. One of his early works is being cited here, 'Framing the Sikh Past', *International Journal of Punjab Studies,* 10: 1–2 (2003), pp. 1–23.

10. For more details on Baba Farid, see Raziuddin Aquil, 'Episodes from the Life of Shaikh Farid-ud-Din Ganj-i-Shakar', pp. 25–46. A separate work by this author on Baba Farid's verses included in the *Guru Granth Saheb* is underway. Also see, Richard M. Eaton, 'The Political and Religious Authority of the Shrine of Baba Farid', in Eaton (ed.), *India's Islamic Traditions, 711–1750*, pp. 263–68.

11. For a discussion on Mughal–Sikh relations in the early eighteenth century, see Muzaffar Alam, *Crisis of Empire in Mughal North India, Awadh and Punjab, 1707–48* (New Delhi: Manohar, 1986).

12. W.H. McLeod, 'Sikhs and Muslims in the Punjab', in Roy (ed.), *Islam in History and Politics*, pp. 170–80.

13. For a continued support to this position, see McLeod, *Guru Nanak and the Sikh Religion*, p. 10.

14. *Siyar-ul-Muta'khkhirin* by Ghulam Husain Tabatabai. Vols. I–III (Lucknow: Munshi Newal Kishore, AH 1248).

15. Partha Chatterjee, 'The Early Modern and Colonial Modern in South Asia'. Also see, Raziuddin Aquil, 'Man of the Moment'.

16. For a biography in Urdu, see S.M. Shahbaz, *Zindagani Be-Nazir*, edited by S.M. Hasnain (New Delhi: Taraqqi Urdu Bureau, 1981).

17. See *Kulliyat-i-Nazir Akbarabadi* (Lucknow: Munshi Newal Kishore, AH 1291).

18. Aquil, 'Episodes from the Life of Shaikh Farid-ud-Din Ganj-i-Shakar'.

19. Maulvi Muhammad Husain Azad, *Qisas-i-Hind* (Lahore, Majlis Taraqqi Adab, 1961).

20. For a discussion of this issue, see chapter four.

21. McLeod, *Guru Nanak and the Sikh Religion,* p. 38.

22. Mohammad Iqbal, *Kulliyat-i-Iqbal* (Delhi: Markazi Maktaba Islami, 2001).

23. For a fuller treatment of the theme, see Raziuddin Aquil, '"*Sab sis nuwa ardas karo, aur har dam bolo wah guru*": Celebrations of Guru Nanak's Career in Classical Urdu Literature', Proceedings of a Seminar on Sufi and Bhakti Convergences, Department of Comparative Literature, Jadavpur University (forthcoming).

24. See chapter two of this book. Also see, Aquil, 'Miracles, Authority and Benevolence'; and Digby, 'The Sufi Shaykh as a Source of Authority'.

25. See, for instance, Annemarie Schimmel, 'The Vernacular Tradition in Persianate Sufi Poetry in Mughal India', in Leonard Lewisohn and David Morgan (eds), *The Heritage of Sufism: Late Classical Persianate Sufism (1501–1750)*, Vol. 3 (Oxford: Oneworld, 1999).

26. For more details see, Aquil, 'Conversion in Chishti Sufi Literature'. Also see, Aziz Ahmad, *Studies in Islamic Culture in Indian Environment*; and Richard M. Eaton (ed.), *India's Islamic Traditions, 711–1750*. More generally, see Christian W. Troll (ed.), 2003.

Muslim Shrines in India: Their Character, History and Significance, with a new forward by Marc Gaborieau (New Delhi: Oxford University Press, 2003).

27. Eaton, *Essays on Islam and Indian History*.

28. Eaton, *The Rise of Islam and the Bengal Frontier*.

29. For similar observations, see Nizami, *Religion and Politics in India During the Thirteenth Century*. Also see Habib, *Politics and Society*.

30. Marlow, *Hierarchy and Egalitarianism in Islamic Thought*.

31. For an important, though somewhat neglected, study, see Usha Sanyal, *Devotional Islam and Politics in British India*.

32. David Gilmartin, *Empire and Islam: Punjab and the Making of Pakistan* (London: Oxford University Press, 1988).

33. Ziyaul Hasan Faruqui, *Deoband and the Demand for Pakistan* (Bombay: Asia Publishing House, 1963). Also see, Barbara D. Metcalf, *Islamic Revival in British India: Deoband 1860–1900* (New Delhi: Oxford University Press, 2002).

34. See, for instance, Haron Muhammed, 'The Dawah Movements and Sufi Tariqat: Competing for spiritual spaces in contemporary South(ern) Africa'. URL: http://www.uga.edu/islam/dawah_tariqat_sa.html.

35. Also see Gary R. Bunt, *Virtually Islamic: Computer-Mediated Communication and Cyber Islamic Environments* (Cardiff: University of Wales Press, 2000).

36. Eaton, 'Introduction', *India's Islamic Traditions*.

37. For an appreciation of Sirhindi's role, see I.H. Qureshi, *Muslim Community of the Indo-Pak Subcontinent*; and his *Ulema in Politics* (Delhi: Renaissance Publication House, 1985). For a criticism of Sirhindi, see S.A.A. Rizvi, *Muslim Revivalist Movements in Northern India*. For more on Shah Waliullah, see S.A.A. Rizvi, *Shah Wali-Allah and His Times*. For a more sophisticated treatment of the question of Islam in medieval India, see Alam, *Languages of Political Islam*. Also see chapter one of this book.

38. Marc Gaborieau, 'The *Jihad* of Sayyid Ahmad Barelwi on the North West Frontier: The Last Echo of the Middle Ages? Or a Prefiguration of Modern South Asia?' in Mansura Haidar (ed.), *Sufis, Sultans and Feudal Orders: Professor Nurul Hasan Commemoration Volume* (New Delhi: Manohar, 2004), pp. 23–43.

39. Sanyal, *Devotional Islam and Politics in British India*.

40. Faruqui, *Deoband and the Demand for Pakistan*.

41. Maulana Husain Ahmad Madani, *Composite Nationalism and Islam*.

42. Ibid., pp. 113, 118.

43. Ibid., p. 150.

44. Ibid., pp. 116–17.

45. Compare this with Barabara D. Metcalf, '"Traditionalist" Islamic Activism: Deoband, Tablighis, and Talibs', Social Science Research Council/After Sept. 11, http://www.ssrc.org/sept11/essays/metcalf_text_only.htm.

46. See chapter two of this text. Also see, Aquil, 'Conversion in Chishti Sufi Literature' and Eaton, *Essays on Islam and Indian History*.

47. Carl W. Ernst and Bruce B. Lawrence, *Sufi Martyrs of Love*, p. 108.

48. Simon Digby, 'Shaikh Abd al-Quddus Gangohi (AD 1456–1537): The Personality and Attitude of a Medieval Indian Sufi', *Medieval India: A Miscellany,* 3 (1975), pp. 1–66; Eaton, *Rise of Islam and the Bengal Frontier*; Aquil, 'Sufi Cults, Politics and Conversion, pp. 190–97; also see chapter two of this book.

49. Ernst and Lawrence, *Sufi Martyrs of Love,* p. 130.

50. Ibid., p. 112.

51. For a more detailed treatment of the theme of Sufism in modern times, see Aquil, 'Refashioning Devotional Islam: Sufi Traditions in the Modern Age' in Shirin Maswood, Ritwika Biswas and Amit Dey (eds), *Between Tradition and Modernity: Aspects of Islam in South Asia* (forthcoming).

Chapter 8: Reason and Faith in Islam

1. Youssef M. Choueiri, *Islamic Fundamentalism*, revised edition (London: Continuum, 2002). One cannot entirely agree with Mahmood Mamdani's position that fundamentalism remains a Christian problem and that the term cannot be applied for Islam and Muslims. See his *Good Muslim, Bad Muslim: Islam, the USA, and the Global War Against Terror* (Delhi: Permanent Black, 2004).

2. See, for instance, T.N. Madan, *Modern Myths, Locked Minds: Secularism and Fundamentalism in India* (New Delhi: Oxford University Press, 1997).

3. Mamdani, *Good Muslim, Bad Muslim*.

4. Robert W. Hefner, 'September 11 and the Struggle for Islam', Social Science Research Council/After Sept. 11, http://www.ssrc.org/sept11/essays/hefner.htm.

5. Olivier Roy, 'Neo-Fundamentalism', Social Science Research Council/After Sept. 11, http://www.ssrc.org/sept11/essays/roy.htm.

6. Partha Chatterjee, 'Anderson's Utopia', *Diacritics*, 29: 4 (1999), pp. 128–34. In this context, also see, Chatterjee's *The Nation and Its Fragments: Colonial and Postcolonial Histories* (Princeton: Princeton University Press, 1993).

7. Roy, 'Neo-Fundamentalism'.

8. Jonathan Benthal, 'Confessional Cousins and the Rest: The Structure of Islamic Toleration', *Anthropology Today*, 21: 1 (2005), pp. 16–20. Najwa Al-Qattan's study of *sijill* documents from the sharia courts of Ottoman Damascus in the eighteenth and nineteenth centuries has shown that legal, cultural and institutional causes contributed to the creation of a complex and relatively fluid and just legal arena in which important aspects of the zimmi, or non-Muslim People of the Book, were 'not governed by the extremes of fortune familiar to us from other sources, and where the Muslims of Damascus—the putative mob—came face to face with their Jewish and Christian neighbours in a public and open sphere that catered to their needs in a fair and orderly manner. It may be kept in mind that zimmi men and women had opted for resolving their disputes through the sharia court on their own initiative. The court did not discriminate on account of their being non-Muslims even in cases in which Muslims were pitted against the zimmis. See Najwa Al-Qattan, 'Dhimmis in the Muslim Court: Legal Autonomy and Religious Discrimination', *International Journal of Middle East Studies*, 31: 3 (1999), pp. 429–44.

9. See in this context Partha Chatterjee's important analysis of the churnings within the communities at the margins of the civil society, in his *The Politics of the Governed: Considerations on Political Society in Most of the World* (New York: Columbia University Press, 2004).

10. For a good general account, see Marshall G.S. Hodgson's majestic three-volume set, *The Venture of Islam: Conscience and History in a World Civilization* (Chicago: University of Chicago Press, 1975–77).

11. For useful brief notes and essays on the various religious sects and intellectual schools, see the entries in the *Encyclopaedia of Islam*, New Edition.

12. Marshall Hodgson can be a good guide for an appreciation of the process; see his *Venture of Islam*.

13. See chapters two and seven of this book.

14. Marlow, *Hierarchy and Egalitarianism in Islamic Thought*.

15. M.M. Sharif (ed.), *A History of Muslim Philosophy* (Lahore: Pakistan Philosophical Congress, 1961), p. 556.

16. Ibid., p. 544.

17. Al-Ghazali, *Tahafut al-Falasifah (Incoherence of the Philosophers)*, English translation by Sabih Ahmad Kamali ((Lahore: Pakistan Philosophical Congress, 1963), pp. 3–5.

18. Ibid., p. 8.

19. Al-Ghazali, *Deliverance from Errors*, an annotated translation by Richard Joseph McCarthy of *al-Munqidh min al-Dalal* and other relevant works of Al-Ghazali (Louiseville, Ky: Fons Vitae, 2000), p. 108; Al-Ghazali, *Incoherence of the Philosophers*, p. 8.

20. Al-Ghazali, *Deliverance from Errors*, p. 109.

21. Ibn Rushd, *Decisive Treatise (Kitab Fasl al-Maqal)*, in *On the Harmony of Religion and Philosophy*, English translation by George F. Hourani (London: Luzac & C., 1976), pp. 166–67.

22. Ibid., pp. 169, 181.

23. Ibid., pp. 171, 175, 178.

24. Ibid., p. 178.

25. Ibid., p. 183.

26. Ibid., p. 185.

27. For more on Jesus and Islam, see Tarif Khalidi (ed. and trans.), *The Muslim Jesus: Sayings and Stories in Islamic Literature*, Convergences: Inventories of the Present Series (Cambridge and London: Harvard University Press, 2001).

28. On these questions, see Saïd Amir Arjomand, 'Perso-Indian Statecraft, pp. 455–73.

29. These hopes and expectations have been forcefully put forward by the Delhi-based sociologist, Satish Saberwal, in numerous writings and personal communications. Many of my own formulations here are derived from his insights. For samples of his writings, see his, 'Anxieties, Identities, Complexity, Reality', in Mushirul Hasan (ed.), *Will Secular India survive?* (Gurgaon: ImprintOne, 2004), pp. 93–124. Also see Satish Saberwal, 'Introduction: Civilization, Constitution, Democracy', in Zoya Hasan, E. Sridharan and R. Sudershan (eds), *India's Living Constitution: Ideas, Practices, Controversies* (Delhi: Permanent

Black, 2002), pp. 1–30; and his *Spirals of Contention: Why India was Partitioned in 1947* (New Delhi: Routledge, 2008).

30. Magnus Marsden, 'Muslim Village Intellectuals: The Life of the Mind in Northern Pakistan', *Anthropology Today*, 21: 1 (2005), pp. 10–15. For the connections between the Pakistani madrasas, the Taliban and the so-called terror networks, see Barbara D. Metcalf, '"Traditionalist" Islamic Activism'. Also see her 'Introduction' to Maulana Husain Ahmad Madani, *Composite Nationalism and Islam*, pp. 23–54.

31. See Hasan, Sridharan et al. (eds), *India's Living Constitution: Ideas, Practices, Controversies*.

Timeline

570–632	Life of Prophet Muhammad and the rise of Islam in Arabia
632–661	Period of the rightly-guided caliphs (Abu Bakr, Umar, Usman and Ali)
661–750	Umayyad Caliphate (based in Damascus)
711–12	Arab conquest of Hind
750–1258	Abbasid Caliphate (based in Baghdad)
971–1030	Sultan Mahmud of Ghazna
980–1037	Life of Ibn Sina (Avicenna)
1058–1111	Life of Imam Ghazali
1126–1198	Life of Ibn Rushd (Averroes)
1141–1236	Life of Muin-ud-Din Chishti (Khwaja Gharib Nawaz)
1162–1227	Life of Genghis Khan
1173–1235	Life of Qutb-ud-Din Bakhtiyar Kaki, successor of Muin-ud-Din Chishti
1175–1266	Life of Chishti Sufi Farid-ud-Din Ganj-i-Shakar (Baba Farid), successor of Qutb-ud-Din Bakhtiyar Kaki
1192	Second Battle of Tarain (Turks led by Muhammad Ghauri defeat Prithviraj Chauhan)
1193	Beginning of the construction of Qutb Minar in Delhi
1206–1290	The Delhi Sultanate under the early Turks

1238–1325	Life of Hazrat Nizam-ud-Din Auliya, successor of Chishti Sufi Baba Farid
1253–1325	Amir Khusrau, poet, courtier and disciple of Hazrat Nizam-ud-Din Auliya
1285–1357	Life of Ziya-ud-Din Barani, courtier, historian, political thinker and disciple of Hazrat Nizam-ud-Din Auliya
1290–1320	Khalji dynasty of Delhi Sultans
1320–1413	Tughluq dynasty of Delhi Sultans
1398	Sacking of Delhi by Timur
1414–1451	Sayyid rulers of the Delhi Sultanate
1451–1526	Lodi Afghan Sultans of Delhi and Agra
1469–1539	Life of Guru Nanak
1483–1530	Life of Zahir-ud-Din Muhammad Babur, founder of Mughal empire in India
1486–1545	Life of Afghan empire-builder, Sher Shah Sur
1526	The First Battle of Panipat (Babur defeats Ibrahim Lodi)
1540–1615	Life of Abdul Qadir Badauni, the author of *Muntakhab-ut-Tawarikh*, a critique of Akbar's reign
1551–1602	Life of Abul Fazl, the author of *Akbarnama*, a celebrated account of Akbar's reign
1556–1605	The reign of Mughal emperor Jalal-ud-Din Muhammad Akbar
1562–1572	The mausoleum of Akbar's father, Humayun, built in Delhi
1564–1624	Life of Shaikh Ahmad Sirhindi, Naqshbandi Sufi and Sunni revivalist
1630–1653	The period of the construction of Taj Mahal at Agra, by Shah Jahan (ruled 1628–1658) as a tribute to his wife, Mumtaz Mahal
1639–1648	The construction of the Red Fort (Lal Qila) of Delhi
1658–1707	The reign of Mughal emperor Muhi-ud-Din Muhammad Aurangzeb Alamgir
1703–1762	Life of Shah Waliullah Muhaddis Dehlawi

1707–1857	Period of the later Mughals
1757	The battle of Plassey and beginning of the rule of the English East India Company
1817–1898	Life of Sir Syed Ahmad Khan of Aligarh
1856–1921	Life of Imam Ahmad Raza Khan of Bareilly (leader of Sufi movement in modern times)
1866	Foundation of Darul Uloom, Deoband
1857	The Sepoy Mutiny, celebrated as the 'first war of India's independence' from the British colonial rule
1879–1957	Life of Maulana Husain Ahmad Madani, Deobandi Islamic scholar
1903–1979	Life of Maulana Syed Abul Ala Maududi, founder of Jama'at-i-Islami
1947	Independence and the Partition of the Subcontinent into India and Pakistan
1948	Mahatma Gandhi shot dead by a communal fanatic, Nathu Ram Godse
1971	The emergence of Bangladesh
1992	The demolition of the historic Babri Mosque at Ayodhya, claimed by sections of extremist Hindus as the exact birthplace of Ram
1996	The rise of the Taliban, radical Sunni Islamists in Afghanistan
2001	America attacked by suspected Al Qaida militants
2002	Communal riots in Gujarat

Glossary*

adab	:	civilities, good manners, ceremonies, politeness; salutations, respects; literature
adl	:	justice, equity, rectitude, integrity
agah	:	aware, wary; intelligent, knowing, acquainted with; prudent; vigilant, attentive
ahl-i-kitab	:	believers in a revealed religion; Christian, Jews, Zoroastrians
akhlaq	:	manners; virtues, good qualities; morals, ethics
alim	:	theologian, learned, intelligent, wise (see also, plural *ulama*)
amir	:	noble, chief, lord; a person of rank or distinction (see also, plural *umara*)
amr bil ma'ruf	:	recommending right in Islam
angan	:	courtyard

*This glossary has been prepared with the help of the following dictionaries: F. Steingass, *Comprehensive Persian-English Dictionary*, reprint (Delhi: Munshiram Manoharlal, 1996); also see, the online version at: http://dsal.uchicago.edu/dictionaries/steingass/ (Digital Dictionaries of South Asia, University of Chicago); Bashir Ahmad Qureshi, *Practical Standard 21st Century Dictionary, Urdu into English*, revised and enlarged by Abdul Haq (Delhi: Farid Book Depot, 2004); R.S. Mcgregor (ed.), *Oxford Hindi-English Dictionary*, reprint (New Delhi: Oxford University Press, 1999)

aqil : prudent, judicious, intelligent, sensible, wise, sagacious
aql : intellect, reason
ardas : Sikh form of worship, prayer (possibly from Persian *arz-dasht*—petition, request, entreaty; supplication)
ashraf : nobles, grandees, gentlemen, men of high extraction; refined, courteous, urbane
atal : determined, resolved, firm
atma : soul
azmat : magnificence, pride, pomp, grandeur
baal : hair
baba : holy-man
bachcha : child
badshah : king, emperor, monarch
bakhshish : liberality; generosity; to give, grant, bestow; to remit; to pardon, forgive
balbir : strong or powerful hero
bali : powerful, mighty
baligh : attaining or having attained puberty; an adult; of mature age
batil : false, wrong, untrue, idle, absurd, futile
bayr : animosity, hostility, ill-will, grudge
bhadwa : pimp, shameless man
bhonsri : vagina
bidat : departure from established norms of religiosity, heresy, schism; strife, quarrel
bigha : a land-measure equal to about five-eighths of an acre
bistar : bed
budhapa : old age
buzurg : a saint, adult, elder; powerful, grand, magnificent
chaman : orchard, fruit-garden; a meadow, green field, verdant plain
chandal : wretch, miscreant, low-caste
chilla-i-makus : Sufi practice of hanging oneself upside down for forty nights
chut : vulva

dam	:	a small coin
daram	:	a silver coin
darbar	:	a ruler's court
dargah	:	Sufi shrine, tomb
dar-ul-aman	:	a country of safety, land of peace
dar-ul-harb	:	an enemy country
dar-ul-islam	:	abode of Islam
dilkhwah	:	object of longing, heart's desire; a beloved object
din	:	faith, religion, Islam
diwana	:	mad, insane, ecstatic, foolish
dosti	:	friendship, love, affection
faluda	:	a dish made of starch, honey, and water, sweet flummery
faqir	:	mendicant, dervish, poor
farman	:	royal order or command
fatwa	:	a judicial decree pronounced by a *mufti* (for whom see below); judgment, sentence
fath-nama	:	dispatches announcing victory in a battle
fiqh	:	knowledge, especially of theology and jurisprudence
firangi	:	Frank, European
firni	:	a dish made of ground rice, milk and sugar
firqa	:	a body, sect, clan, community
fitna	:	sedition, insurrection, discord, riot; war, anarchy, calamity; crime, sin, wickedness
fuqaha	:	jurisconsults, scholars of law
gand	:	anus
gandu	:	catamite
geet	:	song
ghanimat	:	good fortune, anything acquired without trouble or gratuitously, booty
gharib	:	poor, needy, humble, stranger
ghayr-muslim	:	non-Muslim
ghazal	:	poetry of love; an ode, a short poem, a sonnet
ghazi	:	conqueror, hero, victorious soldier of Islam
gor	:	grave, tomb
gunah	:	sin, crime, error, vice, fault; punishment, chastisement, retribution

guru	: spiritual guide, religious leader
hadis	: tradition or report relating to the sayings and actions of Prophet Muhammad
haji	: one who has performed the pilgrimage to Mecca
hajj	: performing the pilgrimage to Mecca
haal	: state, situation, condition, ecstasy
Hanafi	: follower of Abu Hanifa, founder of one of the schools of Islamic jurisprudence
Hanbali	: follower of Ibn Hanbal, founder of one of the schools of Islamic jurisprudence
hanumant	: equivalent to Hanuman, powerful monkey chief or deity who supported Ram's Lanka campaign
haqq	: truth, reality, justness, justice; acting justly, uprightly; Islam
haram	: unlawful, forbidden, prohibited
haveli	: mansion, house, dwelling, habitation
hom	: offering oblations to fire, sacrifice by fire, burnt sacrifice
ibadat	: divine worship, prayer, pious work
ibadat-khana	: a house of worship
ihtisab	: forbidding disorderly conduct, superintendence of weights and measures in the market, moral policing, duties of the *muhtasib* (for whom see below)
ijtihad	: fresh interpretation of Islamic law; legal and theological decision; office or authority of the *mujtahid* (for whom see below)
ilm-i-manqulat	: traditional learning and knowledge of Islam
ilm-i-maqulat	: scholarship based on reason and rational inquiry
imam	: leader; one who leads the prayer in the mosque
imam-i-adil	: a just leader; and exemplar
inam	: conferring a favour, reward, prize, grant of rent-free land (also see *madad-i-ma'ash*)
iqtadar	: holder of an assignment of land; power, authority, control

Ja'fari	:	a Shi'ite school of Islamic jurisprudence, named after Imam Ja'far Sadiq
jagir	:	possessing or occupying a place, land assignment
jamatkhana	:	dwelling place of a Sufi, hospice (also see *khanqah*)
jayez	:	lawful, legal, allowable, permissible, tolerable
jhaanth	:	pubic hair
jihad	:	struggle, endeavour, effort, battle, combat; war against infidels (*jihad-i-asghar*, lesser *jihad*); war against one's own lusts (*jihad-i-akbar*, greater *jihad*)
jizya	:	capitation tax (initially paid by Jews and Christians in an Islamic regime), tribute
joban	:	bloom of youth, female beauty
juddha	:	fighter, warrior, soldier, combatant, champion
kafir	:	infidel; one denying Allah's authority (also see *kufr*)
Kalam	:	Islamic scholastic theology; metaphysics
kalima	:	Muslim confession of faith (There is no god but Allah, and Muhammad is His Prophet)
kamil	:	perfect (*insan-i-kamil*, perfect man, a Sufi ideal)
karamat	:	miracle of a Sufi
khalifa	:	spiritual successor of a Sufi; caliph
khalsa	:	religious community of the Sikhs
khanqah	:	hospice of Sufis and *darwishes*
kharaj	:	tribute, tax, revenue
khatib	:	a preacher, especially of the Friday sermon in a mosque (see also *khutba*)
khilafat	:	caliphate
khuda	:	God, Allah
khulafa-i-rashidun	:	the four rightly-guided caliphs, the immediate successors of the Prophet
khutba	:	sermon, especially preached in the mosques on Fridays
khwab	:	dream, sleep
khwaja	:	Sufi master, preceptor; a man of distinction
kitabat	:	calligraphy

kotwal	:	magistrate; superintendent of police
kufr	:	infidelity
kulliyat	:	collected works of a poet or author
la ilaha illallah	:	there is no god but Allah (see also *kalima*)
langota	:	loin-cloth
lauda	:	penis
launde-baz	:	sodomite, paederast
lutf-o-karam	:	graciousness, generosity
maal	:	property, belonging
madad-i-ma'ash	:	revenue-free land grants
madrasa	:	seminary, school, college, university
mahasur	:	mighty warrior
mahdi	:	guide, renovator; the twelfth Shi'ite Imam who is believed to be in hiding and is expected to re-appear in order to purify Islam
mahzar	:	a register, record, decree; any document attested by witnesses, testimony; inquest
makruh	:	distasteful, unpleasant; disapproved in Islamic law, but not invalidated by it
maktab	:	school for beginners
maktubat	:	letters (written by Sufis to their disciples)
malfuzat	:	words, sayings, utterances (especially those relating to the Sufis)
Maliki	:	follower of Imam Malik, founder of one of the schools of Islamic jurisprudence
malik-us-shuara	:	poet-laureate
mansab	:	rank, post, dignity, office, ministry, magistracy; a high place
mansabdar	:	a ranked Mughal official
maqsud	:	wish, intention, design, aim, view, purpose, drift, desire, scope, object
maqtul	:	killed, slain, slaughtered
mard-i-kamil	:	perfect man
marifat	:	divine or spiritual knowledge
marsiya	:	an elegy, dirge; a funeral oration sung during Muharram in commemoration of the Prophet's grandsons, Hasan and Husain
masand	:	agent of the Sikh Gurus
mazahib	:	schools of Islamic jurisprudence

millat	:	community; faith, creed; a nation, people
miskin	:	poor, destitute, indigent
muajiza	:	Prophetic miracles
mubah	:	allowed, lawful, allowable (in Islamic law)
mudarris	:	a *madrasa* teacher
mufti	:	an expounder of Muslim law, giver of a *fatwa*
muhtasib	:	censor official
mujtahid	:	an authoritative interpreter of Muslim law; title given to the highest ecclesiastical dignitaries
mulla	:	schoolmaster, doctor, learned man, theologian
munh	:	mouth
muqtai	:	holder or possessor of land assignment (also see *iqtadar*)
murad	:	desire, wish, will, intention
murid	:	disciple of a Sufi
murtad	:	apostate
mutah	:	short-term marriage contract
muttaqi	:	God-fearing, pious, abstemious, temperate, sober, cautious
na'̒t	:	the praise of the Prophet
naach	:	dance
nadim	:	boon companion of a king
nahi anal munkar	:	to forbid wrong or falsehood
naib	:	deputy
namaz	:	one of the fundamental pillars of Islam, a pre-eminent form of Muslim prayers preferably performed in mosques
naql	:	tradition, report, account, tale, story
nasihat	:	counsel, advice, exhortation, admonition, reprimand
nazr	:	evil eye
nikah	:	marriage
nirbah	:	subsistence, fulfilling, accomplishing, continued existence
niyabat-i-khudai	:	God's deputy or lieutenant
padri	:	Christian priest
paibos	:	kissing the feet of a ruler or of Sufi master
paigham-i-haq	:	message of truth or God

pan bhatta : betel-allowance
panth : community of the Sikhs
parmatma : God
pir : Sufi master
prachin : ancient
pranayam : yogic practice of breath-control
punch : tail
qaum : people, community, nation, tribe, sect
qaumi geet : national song
qawwali : singing and playing musical instruments, especially pertaining to Sufi circles
qazi : judge
qinat : contentment
rafzi : a disparaging epithet for the Shias
rahbar : guide, escort
raushan : light, splendid, luminous, bright, serene, resplendent
rekhta : mixed language, gibberish, early Urdu
sabr : patience, toleration, endurance
sada : call, cry, invitation
sadr : a high ecclesiastical official
sahaba : companions of Prophet Muhammad
salat : prayers (see *namaz*)
sama : a blend of music, song and dance performed in Sufi circles (see also *qawwali*)
sanyasi : one who has supposedly abandoned all worldly possessions and affections; an ascetic or religious mendicant
sawab : recompense, reward, premium; requital; a good work (as worthy of reward)
sayyid : people claiming to be descendants of Prophet Muhammad
sehr : practising sorcery, magic, enchantment, necromancy; a spell
Shafi'i : follower of Imam Shafi'i, founder of one of the schools of Islamic jurisprudence
shahadat : martyrdom
shahid : martyr
shahr-e ashob : poem describing a ruined city

shaitani	:	derived from Satan; Satanic
shariat	:	Islamic law
sheikh	:	Sufi master (see also *khwaja*)
shirk	:	companions or partners of God, polytheism, idolatry, paganism, infidelity
shirni	:	sweets made of ground rice, milk and sugar
shuddhi	:	purification and bringing a convert back to the Hindu fold
sijda	:	prostration before a king or Sufi
sikka	:	coins
silsila	:	Sufi lineage, order
sipahi	:	soldier
sis	:	head (*sis niwana*: bow, yield, submit)
subhani	:	divine; relating to God
sulh-i-kul	:	peace with all; perfect peace
sultan-i-adil	:	just ruler
sunna	:	traditions, practice of the Prophet
tafzili	:	one who privileges Ali from amongst the four immediate successors of the Prophet
taib	:	repentant; returning to God
takfir	:	accusing of infidelity, calling or making one an unbeliever
takhallus	:	nom de plume
talim	:	emphasis on exclusive religious authority of the 'infallible' Shi'ite Imam
tamiz	:	discernment, discretion; discrimination between right and wrong, truth and falsehood
taqiyya	:	a doctrinally sanctioned precautionary concealing of religious beliefs
taqlid	:	blind conformity to one of the *mazahib* or schools of jurisprudence in Islam
tariqa	:	Sufi path or order
tark-i-duniya	:	Sufi's renunciation from the world
tasawwuf	:	Sufism; Islamic mysticism
tauhid	:	people's unity; unity of God
tawakkul	:	trust in God; resignation to the divine will; faith, reliance
tazkira	:	biographies; hagiographies
tedha	:	crooked

ulama	:	learned men, scholars, theologians
umara	:	nobles (singular, *amir*)
umma	:	people, nation, sect, religious community, creed, follower, co-religionist
ummid	:	hope, expectation, dependence, trust, desire,
unt	:	camel
urs	:	death anniversary of a Sufi
wah guru	:	wonderful teacher or Guru, a common form of chanting the praise of God in Sikhism
wahdat	:	unity
wahdat-ul-wujud	:	unity of existence
wahdat-us-shuhud	:	unity of witness
wahi	:	prophetic revelation
wajib	:	necessary, obligatory, binding
watan	:	home-land
wazir	:	minister
wilayat	:	territory under spiritual authority of a Sufi
yahud-o-nasara	:	Jews and Christians, perceived as conventional enemies of Islam
zakat	:	religious tax on Muslims
zamin	:	land, earth
zar	:	gold, money, wealth, riches
zawabit-i-mulki	:	non-religious regulations for ruling the Sultanate
zewar	:	jewellery, ornaments
zikr	:	continual prayers or repetitions of the names, praise or glorification of God
zillullah	:	shadow of God; title adopted by Muslim rulers and Sultan
zimmis	:	People of the Book such as Jews, Christians, Zoroastrians who could earn protection for themselves in an Islamic regime by paying *jizya*, for which see above
zira	:	cumin-seed
zunnar	:	brahminical sacred thread

Select Bibliography

Abbas, Fauzia Zareen. 1987. *Abdul Qadir Badauni as a Man and Historiographer*. Delhi: Idarah-i Adabiyat-i Delli.

Abdur Rahman, Syed Sabahuddin. 1964. *Hindustan ke Salatin, Ulama aur Mashaikh ke Talluqat par ek Nazr*. Azamgarh: Darul Musannefin.

Abel, A. 1991a. 'Dar al-harb', *Encyclopaedia of Islam* (New Edition), Vol. II, Leiden: Brill, p. 126.

——. 1991b. 'Dar al-Islam', *Encyclopaedia of Islam* (New Edition), Vol. II, Leiden: Brill, pp. 127–28.

Abul Fazl, *Akbarnama*, English translation by H. Beveridge, Vols. I–III, reprint (Delhi: Rare Books, 1972–73).

——. *Ain-i-Akbari*, English translation by H. Blochmann (Vol. I) and H.S. Jarrett (Vols. II and III), reprint (Delhi: Oriental Reprint, 1977–78).

Adab-us-Salihin (titled *Uswat-us-Salihin*), Abdul Haqq Muhaddis Dehlawi. Urdu translation by Abdur Rahman Jami. Delhi: Adabi Duniya, 2006.

Ahmad, Aziz. 1964. *Studies in Islamic Culture in the Indian Environment*. Oxford: Clarendon Press.

——. 2003. 'Epic and Counter-Epic in Medieval India', first published in 1963, reprinted in Richard M. Eaton (ed.). *India's Islamic Traditions, 711–1750*. New Delhi: Oxford University Press, pp. 37–49.

Akhbar-ul-Akhyar, Shaikh Abdul Haqq Muhaddis Dehlawi. Ms., IO Islamic 1450, OIOC, British Library, London. Urdu trans., Subhan Mahmud and Muhammad Fazil. Delhi: Adabi Duniya, 1990.

Alam, Muzaffar and Sanjay Subrahmanyam (eds). 1998. *The Mughal State, 1526–1750*. New Delhi: Oxford University Press.

Alam, Muzaffar. 1986. *The Crisis of Empire in Mughal North India, Awadh and the Punjab, 1707–48*. New Delhi: Oxford University Press.

____. 1996. 'Assimilation from a Distance: Confrontation and Sufi Accommodation in Awadh Society', in R. Champakalakshmi and S. Gopal (eds), *Tradition, Dissent and Ideology, Essays in Honour of Romila Thapar*. New Delhi: Oxford University Press, pp. 164–91.

____. 2004. *The Languages of Political Islam in India, c. 1200–1800*. New Delhi: Permanent Black.

Alam, Muzaffar, F. Nalini Delvoye and Marc Gaborieau (eds). 2000. *The Making of Indo-Persian Culture*. New Delhi: Manohar.

Alavi, Seema (ed.). 2002. *The Eighteenth Century in India*. New Delhi: Oxford University Press.

Al-Azmeh, Aziz. 1997. *Muslim Kingship: Power and the Sacred in Muslim, Christian and Pagan Polities*. London and New York: I.B. Tauris.

Ali, M. Athar. 1997. *The Mughal Nobility under Aurangzeb*. New Delhi: Oxford University Press.

____. 2006. 'Translations of Sanskrit Works at Akbar's Court' and '*Sulh-i-Kul* and the Religious Ideas of Akbar', in *Mughal India: Studies in Polity, Ideas, Society, and Culture*. [Collection of Athar Ali's essays] New Delhi: Oxford University Press.

Al-Ghazali, *Tahafut al-Falasifah (Incoherence of the Philosophers)*, English translation by Sabih Ahmad Kamali (Lahore: Pakistan Philosophical Congress, 1963).

____. *Deliverance from Errors*, an annotated translation by Richard Joseph McCarthy of *al-Munqidh min al-Dalal* and other relevant works of Al-Ghazali (Louiseville, Ky: Fons Vitae, 2000).

Al-Qattan, Najwa. 1999. 'Dhimmis in the Muslim Court: Legal Autonomy and Religious Discrimination', *International Journal of Middle East Studies*, 31: 3, pp. 429–44.

Amin, Shahid. 2002. 'Alternative Histories: A View from India', SEPHIS–CSSSC lecture, Amsterdam/Kolkata.

Anooshahar, Ali. 2008. 'The King who would be Man: The Gender Roles of the Warrior King in Early Mughal History', in *Journal of the Royal Asiatic Society*, 18, pp. 327–40.

Ansari, A.S. Bazmee. 'Bulandshahr (Baran)', *Encyclopaedia of Islam*, New Edition, Vol. 1, pp. 1299–1300.

Aquil, Raziuddin. 2008. 'The Study of Islam and Indian History at the Darul Musannefin, Azamgarh', in Raziuddin Aquil and Partha

Chatterjee (eds.), *History in the Vernacular*. Ranikhet: Permanent Black.

_____. 1997–98. 'Conversion in Chishti Sufi Literature (13th–14th Centuries)', *Indian Historical Review,* 24: 1–2, pp. 70–94.

_____. 2003a. 'Miracles, Authority and Benevolence: Stories of *Karamat* in Chishti Sufi Literature of the Delhi Sultanate', in Anup Taneja (ed.). *Sufi Cults and the Evolution of Medieval Indian Culture*. New Delhi: ICHR and Northern Book Centre, pp. 109–38.

_____. 2003b. 'Episodes from the Life of Shaikh Farid-ud-Din Ganj-i-Shakar', *International Journal of Punjab Studies,* 10: 1–2, pp. 25–46.

_____. 2007. *Sufism, Culture and Politics: Afghans and Islam in Medieval North India*. New Delhi: Oxford University Press.

Arjomand, Saïd Amir. 2001. 'Perso-Indian Statecraft, Greek Political Science and the Muslim Idea of Government', *International Sociology,* 16: 3, pp. 455–73.

_____. 2004. 'Transformation of the Islamicate Civilization: A Turning-Point in the Thirteenth Century?', *Medieval Encounters,* 10: 1–3, pp. 213–45.

Asher, Catherine B. and Cynthia Talbot. 2006. *India Before Europe*. Cambridge: Cambridge University Press.

Asher, Catherine. 1992. *Architecture of Mughal India.* Cambridge: Cambridge University Press.

Azad, Muhammad Husain. 1961. *Qisas-i-Hind*, reprint. Lahore: Majlis Taraqqi Adab.

_____. 1986. *Aab-e-Hayat*, reprint. Lucknow: Uttar Pradesh Urdu Academy.

Bagley, F.R.C. 1964. *Ghazali's Book of Counsel for Kings*. Oxford: Oxford University Press.

Ballantyne, Tony. 2003. 'Framing the Sikh Past', *International Journal of Punjab Studies,* 10: 1–2, pp. 1–23.

Barnett, Richard B. (ed.). 2002. *Rethinking Early Modern India*. New Delhi: Manohar.

Benthal, Jonathan. 2005. 'Confessional Cousins and the Rest: The Structure of Islamic Toleration', *Anthropology Today*, 21: 1, pp. 16–20.

Bhattacharya, Neeladri. 2008. 'Predicament of Secular Histories', *Public Culture*, 20: 1, pp. 57–73.

Bjorkman, W. 'Kafir', *Encyclopaedia of Islam*, New Edition, Vol. 4, pp. 407–09.

Bose, Brinda and Subhabrata Bhattacharyya (eds). 2007. *The Phobic and the Erotic: The Politics of Sexualities in Contemporary India*. London/ New York/Calcutta: Seagull Books.

Brown, Katherine Butler. 2007. 'Did Aurangzeb Ban Music? Questions for the Historiography of his Reign', *Modern Asian Studies*, 41: 1, pp. 77–120.

Bunt, Gary R. 2000. *Virtually Islamic: Computer-Mediated Communication and Cyber Islamic Environments*. Cardiff: University of Wales Press.

Busch, Allison. 2005. 'Literary Responses to the Mughal Imperium: The Historical Poems of Kesavdas', *South Asia Research*, 25: 1, pp. 31–54.

Cahen, Cl. 'Dhimma', *Encyclopaedia of Islam*, New Edition, Vol. 2, pp. 227–31.

Chandoke, Neera. 1999. *Mapping Histories: Essays Presented to Ravinder Kumar*. New Delhi: Tulika.

Chandra, Satish. 2003. *Essays on Medieval Indian History*. New Delhi: Oxford University Press.

Chatterjee, Partha. 1983. 'Peasants, Politics and Historiography: A Response', *Social Scientist*, 11: 5, pp. 58–65.

____. 1993. *The Nation and Its Fragments: Colonial and Postcolonial Histories*. Princeton: Princeton University Press.

____. 1999. 'Anderson's Utopia', *Diacritics*, 29: 4, pp. 128–34.

____. 2004a. 'The Early Modern and Colonial Modern in South Asia: A Proposal for a Distinction'. Paper presented at the Centre for Studies in Social Sciences, Calcutta.

____. 2004b. *The Politics of the Governed: Considerations on Political Society in Most of the World*. New York: Columbia University Press.

Choueiri, Youssef M. 2002. *Islamic Fundamentalism*, revised edition. London: Continuum.

Cook, M. 'Al-Nahy an al-Munkar', *Encyclopaedia of Islam*, New Edition, Vol. XII, Supplement, Leiden: Brill, pp. 644–46.

Currie, P.M. 1989. *The Shrine and Cult of Muin al-Din Chishti of Ajmer*. New Delhi: Oxford University Press.

Darling, Linda T. 2002. '"Do Justice, Do Justice, For That is Paradise": Middle Eastern Advice for Indian Muslim Rulers', *Comparative Studies of South Asia, Africa and the Middle East,* 22: 1–2, pp. 3–19.

Datta, Rajat (ed.). 2008. *Rethinking a Millennium: Perspectives on Indian History from the Eighth to the Eighteenth Century, Essays for Harbans Mukhia*. Delhi: Aakar Books.

Digby, Simon. 1975. 'Shaikh Abd al-Quddus Gangohi (AD 1456–1537): The Personality and Attitude of a Medieval Indian Sufi', *Medieval India: A Miscellany,* 3, pp. 1–66.

———. 1983. 'Early Pilgrimages to the Graves of Muinuddin Sijzi and other Indian Chishti Shaikhs', in M. Israel and N.K. Wagle (eds). *Islamic Society and Culture: Essays in Honour of Aziz Ahmad*. New Delhi: Manohar, pp. 95–100.

———. 1986. 'The Sufi Shaykh as a Source of Authority in Medieval India', *Purushartha,* 9, pp. 55–77.

———. 1990. 'The Sufi Shaikh and the Sultan: A Conflict of Claims to Authority in Medieval India', *Iran,* 28, pp. 71–81.

———. 2001. *Sufis and Soldiers in Awrangzeb's Deccan: Malfuzat-i-Naqshbandiyya*. New Delhi: Oxford University Press.

Eaton, Richard M. 1978. *Sufis of Bijapur, 1300–1700, Social Roles of Sufis in Medieval India*. Princeton: Princeton University Press.

———. 1994. *The Rise of Islam and the Bengal Frontier, 1204–1760*. New Delhi: Oxford University Press.

———. 2002. *Essays on Islam and Indian History*. New Delhi: Oxford University Press.

——— (ed.). 2003. *India's Islamic Traditions, 711–1750*. New Delhi: Oxford University Press.

Ernst, Carl W. 1992. *Eternal Garden: Mysticism, History and Politics at a South Asian Sufi Centre*. Albany: State University of New York Press.

Ernst, Carl W. and Bruce B. Lawrence. 2002. *Sufi Martyrs of Love: The Chishti Order in South Asia and Beyond*. New York: Palgrave Macmillan.

Faruqi, Ihsanul Haq. 1963. *Sultan-ut-Tarikin*. Karachi: Dairah Mu'inul Ma'arif.

Faruqui, Ziyaul Hasan. 1963. *Deoband and the Demand for Pakistan*. Bombay: Asia Publishing House.

Fatawa-i-Jahandari, Ziya-ud-Din Barani. 1972. Edited by Afsar Salim Khan. Lahore.

Fawa'id-ul-Fu'ad, Conversations of Shaikh Nizam-ud-Din Auliya. 1990. Compiled by Amir Hasan Sijzi. Persian text with an Urdu translation by Khwaja Hasan Sani Nizami. New Delhi: Urdu Academy.

Foucault, Michel. 1991. 'Governmentality', in Graham Burchell et al. (eds), *The Foucault Effect: Studies in Governmentality*. London: Harvester, pp. 87–104.

____. 2003. *'Society Must Be Defended'. Lectures at the College De France, 1975–76*. Edited by Mauro Bertani and Alessandra Fontana, translated by David Macey. New York: Picador.

Friedmann, Yohanan. 2003. 'Islamic Thought in Relation to the Indian Context', first published in 1986, reprinted in Richard M. Eaton (ed.), *India's Islamic Traditions, 711–1750*. New Delhi: Oxford University Press, pp. 50–63.

Gaborieau, Marc. 2004. 'The *Jihad* of Sayyid Ahmad Barelwi on the North West Frontier: The Last Echo of the Middle Ages? Or a Prefiguration of Modern South Asia?', in Mansura Haidar (ed.), *Sufis, Sultans and Feudal Orders: Professor Nurul Hasan Commemoration Volume*. New Delhi: Manohar, pp. 23–43.

Ghazali, Imam. 1982. *Ihya Ulum-id-din*, Vols. I–IV. Translated into English by Maulana Fazlul Karim. Delhi: Kitab Bhavan.

Gilmartin, David and Bruce B. Lawrence. eds. 2002. *Beyond Turk and Hindu: Rethinking Religious Identities in Islamicate South Asia*. New Delhi: India Research Press.

Gilmartin, David. 1988. *Empire and Islam: Punjab and the Making of Pakistan*. London: Oxford University Press.

Green, Nile. 2006. *Indian Sufism since the Seventeenth Century: Saints, Books and Empires in the Muslim Deccan*. London: Routledge.

Grehan, James. 2004. 'The Mysterious Power of Words: Language, Law, and Culture in Ottoman Damascus (17th–18th Centuries)', *Journal of Social History*, 37: 4, pp. 991–1015.

Grewal, J.S. 1990. *The Sikhs of the Punjab*. Cambridge: Cambridge University Press.

____. 1996. *Sikh Ideology, Polity and Social Order*. New Delhi: Manohar.

____. (ed.). 2004. *The Khalsa: Sikh and Non-Sikh Perspectives*. New Delhi: Manohar.

Habib, Irfan (ed.). 1997. *Akbar and His India*. New Delhi: Oxford University Press.

Habib, Mohammad and Afsar Umar Salim Khan. n.d. *The Political Theory of the Delhi Sultanate (Including translation of Ziauddin Barani's Fatawa-i-Jahandari, circa, 1358–9 AD)*. Allahabad: Kitab Mahal.

Habib, Mohammad and K.A. Nizami (eds). 1992. *A Comprehensive History of India, Vol. V, Part One, The Delhi Sultanate*, first published 1970. New Delhi: Peoples Publishing House.

Habib, Mohammad. 1974 and 1981. *Politics and Society During the Early Medieval Period, Collected Works of Mohammad Habib*, Vols. I and II. Edited by K.A. Nizami. New Delhi: Peoples Publishing House.

Habibullah, A.B.M. 1961. *The Foundation of the Muslim Rule in India*, revised edition. Allahabad: Central Book Depot.

Haidar, Mansura (ed.). 2004. *Sufis, Sultans and Feudal Orders: Professor Nurul Hasan Commemoration Volume*. New Delhi: Manohar.

Hall, Dianne. 2006. 'Words as Weapons: Speech, Violence, and Gender in Late Medieval Ireland', *Éire-Ireland*, 41: 1, pp. 122–141.

Hall, Stuart. 1992. 'Cultural Studies and its Theoretical Legacies', in Lawrence Grossberg, Cary Nelson and Paula Treichler (eds), *Cultural Studies*. New York and London: Routledge, pp. 277–94.

Haqq, M. Enamul. 1975. *A History of Sufi-ism in Bengal*. Dacca: Asiatic Society of Bangladesh.

Hardy, Peter. 'Barani', *Encyclopaedia of Islam*, New Edition, Vol. 1, pp. 1036–37.

Hasan, Mohibbul (ed.). 1968. *Historians of Medieval India*. Meerut: Meenakshi Prakashan.

Hasan, Mushirul and Asim Roy (eds). 2005. *Living Together Separately*. New Delhi: Oxford University Press.

Hasan, S. Nurul. 2005. 'The *Mahzar* of Akbar's Reign', in *Religion, State, and Society in Medieval India*. Edited and introduced by Satish Chandra. New Delhi: Oxford University Press.

Hefner, Robert W. 'September 11 and the Struggle for Islam', Social Science Research Council/After Sept. 11, http://www.ssrc.org/sept11/essays/hefner.htm.

Hodgson, Marshall G.S. 1975–77. *The Venture of Islam: Conscience and History in a World Civilization*. Chicago: University of Chicago Press.

Hunter, W.W. 2002. *The Indian Musalmans*, with an Introduction by Bimal Prasad. New Delhi: Rupa & Co.

Husain, Agha Mahdi. 1976. *Tughluq Dynasty*. Delhi: S. Chand.

Hussain, Syed Ejaz. 2003. *The Bengal Sultanate: Politics, Economy and Coins (AD 1205–1576)*. New Delhi: Manohar.

Ibn Rushd, *Decisive Treatise (Kitab Fasl al-Maqal)*, in *On the Harmony of Religion and Philosophy*, English translation by George F. Hourani (London: Luzac & C., 1976).

Iqbal, Mohammad. 2001. *Kulliyat-i-Iqbal Urdu*. Delhi: Markazi Maktaba Islami.

Jackson, Peter. 1999. *The Delhi Sultanate: A Political and Military History*. Cambridge: Cambridge University Press.

Jalibi, Jamil. 1989. *Tarikh Adab Urdu*. Delhi: Educational Publishing House.

Jawahir-i-Faridi. Ali Asghar. Lahore: Victoria Press, 1884.

Juneja, Monica (ed.). 2001. *Architecture in Medieval India: Forms, Contexts, Histories*. New Delhi: Permanent Black.

Karamustafa, Ahmet T. 2007. *Sufism: The Formative Period*, The New Edinburgh Islamic Surveys. Edinburgh: Edinburgh University Press.

Khalidi, Tarif (ed. and trans.). 2001. *The Muslim Jesus: Sayings and Stories in Islamic Literature*, Convergences: Inventories of the Present Series. Cambridge and London: Harvard University Press.

Khan, Dominique-Sila and Zawahir Moir. 2006. 'Coexistence and Communalism: The Shrine of Pirana in Gujarat', in Asim Roy (ed.), *Islam in History and Politics: Perspectives from South Asia*. New Delhi: Oxford University Press, pp. 147–69.

Khan, Iqtidar Alam (ed.). 1999. *Akbar and His Age*. New Delhi: ICHR and Northern Book Centre.

____. 1997. 'Akbar's Personality Traits and World Outlook—A Critical Appraisal', in Irfan Habib (ed.), *Akbar and His India*. New Delhi: Oxford University Press, pp. 79–96.

____. 2003. 'The Nobility under Akbar and the Development of his Religious Policy, 1560–80', in Richard M. Eaton (ed.), *India's Islamic Traditions, 711–1750*. New Delhi: Oxford University Press.

Khan, Sir Syed Ahmad. 2000. *Asar-us-Sanadid*, with an Introduction by Tanwir Ahmad Alavi. New Delhi: Urdu Academy.

Khayr-ul-Majalis, Conversations of Shaikh Nasir-ud-Din Chiragh-i-Dehli. 1959. Compiled by Hamid Qalandar. Edited by K.A. Nizami. Aligarh: Muslim University.

Khaza'in-ul-Futuh, Amir Khusrau. 1953. Edited by M. Wahid Mirza. Calcutta.

Khazinat-ul-Asfiya, Vol. I, Maulwi Ghulam Sarwar. n.d. Kanpur.

Kulliyat-i-Nazir Akbarabadi. AH 1291. Lucknow: Munshi Newal Kishore Press.

Kumar, Sunil. 2007. *The Emergence of the Delhi Sultanate, 1192–1286*. Delhi: Permanent Black.

Lal, Ruby. 2005. *Domesticity and Power in the Early Mughal World*. Cambridge: Cambridge University Press.

Lambton, A.K.S. 1981. *State and Government in Medieval Islam: An Introduction to the Study of Islamic Political Theory*. Oxford: Oxford University Press.

Latif, Sk. Abdul. 1993. *The Muslim Mystic Movement in Bengal, 1301–1550*. Calcutta: K.P. Bagchi.

Lawrence, Bruce B. 1984. 'Early Indo-Muslim Saints and Conversion', in Y. Friedmann (ed.), *Islam in Asia,* Vol. I, South Asia. Jerusalem: Max Schloessinger Memorial Foundation.

Lefevre, Corinne. 2007. 'Recovering a Missing Voice from Mughal India: The Imperial Discourse of Jahangir (r. 1605–1627) in his Memoirs', *Journal of the Economic and Social History of the Orient*, 50: 4, pp. 452–89.

Madan, T.N. 1997. *Modern Myths, Locked Minds: Secularism and Fundamentalism in India*. New Delhi: Oxford University Press.

Madani, Maulana Husain Ahmad. 2005. *Composite Nationalism and Islam*. Translated by Mohammad Anwer Hussain and Hasan Imam. New Delhi: Manohar.

Mamdani, Mahmood. 2004. *Good Muslim, Bad Muslim: Islam, the USA, and the Global War Against Terror*. Delhi: Permanent Black.

Marlow, Louise. 1997. *Hierarchy and Egalitarianism in Islamic Thought*, Cambridge Series in Islamic Civilization. Cambridge: Cambridge University Press.

Marsden, Magnus. 2005. 'Muslim Village Intellectuals: The Life of the Mind in Northern Pakistan', *Anthropology Today*, 21: 1, pp. 10–15.

Marshall, P.J. (ed.). 2003. *The Eighteenth Century in Indian History, Evolution or Revolution?* New Delhi: Oxford University Press.

McLeod, W.H. 1998. *Guru Nanak and the Sikh Religion*, first published 1968. New Delhi: Oxford University Press.

———. 2006. 'Sikhs and Muslims in the Punjab', in Asim Roy (ed.), *Islam in History and Politics: Perspectives from South Asia*. New Delhi: Oxford University Press, pp. 170–80.

Metcalf, Barabara D. '"Traditionalist" Islamic Activism: Deoband, Tablighis, and Talibs', Social Science Research Council/After Sept. 11, http://www.ssrc.org/sept11/essays/metcalf_text_only.htm.

———. 2002. *Islamic Revival in British India: Deoband 1860–1900*. New Delhi: Oxford University Press.

———. 2004. *Islamic Contestations: Essays on Muslims in India and Pakistan*. New Delhi: Oxford University Press.

Muhammed, Haron. 'The Dawah Movements and Sufi Tariqat: Competing for spiritual spaces in contemporary South(ern) Africa', http://www.uga.edu/islam/dawah_tariqat_sa.html.

Mujeeb, M. 1972. 'The Qutb Complex as a Social Document', in M. Mujeeb, *Islamic Influence on Indian Society*. Meerut: Meenakshi Prakashan.

———. 1985. *Indian Muslims*. New Delhi: Munshiram Manoharlal.

Mukherjee, Tilottama. 2004. 'Markets, Transport and the State in the Bengal Economy, *c*. 1750–1800'. Ph.D. thesis, University of Cambridge.

Mukhia, Harbans. 1976. *Historians and Historiography During the Reign of Akbar*. Delhi: Vikas Publications.

———. 1999. 'The Celebration of Failure as Dissent in Urdu Ghazal', *Modern Asian Studies*, 33, pp. 861–81.

———. 2004. *The Mughals of India*. Oxford: Blackwell.

Muntakhab-ut-Tawarikh, Vols. I–III, Mulla Abdul Qadir Badauni. 1864–9. Persian text edited by Ahmad Ali, Kabir al-Din Ahmad and W. Nassau Lees. Calcutta: Bibliotheca Indica.

Muntakhabu't-Tawarikh, by 'Abdu'l-Qadir ibn i Muluk Shah known as Al-Badaoni, Vol. II: 'The Reign of Akbar, from 963 to 1004 AH', translated into English by W.H. Lowe, first published 1899 (Delhi: Idarah-i Adabiyat-i Delli, 1973).

Murphey, Anne. 2007. 'History in the Sikh Past', *History and Theory*, 46, pp. 345–65.

Naim, C.M. 2004. 'Popular Jokes and Political History: The Case of Akbar, Birbal and Mulla Do-Piyaza', and 'Homosexual (Pederastic) Love in Pre-Modern Urdu Poetry', in C.M. Naim, *Urdu Texts and Contexts*. Delhi: Permanent Black.

Nizami, K.A. 1953. *Hayat-e Sheikh Abdul Haqq Muhaddis Dehlawi*. Delhi: Nadwatul Musannefin.

———. 1955. *The Life and Times of Shaikh Fariduddin Ganj-i-Shakar*. Aligarh: Muslim University.

———. 1991a. *The Life and Times of Shaikh Nizamuddin Auliya*. Delhi: Idarah-i-Adabiyat-i Delli.

———. 1991b. *The Life and Times of Shaikh Nasiruddin Chiragh*. Delhi: Idarah-i-Adabiyat-i Delli.

———. 2002. *Religion and Politics in India During the Thirteenth Century*. New Delhi: Oxford University Press.

Qamaruddin. 1985. *The Mahdawi Movement in India*. Delhi: Idarah-i-Adabiyat-i Delli.

Qasimi, Ata-ur-Rahman. 1995. *Dilli ki Tarikhi Masajid*. Delhi: Maulana Azad Academy.

Qiwam-ul-Aqa'id, Muhammad Jamal Qiwam. 1994. Translated from Persian into Urdu by Nisar Ahmad Faruqui. Rampur: Idarah Nashar-o-Isha'at.

Quddusi, Aijazul Haq. 1961. *Shaykh Abdul Quddus aur un ki Ta'limat*. Karachi: All Pakistan Educational Conference.

Qureshi, I.H. 1985a. *Ulema in Politics*. Delhi: Renaissance Publication House.

____. 1985b. *The Muslim Community of the Indo-Pak Subcontinent, 610–1947*. Delhi: Renaissance Publication House.

Rizvi, S.A.A. 1978. *A History of Sufism in India*, Vol. I, *Early Sufism and its History in India to 1600 AD*. New Delhi: Munshiram Manoharlal.

____. 1980. *Shah Wali-Allah and His Times*. Canberra: Ma'rifat Publishing House.

____. 1993. *Muslim Revivalist Movements in Northern India in the Sixteenth and Seventeenth Centuries*. New Delhi: Munshiram Manoharlal.

Robinson, Chase F. 2003. *Islamic Historiography*. Cambridge: Cambridge University Press.

Roy, Olivier. 'Neo-Fundamentalism', Social Science Research Council/ After Sept. 11, http://www.ssrc.org/sept11/essays/roy.htm.

Saberwal, Satish. 2002. 'Introduction: Civilization, Constitution, Democracy', in Zoya Hasan, E. Sridharan and R. Sudershan (eds), *India's Living Constitution: Ideas, Practices, Controversies*. Delhi: Permanent Black, pp. 1–30.

____. 2004. 'Anxieties, Identities, Complexity, Reality', in Mushirul Hasan (ed.), *Will Secular India Survive?* Gurgaon: ImprintOne, pp. 93–124.

____. 2008. *Spirals of Contention: Why India Was Partitioned in 1947*. New Delhi: Routledge.

Said, Edward W. 2001. *Orientalism: Western Conceptions of the Orient*. New Delhi: Penguin Books.

Sangari, Kumkum. 1999. 'Tracing Akbar: Hagiographies, popular narrative traditions, and the subject of conversion', in Neera Chandoke (ed.), *Mapping Histories: Essays Presented to Ravinder Kumar*. New Delhi: Tulika.

Sanyal, Usha. 1996. *Devotional Islam and Politics in British India—Ahmad Riza Khan and his Movement, 1870–1920*. New Delhi: Oxford University Press.

Sarkar, Jadunath (ed.). 1973. *The History of Bengal, Muslim Period, 1200–1757*. Patna: Academica Asiatica.

Sarker, Kobita. 2007. *Shah Jahan and his Paradise on Earth: The Story of Shah Jahan's Creations in Agra and Shahjahanabad in the Golden Days of the Mughals*. Kolkata: K.P. Bagchi.

Schimmel, Annemarie. 1999. 'The Vernacular Tradition in Persianate Sufi Poetry in Mughal India', in Leonard Lewisohn and David Morgan (eds), *The Heritage of Sufism: Late Classical Persianate Sufism (1501–1750)*, Vol. 3. Oxford: Oneworld.

———. 2005. *The Empire of the Great Mughals: History, Art and Culture*. Translated from German by Corinne Attwood. Edited by Burzine K. Waghmar, with a foreword by Francis Robinson. New Delhi: Oxford University Press.

Sennett, Richard. 1994. *Flesh and Stone*. London: Faber and Faber.

Shahbaz, S.M. 1981. *Zindagani Be-Nazir*. Edited by S.M. Hasnain. New Delhi: Taraqqi Urdu Bureau.

Sharif, M.M. ed. 1961. *A History of Muslim Philosophy*. Lahore: Pakistan Philosophical Congress.

Sharma, Sunil. 2000. *Persian Poetry at the Indian Frontier: Mas'ud Sa'd Salman of Lahore*. New Delhi: Permanent Black.

———. 2005. *Amir Khusraw: The Poet of Sultans and Sufis*. Oxford: Oneworld.

Shokoohy, Mehrdad. 2003. *Muslim Architecture of South India: The Sultanate of Ma'bar and the Traditions of Maritime Settlers on the Malabar and Coromandel Coasts; Tamil Nadu, Kerala and Goa*. London and New York: Routledge Curzon.

Siddiqui, I.H. 1961. *Afghan Despotism in India*. Aligarh: Three Men.

Siyar-ul-Arifin, Shaikh Jamali. Ms., IO Islamic 1313, OIOC, British Library, London.

Siyar-ul-Auliya, Amir Khwurd. 1978. Islamabad: Markaz Tahqiqat-i-Farsi Iran wa Pakistan.

Siyar-ul-Muta'khkhirin, Vols. I–III, Ghulam Husain Tabatabai. AH 1248. Lucknow: Munshi Newal Kishore.

Sreenivasan, Ramya. 2007. *The Many Lives of a Rajput Queen, Heroic Pasts in India, c. 1500–1900*. Delhi: Permanent Black.

Steingass, F. 1996. *A Comprehensive Persian–English Dictionary*. New Delhi: Munshiram Manoharlal.

Storey, C.A. 1970. *Persian Literature: A Bio-Bibliographical Survey*, Vol. I, Part I. London: Luzac.

Subrahmanyam, Sanjay. 2001. *Penumbral Visions: Making Polities in Early Modern South India*. New Delhi: Oxford University Press.

Tabaqat-i-Nasiri, Vol. I, Minhaj-us-Siraj. 1963–64. Edited by Abdul Hayy Habibi. Kabul: Historical Society of Afghanistan.

Talbi, M. 'Ibn Khaldun', *Encyclopaedia of Islam*, New Edition, Vol. 3, pp. 825–31.

Tarikh-i-Firuz-Shahi, Ziya-ud-Din Barani. British Museum Ms. 6376, OIOC, British Library, London.

Tarikh-i-Mubarak-Shahi, Yahya bin Ahmad bin 'Abdullah Sarhindi. 1931. Edited by M. Hidayat Hosain. Calcutta: Asiatic Society,

Thapar, Romila. 2004. *Somanatha: The Many Voices of a History*. New Delhi: Viking.

The Delhi Omnibus. 2002. *Delhi: A Historical Sketch* and *Twilight of the Mughuls: Studies in Late Mughal Delhi* by Percival Spear, *Delhi between Two Empires 1803–1931* by Narayani Gupta and *Delhi through the Ages: Selected Essays in Urban History, Culture and Society*, edited by R.E. Frykenburg. New Delhi: Oxford University Press.

Troll, Christian W. (ed.). 2003. *Muslim Shrines in India: Their Character, History and Significance*, with a new forward by Marc Gaborieau. New Delhi: Oxford University Press.

Tusi, Nizam-ul-Mulk. *The Book of Government or Rules for Kings, The Siyasat-nama* or *Siyar al-Muluk* of *Nizam-ul-Mulk*. 1960. Translated from Persian by Hubert Darke. London: Routledge & Kegan Paul.

Tyan, E. 'Djihad', *Encyclopaedia of Islam*, New Edition, Vol. II, pp. 538–40.

Vaudeville, Charlotte. 1993. *A Weaver Named Kabir—Selected Verses with a Detailed Biographical and Historical Introduction*. New Delhi: Oxford University Press.

Zatalli, Jafar. 2003. *Zatal-nama (Kulliyat-i-Jafar Zatalli)*. Edited by Rashid Hasan Khan. New Delhi: Anjuman Taraqqi Urdu (Hind).

Zelliot, Eleanor. 2003. 'A Medieval Encounter Between Hindu and Muslim: Eknath's Drama-Poem *Hindu-Turk Samvad*', in Richard M. Eaton (ed.), *India's Islamic Traditions, 711–1750*. New Delhi: Oxford University Press, pp. 64–82.

Index

Abbasid Caliphate, 14, 25, 36, 37, 61, 111, 128, 130, 177, 199, 201–03
  bureaucracy, 201
  disintegration, 201
Abdun Nabi, Sheikh, 77–79, 82–85, 90, 93, 98, 100, 102–04
Abdur Rahman, Syed Sabahuddin, 149–50
Ab-i-Hayat, 166
Abu Bakr, 154
Abul Fateh, Hakim, 86, 87, 97
Abul Fazl, 9, 22, 76–77, 81, 84, 86, 87, 95, 97–98, 100, 104–05, 107, 110
  Ain-i-Akbari, 9, 76
  Akbarnama, 76
  as Allami, 77
Abul Hasan Tana-Shah, ruler of Golconda, 148
Adl, Sayyid Muhammad Mir, 86
Advaita Hinduism, 27
Afghanistan, American belligerence, 193
Afghans, 2, 10, 11, 18, 21, 73
Afrasiyab, 38
Afsar Umar Salim Khan, 52, 60
Agamben, Giorgio, 13
Ahl-i-Hadis, 212
ahl-i-kitab (People of the Book), 33, 92
Ahl-i-Sunnat wal Jama‘at, 183, 212
Ahmad, Aziz, 159
Ahmad, Maulvi Mahbub, 172
Ahmad, Nizam-ud-Din, 110
Ahmadiya/Qadiyani, 183
Aimanabad, 171
Akbar, Jalal-ud-Din Muhammad (r. 1556–1605 CE), 4, 11, 19–22, 30, 76–111, 143, 153, 155, 159–60
  policy of *sulh-i-kul*, 20, 69, 167
Akbarabadi, Nazir, 164–65, 166–67, 175
akhlaq and *adab*, 6–9, 14, 33, 111, 133
Akhlaq-i-Nasiri, 8
Al Qaida, 194
Alam, Muzaffar, 6–7, 11, 13
Ali, Hazrat, caliph, 59, 114, 154, 200, 201

Ali, Qazi, 103–04
Aliman, Huzaifa ibn, 114–15
al-Nasir (Abbasid caliph), 37
Amin, Imam Hafiz Muhammad, 99
Anderson, Benedict, 196
Angad, Guru, 174
animism or shamanism, 32
Arabs, 53, 66, 97, 201
Aristotle, 15, 201, 205, 207, 211
Arthashastra, 14
Asaf Khan, 81
Asghar, Ali
  Jawahir-i-Faridi, 38
Asna-Asharis, 212
Atharva Veda, 88
Aurangzeb, Alamgir (r. 1658–1707 CE), 19–22, 110, 129, 136–40, 147–51, 160, 167
Azad, Maulana Abdul Kalam, 184
Azad, Muhammad Husain, 166–74
Aziz, Umar bin Abdul, 69

Babur, Zahir-ud-Din Muhammad, 167, 171
  invasions in Punjab, 172
Badauni, Abdul Qadir, 17, 69–70, 76–100, 102–08, 110–11, 116, 143
  Muntakhab-ut-Tawarikh, 22, 76
  Najat-ur-Rashid, 142
Badr-ud-Din, Sheikh, 88
Bahadur Shah, 138, 144, 145
Baihaqi, 53
Bakhshi, Nizam-ud-Din, *Tabaqat-i-Akbari*, 110
Bakhtiyar, Sheikh Jamal, 89
Bala, 171, 172
Balban, Ghiyas-ud-Din, 37–38, 54
Banda Bahadur, 163, 174
Barani, Ziya-ud-Din, 13, 17, 33–34, 37, 44, 48–75, 111, 129
  Akhbar-ul-Akhyar, 59
  conception of Islam, 56
  Fatawa-i-Jahandari, 7, 13, 17, 49–50, 52, 57, 59–62
  Hasratnama, 58–59
  Inayat Nama-i-Ilahi, 57
  Masir-i-Sadat, 57
  Salat-i-Kabir, 57
  Sana-i-Muhammadi, 57
  Tarikh-i-Firuz Shahi, 50, 53, 57, 58, 59, 68
Barelwi Muslims, 182–84, 189
Barelwi, Ahmad Raza Khan, 181–84, 187–88, 212
Basari, Hasan, 25
Basari, Rabiya, 25
Bed Atharban (*Atharva Veda*), 88
Bedil, Mirza, 139
Beg, Mirza Khudayar, 145
Beg, Mirza Ulugh, 98
Beg, Mirza Zulfiqar, 145
Beg, Muhammad Yar, 145
Benthal, Jonathan, 198
Bhakkar, 82
Bhakti, 3, 16, 23, 74, 157*ff*. *See also* Sufism
Bhangu, Ratan Singh
  Guru Panth Prakash, 161
Bhawan, Sheikh, 88
Birbal, 87, 95, 103
Bohras, 212
Brahmins, 46, 61, 64, 91, 179, 184
brotherhood, notion in Islam, 180
Brown, Katherine, 22
Buddhism, 32, 175, 186

Bukhara, 33
Bundela, Bir Singh, 107
Bustami, Bayazid, 25, 26

Chauhan, Prithviraj, 11, 34–35
Chenghis Khan, 32
Chibber, Kesar Singh
Bansavalinama Dasan Patshahian Ka, 161
Chishti Sufis, 10–12, 23, 26, 27, 29–48, 51, 56–59, 74, 78, 80, 88–89, 102, 126, 161–62, 165, 174–75, 178, 188–89
Chishti, Abdur Rahman
Mirat-ul-Asrar, 12
Chishti, Islam, 80, 88
Chishti, Muin-ud-Din, 26, 34–37, 38, 47, 80, 89, 102, 175, 188
Fawaid-ul-Fuad, 43
Khayr-ul-Majalis, 43
Chishti, Salim, 78
Chitral, Pakistan, 211
Choueiri, Youssef M., 193
Christianity, 32, 33, 65–66, 95, 147, 186, 208, 210, 211
colonialism, 52, 188
and modernity, 19, 189
communal relations, 74
communalism, 1, 19, 51, 74
communication technology, 189
conversion to Islam, 75–75, 179–80
forced, 3
role of Sufis, 12, 28–30, 35, 43, 46–47, 158, 179, 188
cow slaughter issue, 184
cultural forms, 10, 15, 21

Dabistan-i-Mazahib, 176
Daniyal, Prince, 89
Dard, Khwaja Mir, 134
Dar-ul-Ulum Deoband, 24, 181, 183, 184, 185, 187, 197, 212
Daulat Khan, Nawab of Sultanpur, 167, 169, 170
Daulatabad, 42
Dawwani, Jalal-ud-Din
Akhlaq-i-Jalali, 8
Dayananda, Swami, 186
Deb Chand, raja of Manjhola, 87
Deccan, political conditions, 20
Dehlawi, Abdul Haqq Muhaddis, 12, 22, 31, 59, 108, 109–12, 119, 121–22, 124–25, 127
Adab-us-Salihin, 109, 111
Akhbar-ul-Akhyar, 12, 109
Madarij-i-Nubuwwat, 110
Tarikh-i-Haqqi, 110
Delhi Sultanate, 1, 7, 13, 26, 29–31, 38, 42, 43, 130, 135, 178
Muslims and *kafirs* in, 49*ff*
demographic dislocations, 2
Deoband. *See* Dar-ul-Ulum Deoband
Devgiri. *See* Daulatabad
doctrinal unity, 208

East India Company, 164
Eaton, Richard M., 3
egalitarianism, 180, 204
Eknath, 74

Faizi, 88, 89, 95, 99, 110
Fakhr-i-Mudabbir, 17
Adab-ul-Harb, 7
falsehood, 66, 68, 186
fanaticism, 16, 52, 131, 149
Al-Farabi, 200, 201, 204, 205, 207

Farid-ud-Din Ganj-i-Shakar, Sheikh (Baba Farid), 23, 26, 38, 40–41, 89, 161–66, 176
Farrukh-Siyar, 139–40, 152, 167
farz-i-ayn (principle duty), 112
farz-i-kifaya (supplementary obligation), 112
Fateh Ali Khan, 145
Fatima, 200, 201
Fatimid Egypt, 199
Firdausi, 53
fitna (sedition), 120, 214
Foucault, Michel, 14, 210
fundamentalism, 183, 192–96

Gaborieau, Marc, 182
Ganda Singh, 161
Gandhi, M.K., 184
Gangohi, Abdul Quddus, 17, 188
Gesudaraz, Bandanawaz, 42
Ghazali, Imam (d. 1111), 43, 54, 71, 94, 111, 117–18, 122–23, 130–31, 200, 204–07
  Deliverance from Error, 203, 206
  Ihya Ulum al-Din (*Bringing the Religious Sciences to Life*), 111
  Incoherence of the Philosophers, 205
  Kimiya-i-Sadat, 111
  Nasihat-ul-Muluk, 7
Ghazi Khan, 100
Ghaznavi, Badr-ud-Din, 130
Ghaznavids, 31, 32
Ghurid forces, 31, 32, 34
Gilmartin, David, 183
Gobind Singh, Guru (d. 1708), 160, 174
Greek sciences, 72
Grewal, J.S., 159
Gujarati, Itimad Khan, 81
Gurdas, Bhai, 171
Guru Granth Saheb, 27, 160, 162
Gurudaspur, 172

Habib, Mohammad, 13, 52–53, 55, 60–62
  The Political Theory of the Delhi Sultanate, 52, 60
Hadis. *See* Quran and Tradition of Prophet Muhammad
Hairati, 98
Hajj, Mir, 98
Hakim-ul-Mulk, 97, 104
Hall, Stuart, 49
Hallaj, Mansur, 26
Hamadani, Sayyid Ali, 17
Hamid-ud-Din, 34, 36
Hamza, 114
Hanafi school of jurisprudence, 26, 39, 66, 90, 125, 130, 131, 178, 212
Hanbali school of jurisprudence, 66, 212, 125
Hanifa, Imam Abu, 59
Harwani, Usman, 36
Hasan, Amir, 56, 58
Hasan, Nurul, 102
Hellenistic epistemology, 203
hereditary principles, 7, 69
Hidayah (Guidance), 83
Hindu(s), Hinduism, 3, 5, 16–17, 19–22, 32, 47–48, 56, 65, 66, 69, 75, 89, 92, 157, 161, 163, 186, 189, 208
  Advaita, 24
  belief systems, 89
  categorized as *kafirs*, 18, 183–84

majoritarianism, 212
and Muslims, hostility, 20, 161, 170, 173
relations in British India, 184–85
religious struggle, 73
and Sikhism, 157
in the Sultanates, 35, 56
Hindu-Turk Samvad, 74
Humaun, Hakim, 86
Husain Khan Tukariya, 69–70
Husaini, Qazi Ikhtiyar-ud-Din Hasan, *Dastur-ul-Wizarat* or *Akhlaq-i-Humayuni*, 8, 14
Husam-ud-Din, governor of Lakhnauti, 50
Huzaira, Bibi, 38
hypocrisy, 64, 105, 134, 148

Ibn Miskawayh, *Tahzib al-Akhlaq* (or *Kitab al-Taharat*), 8
Ibn Rushd, 201, 203, 204, 206–08, 213
Ibn Sina, 200, 204, 205, 206
Ibn Taimiyya, 69
Ibn-i-Arabi, 10, 26, 93
Fusus-ul-Hikam, 93
identity politics and Sikhs, 157, 161
idol worship, idolatory (*but-parasti*), 17, 27, 35, 47, 63, 68, 81
ijtihad, 18, 100, 131, 204
Iltutmish, Sultan Shams-ud-Din (r.1211–36), 36, 37, 38, 67
Indian Muslims (*sheikh-zadas*), 20, 21
Indian National Congress, 184–85
Indian Ocean trade network, 3
Indian Subcontinent, Islamization, 28–30
Indo-Persian treatise on music, 22
infidelity (*kufr*), infidels (*kafirs*), 17, 35, 47, 62–65, 68, 107, 120, 183–84, 190, 199; and Islam, distinction, 48
intellectual reasoning, 206
Iqbal, Mohammad, 174, 175, 176, 185, 196
iqtadars or *muqtais* (provincial governors), 2
Islam, Islamic
acculturation, 12, 46, 180
and heresies in Mughal India, 76*ff*
Islamicization process, 12, 179–80
law. *See* shariat
norms in the light of Quran, 109–32
and other religious traditions, interaction, 16, 23
refashioning devotional Islam, 177–91
scholasticism, 202
Isami, *Futuh-us-Salatin*, 36
Ismailis, 202, 212
Ismatun Nisa Begam, 145

Ja'fri, 59, 212
Jahangir, 107, 110, 167
Jalal-ud-Din, Maulana of Multan, 85
Jalal-ud-Din, Qazi-ul-Quzzat Qazi, 87, 100
Jalibi, Jamil, 133–34
Jama Masjid, Fatehpur, 99
Jama'at-i-Islami, 212
Jamali, Sheikh, 31
Siyar-ul-Arifin, 12

Jamaluddin, Syed, 150
Jat peasants, 159
Jats, 155
Jews, 33, 66, 185, 193
jihad (holy war) against infidelity, 20, 64, 73, 193
Jilani, Sheikh Abdul Qadir, 10
Jinnah, Mohammad Ali, 185
jizya (discriminatory tax), 18–21, 33, 65, 67–69, 85, 104. *See also* Akbar
Judaism, 186
Juwaini, 200
Juzjani, Minhaj-ud-Din Siraj, 53
  Tabaqat-i-Nasiri, 54

Ka'ba, 170–71
Kabir, 27, 162–63, 173
  division of followers, 162
kafirs. See infidels
Kam Bakhsh, 137–38, 144–45
Karamiyah, 205
Kararani, Sulaiman, 80
Kartarpur, 172
Kashani, Maulana Muhy-ud-Din, 58
Kashifi, Husain Waiz; *Akhlaq-i-Muhsini*, 8
Kayasthas, 11
Khafi Khan, 152
Khalji, Ala-ud-Din (r. 1296–1316), 38, 41, 42, 44, 51, 55, 129
Khalji, Jalal-ud-Din, 67–68
Khalji, Qutb-ud-Din Mubarak Shah (r.1316–1320), 38–39, 44
Khalsa, foundation of, 160–61, 163
Khan Bahadur, Zulfiqar, 140
Khan, Rashid Hasan, 136, 151
Khan-i-Arzu, Siraj-ud-Din Ali (1687–1756), 134
khanqah (hospice) and *dargah* (shrine), 26, 28, 33, 37, 64, 172, 180, 210
Khaqani, Hasan Ali Ibn Ashraf Munshi,
  Akhlaq-i-Hakimi, 9
Khaqani, Nur-ud-Din Qazi
  Akhlaq-i-Jahangiri, 9
kharaj, 65, 68
Khatris, 11
al-Khattab, Umar ibn, 17
Khilafat movement, 184
Khirad-Afza, 92
Khojas, 212
Khusrau Khan, 39
Khusrau, Amir (d. 1325), 44, 45, 47–48, 51, 55–59, 66, 73, 182
  Khazain-ul-Futuh, 55
khutba, 33
Khwarijis, 199
Khwurd, Amir, 31, 34–35, 38, 58–59
  Siyar-ul-Auliya, 12, 56–58, 59
Al-Kindi, 204
kitabat (calligraphy), 181
Koer Singh, *Gurbilas Patshahi Das*, 161
Koka, Mirza Aziz, 78, 82
Krishna Bhakti, 166

Laden, Osama Bin, 157, 198–99
Lahori, Qasim, 152
Lakshmi Das, son of Guru Nanak, 168
langar (community kitchen), 157

Latif, Abdul, 161
Lodi Sultanate, 158, 167
Lodi, Ibrahim, 167

Machiavelli, Niccolo, 14
Madani, Husain Ahmad, 185–87
Mahabharata, 88, 92
Mahdawis, 78, 80, 88
Mahmud, Sultan Nasir-ud-Din (r. 1246–66), 37, 40, 61
Mahmud, Sultan of Ghazna, 50, 62, 151
maktubat, 10, 29
malfuzat, 10, 29, 30, 43
Malik, Imam, 84–85
Malik, Khusrau, 40, 44
Maliki school of jurisprudence, 66, 125, 212
Maliki, Husain Arab, 85
Mamdani, Mahmood, 194–95
Mamluk, 70
Man Singh, 89
mansabdari system, 2, 79
Maraghah, Mongol ruler of, 8
Marathas, 19, 20, 21
Mardana, 171
Marsden, Magnus, 211
Marxism, 15, 31
masands (revenue agents), 160
materialism, 25, 29, 177, 202
al-Mawardi, Abul Hasan
  Ahkam-us-Sultaniya, 7
McLeod, W.H., 163, 165, 172
military technology, 4
Mir Taqi Mir, 134
modernity, 19, 147, 177, 187, 189, 196, 211
Mongols, 2, 7, 32, 70, 130, 201
monotheism, 18, 159, 168
Muazzam, Prince, 138
Mughal empire, Mughals, 2, 18–22, 46, 73, 102, 196
  disintegration/decline, 6, 11, 19
  Islam and heresies, 76*ff*
  norms of conduct, 9, 133–56
  Puritanism and intolerance, 22
  Safavid relationship, 10
  Sikhs, conflict, 23, 160–61, 163–64, 171–72, 175–76
  Sufi-Bhakti milieu, 157–64, 167, 171, 174, 176
Muhammad Khan, Qutb-ud-Din, 103
Muhammad Shah, 167
Muhammad, Prophet, 4, 34, 65, 71, 87, 113–14, 154, 170, 178, 185, 199
muhtasib, 71, 119–21, 124
Muin-ud-Din. *See* Chishti, Muin-ud-Din Bakhtiyar Kaki, Qutb-ud-Din, 26, 36–38, 40, 45
Muiz-ud-Din bin Sam, 31, 35
mujtahid, 78, 84, 99, 101
Murad, Prince, 95
Murjias, 199
Muslim(s)
  Congress alliance, 184
  ethnic and social differentiations, 192
  and *kafirs* in the Delhi Sultanate, 49*ff*
  political domination, 1, 2, 10, 16
  religious struggle, 73
Muslim League, 184
Mutazilas, 43, 72, 126, 199, 200, 206, 207

Muttahida Qaumiyat aur Islam (*Composite Nationalism and Islam*), 185
Muttaqi, Abdul Wahhab, 110

Nadwat-ul-Ulama Lucknow, 197
Nagauri, Hamid-ud-Din, 45
Nagauri, Sheikh Mubarak, 77–78, 100
Nakhshabi, Khwaja Ziya, 59–60
  Silk-us-Suluk, 60
  Tutinama, 60
Nanak, Guru, 23, 24, 27, 158–59, 161–72, 174–77
Naqib Khan, 84
Naqshbandi, 13, 26, 28–30, 46, 108, 110, 182
Nasir-ud-Din Chiragh-i-Dehli (d. 1356), 26, 38, 40, 41
Nizam-ud-Din, 38–39
Nizam-ud-Din Auliya, 26, 34, 38, 40–48, 51, 56–59, 72, 75, 182, 188
Nizam-ul-Mulk, 200
Non-cooperation movement, 184
norms of conduct, violation, 13*ff*
Nuzhat-ul-Arwah, 93

orthodoxy, 8, 33, 77, 106, 160, 200, 210, 213
Ottoman Empire, 102, 186

paibos (kissing of feet), 38
Pakistan, 211
  Talibanization, 212
Panchatantra, 14
Partition of Indian Subcontinent, 163, 187
Persian, 4, 6, 8–11, 14, 22, 27, 29, 50, 53, 73, 80, 88, 92, 95, 109, 111, 134–37, 139, 141, 167, 171, 176, 182
Pharaohs, 47, 77, 93
Plato, 201, 211
political, politics, 2, 9, 18, 50, 107, 152, 193, 195, 199, 201–02, 213
  authorization, 123
  of Delhi Sultanate, 43
  economy, 31
  governmentalization, 166
  ideology of Akbar, 167
  and Islam, 5, 6, 14, 18, 20, 50
  patronage, 15
  power of the Caliphate, 200
  and Sikhism, 161, 164, 176
  and Sufis, 29–30, 159, 180
  violence, 163
polity, secularization, 55
polytheism (*shirk*), 183, 184, 198
Portuguese (*firangi*), 81
pranayam (breath control), 27
Punjab, 23, 2631, 33, 37, 38, 161–66, 172–76, 181, 184, 188
Puratan janam-sakhi, 170
Purushottam, 92

Qadiri, 10, 26, 29, 108, 110
Qarari, Nur-ud-Din, 86
Qasim, Muhammad bin, 66
  conquest of Sindh, 73
qaum (nation), 185
Qisas-i-Hind, 166–67, 176
Quran and the Traditions of the Prophet (*hadis*), 7, 24, 54, 65, 71, 82, 84–87, 93, 101–02, 106, 108, 109–32, 141, 143, 182, 190, 192, 194, 200, 204, 206–07, 209, 213
Qutb Minar, 32

Qutb-ud-Din Aybak, Sultan (r. 1206–10), 32
Qutb-ud-Din Bakhtiyar Kaki, 36
Qutub Din, Hafiz, 172

rahit-namas (Sikh codes of belief and conduct), 163
Rai Pithaura. *See* Chauhan, Prithviraj
Rajputs, 19–21, 35, 73
Ramayan, 88
Razi, Imam, 94
reason (*aql*) and faith in Islam, 87, 116, 192*ff*
Reformation, 208
reformist movements, 28, 189
religion (*din*), religious, 8, 10, 16, 20–21, 91, 172
  and cultural co-existence, 9, 28
  diversities, 3
  hierarchy, 208
  identities, 19
  policies, 19–20
  and politics, interconnections, 15
  religiosity, cults and sects, 3
  and social norms, 23
  state laws, 72
Renaissance Europe, 14
right (*haqq*), 90–91
righteousness, 39, 112, 117, 127, 131, 153, 190, 200
  of Islam, 178–79, 203
Rishi Sufis of Kashmir, 45

Sabha Chand, 145–46
Safavids, 9, 102
Sainapat
  Sri Guru Sobha, 161
Saljuqid, 54
sama or *qawwali*, 27, 30, 39, 45, 58
Sambhaji, 148
Sanai, Ziya, 60
Sant Ghat, 168
Santokh Singh
  Suraj Prakash, 161
Sarhindi, Haji Ibrahim, 86, 88
Sarhindi, Sheikh Abdulla Niyazi, 80
Sarkar, Jadunath, 150
Sarwar, Ghulam
  Khazinat-ul-Asfiya, 12
Sassanid Persia, 72
Satnamis, 155
Sauda, Muhammad Rafi, 134, 152
Saudi Arabia, 183
Sayyids, 64
sectarian divisions amongst Muslims, 3, 18, 177
secularism, 1, 11–13, 15,19, 24, 28, 32, 38, 46, 47, 51–52, 55, 72, 90–91, 128–29, 149, 181, 187, 189, 193, 207, 212–13
separatism, 1, 5, 19, 73, 159, 175–76, 185, 187
Shafi'i school of jurisprudence, 90, 125, 212
Shafi'i, Imam, 56, 58–59, 61, 66
Shah Jahan, 110, 140, 153, 167
Shahbaz Khan, 103
Shahid, Sayyid Ahmad, 182
shariat (Muslim law), 2, 6–8, 14, 16, 18, 28, 32, 33, 35, 43, 93, 118, 124, 131, 141, 199, 210, 213
Shattaris, 45
Shi'ite state of Golconda, 21
Shi'ite Safavids (*qizilbash*), 81
Shias, Shi'ite, 84–87, 90, 98, 106, 126, 154, 199, 200, 201–02, 212
Shibli Numani, Allama, 149–50

Shivaji, 148, 150
shuddhi movement, 184
sijda (prostration), 38, 94
Sijzi, Khwaja Muin-ud-Din, 11
Sikandar Hasan, ruler of Bijapur, 148
Sikhism, 3, 23–24, 27–28, 155
and Islam, relation, 28, 157–77
sinful trades and professions, 71
Sirhindi, Sheikh Ahmad, 13–14, 17, 28, 46, 67, 106, 108, 110, 182
Socrates, 201
Sri Chand, son of Guru Nanak, 168
state, statecraft
  Indian, 14
  Indo-Persian, 15
  secularization, 193
  and Sufi orders, relation, 29, 178
Sufis, Sufism, 3, 6, 10–12, 15, 18, 23, 49, 51, 56–59, 62–64, 74–75, 77,80, 93–94, 96, 105–06, 109–10, 130, 133–35, 141, 151, 154–55, 201–03, 213
  and Bhakti interactions, 16, 23, 157*ff*
  decline, 189
  and emergence of Islam in Indian Subcontinent, 25*ff*
  meditation practices, 27
  in politics, 29–30
  relations with non-Muslims and Hindus, 30, 43, 178
Sughra, Sheikh-ul-Islam Najm-ud-Din, 36
Suhrawardis, 26, 29–30, 44–46, 178
Suhrawardy, Ilm-ud-Din, 45
Sulaiman, Mirza of Badakshan, 80
Sultanate period, 2, 9–10, 13, 15, 29, 46, 170, 180
Sultanpuri, Makhdum-ul-Mulk Abdullah, 77, 78, 81–82, 85, 90, 93, 97–98, 100, 102
Sunami, Ziya-ud-Din, 130
Sunni Muslims, 4, 6, 7, 20, 22, 23, 25, 43, 55, 71–72, 89, 108, 130, 133, 169, 177, 178, 199–201, 203
  four schools of jurisprudence, 56, 59, 125, 128, 200, 212
Sur regime, 158
syncretism and synthesis, 158, 162

Tabari, 53
Tablighi Jama'at, 183, 212
Tabtabai, Ghulam Husain, *Siyar-ul-Muta'khkhirin*, 163–64
Taj-ud-Din, Sheikh, 93–94
Taliban, 187, 193–94, 211–12
Talwandi, 167
Tarain battle, 1192, 31, 34
Tartars, 33
tasawwuf (Islamic mysticism), 110
tauhid, the unity of God, 46, 175
Taunsawi, Sulayman, 188
tazkiras, 10, 29, 30, 43, 45, 58, 179
Tegh Bahadur, Guru, 174
Teja Singh, 161
temples, demolition, 73
terrorism, 190, 194
Timur, 42, 98
travel documents (*ahd-nama*), 81
Trinity, 95
truth, Truth, 47, 62–63, 65–68, 90–91, 95, 100, 105, 107, 111–

12, 117, 121, 170, 172, 174–75, 177, 179, 199, 203–04, 206, 208
Tughluq, Firuz Shah (r. 1351–88), 42, 51, 53, 57, 129
Tughluq, Ghiyas-ud-Din (r. 1320–25), 38–40, 44–45, 58
Tughluq, Muhammad (r. 1325–51), 33, 36, 39–42, 51, 57, 70
Turanis (Central Asians), 21
Turks, 2, 10, 13, 18, 32, 73
  invasion of Hindustan, 2, 34
Tusi, Khwaja Nasir-ud-Din, 8, 14
  Akhlaq-i-Nasiri, 8
Tusi, Nizam-ul Mulk, 55, 71
  Siyasat-nama or Siyar-ul-Muluk, 7
two-nation theory, 175

ulama, 7, 15, 18, 20, 23, 26, 28–30, 32, 39, 42, 45, 59, 63, 74, 77, 80, 93, 129, 131, 178, 200, 204, 209
Ulugh Khan. *See* Balban
Umar, caliph, 72, 115, 154
Ummayad caliph, 25, 69, 86, 199
United States
  9/11, 192, 194–95
  foreign policy, 195, 199
  and Islamic terrorism, 194
Urdu, 11, 24, 27, 133–36, 139, 144, 149, 151–53, 158, 164–66, 174, 176, 182, 184–85
Usman, 154
Usuli, Ala-ud-Din, 130
Utbi, 53
Uzbegs, 102

Vatrisha Simhasana (*Sinhasan Batisi*), 92
Vedas, 87

wahdat-ul-wujud doctrine (unity of being), 10, 26, 27, 28, 45–46, 93, 158, 175
wahdat-us-shuhud, 28
Wahhabis, 181, 183, 185, 193, 212
Waliullah, Shah, 14, 182
Waqifiyah, 205
West European Civilizations, 15
wisdom (*hikmat-i-amli*), 8
World Wide Web (WWW), 181, 189, 198
wujudi doctrine, 46, 175

Yaqub, Qazi, 84
Yazdi, Mulla Muhammad, 87, 97, 104–05
yogic practices, 16
Yusuf, Abu Yaqub, 208

Zahid, Kamal-ud-Din, 130
Zakariya, Baha-ud-Din, 26, 45, 93
zaminbos (kissing the ground), 94
Zardust, 96
Zarradi, Fakhr-ud-Din, 45
Zatalli, Mir Muhammad Jafar, 133–56
zawabit-i-mulki (state regulations), 13, 32, 72, 129
zikr (remembrance of God), 30, 44, 45
zimmis, 35, 65–66, 68–70, 190
Zoroastrians, 33, 65